Ken Sparks, Ph.D., is a former world class middle distance runner and member of the World Record two-mile relay team from the University of Chicago Track Club. He is also an exercise physiologist and Director of Rehabilitative Care at Saint Vincent Charity Hospital and Health Center in Cleveland, Ohio.

Garry Bjorklund was an outstanding runner while attending the University of Minnesota, earning All-American honors in both cross country and track. He was also a member of the 1976 Montreal Olympic Team running in the 10,000 m. Garry is a veteran marathon runner and has a personal best of 2:10:20 in that event.

LONG-DISTANCE TO TRAINING

BUILD YOUR ENDURANCE, STRENGTH & EFFICIENCY

RUNNER'S GUIDE AND RACING

Ken Sparks
Garry Bjorklund

A SPECTRUM BOOK

Prentice-Hall, Inc., Englewood Cliffs, New Jersey 07632

Library of Congress Cataloging in Publication Data

Sparks, Ken.
    Long-distance runner's guide to training and racing.

    "A Spectrum Book."
    Includes bibliographies and index.
    1. Running--Training. 2. Running races.
I. Bjorklund, Garry. II. Title.
GV1061.5.S63 1984   796.4'26   83-24711
ISBN 0-13-540229-8
ISBN 0-13-540211-5 (pbk.)

ISBN 0-13-540229-8

ISBN 0-13-540211-5 {PBK.}

LONG-DISTANCE RUNNER'S GUIDE TO TRAINING AND RACING
BUILD YOUR ENDURANCE, STRENGTH AND EFFICIENCY
Ken Sparks   Garry Bjorklund

This book is available at a special discount when ordered in bulk quantities.
Contact Prentice-Hall, Inc., General Publishing Division, Special Sales, Englewood
Cliffs, N. J. 07632.

© 1984 by Prentice-Hall, Inc., Englewood Cliffs, New Jersey 07632

A SPECTRUM BOOK

10 9 8 7 6 5 4 3

Printed in the United States of America

Prentice-Hall International, Inc., *London*
Prentice-Hall of Australia Pty. Limited, *Sydney*
Prentice-Hall of Canada Inc., *Toronto*
Prentice-Hall of India Private Limited, *New Delhi*
Prentice-Hall of Japan, Inc., *Tokyo*
Prentice-Hall of Southeast Asia Pte. Ltd., *Singapore*
Whitehall Books Limited, *Wellington, New Zealand*
Editora Prentice-Hall do Brasil Ltda., *Rio de Janeiro*

There are many persons to whom I am indebted for their influence in my personal research and running, such as Dr. Dave Costill for his faith in my research ability, and Ted Hayden, coach of the University of Chicago Track Club, for his belief in my ability and his confidence in my maturity.

I would also like to thank my parents who made it all possible. I am dedicating this book to my wife Debbie, who gave me all the loving support I could ask for, and my son Chad, who will someday carry on the running tradition.

Ken Sparks

Contents

Preface xi

1

Introduction To Training 1
The Aerobic System 3
The Anaerobic System 7
Percentage of Body Fat in Runners 10
Muscle Cell Composition 11

2

Training for Endurance 18
Runner's Jargon 17
General Training Guidelines 21
Warmup / Cooldown
Types of Training 22
Long Slow Distance (LSD) / Fast Distance
(Tempo Running) / Interval (High Intensity Training) / Fartlek
Training / The Magic of a Marathon Race

Training the Young Runner 33

Overtraining (Signs and Symptoms) 34
Symptoms of Overstress

The Psychological Aspects of Training 35
Relaxation / Preparing for a Race

Training Tips 43

3

The Development of Strength 47
Muscle Structure 51
Improving Strength 52
Isometric Programs / Isotonic Programs
Specific Muscle Groups Need Improvement
in Runners 55
Exercises 57
Two-Arm Front Curl / Triceps Extension
(lying on a bench) / Triceps Extension (standing) / Two Arm
Standing Press (barbell press) / Arm Pullover / High
Pull-Ups / Lateral Arm Raise / Bench Press / Half
Squat / Heel Raise / Knee Extension (Extension, Flexion
Machine) / Knee Flexion (Flexion, Extension Machine)
Isokinetic Programs 74
Circuit Weight Training 75

4

Stretching 83
Static Stretching Versus Ballistic Stretching 85
Stretching Program for Runners 86
Exercises 87
Hamstring Stretch / Hurdle Stretch / Achilles
Stretcher / Stride Stretcher / Quadricep or Thigh
Stretcher / Low Back and Hamstring Stretcher / Heel Cord
Stretcher / Side Stretcher / Back-Over / Lower Leg
Stretch / Shoulder and Upper Back Stretcher / Groin
Stretcher
Strengthening Exercises 99
Bent-Knee Sit-Ups / Half Curl-up / Push-Ups / Pull-
Ups / Alternating Prone-Lifts

5

Altitude Training 109
Adaptation to Altitude 112

6

Thermoregulation and Electrolyte Replacement 123

Water Loss and Dehydration 125
Fluid Ingestion 127
Electrolyte Solutions
Fluid Replacement
Running in the Heat
Acclimatization to Running in the Heat

7

Nutrition 141

Carbohydrates 143
Fats 143
Protein 144
Fuel for Exercise 144
Vitamins 147
Fat Soluble Vitamins / Water Soluble Vitamins
Minerals 151
Carbohydrate Loading 152
Diet Following a Long Run or Marathon 160
Misconceptions About Diet 161

8

Injury Treatment and Prevention 165

The Running Stride 166
Types of Injuries 168
Injuries of the Ankle and Foot / Injuries of the Lower
Leg and Knee / Low Back Pain and Hamstring Muscle Injury
Orthodic Devices 186
The Running Shoe 188
Running Injuries Are for Real 190

9

Drugs and Sport 195

Blood Doping 197
Oxygen 197
Amphetamines 198
Caffeine 198
Analgesics (Pain Killers) 199

Anabolic Steroids 200
Alcohol and Marijuana 201
Vitamins: Needed or Not? 201
Hypnosis and Transcendental Meditation 202
Summary 202

10

Runners' Biographies 205

William Andberg / Jon Anderson / David Babriacki / Dick
Beardsley / Garry Bjorklund / Doug Brown / Amby
Burfoot / Patti Lions Catalano / Nancy Conz / Philip
Coppess / Jim Crawford / John
Dimick / Benji "Zonker" Durden / Lee Fiddler / Steve
Flannagan / Tom Fleming / Ray Flynn / Jeff Galloway / Don
Kardong / Alex Kasich / Herb Lindsay / John
Lodwick / Kevin McCarey / Henry Marsh / Stan
Mavis / Greg Meyer / Lorraine Moller / Kenny
Moore / Marcus James "Mark" Nenow / Lionel Ortega / Kirk
Pfeffer / Hank Pfeifle / Mike Pinocci / Steve
Plasencia / Miguel Santiago "Mike" Roche / Bill
Rodgers / Marge Rosasco / Alberto Salazar / Frank
Shorter / Jon Sinclair / Charles "Chuck" Smead / Ken
Sparks / Tony Staynings / Mary Decker / Ron
Tabb / Pablo Charley Vigil / Jeff Wells

Preface

Thousands of men and women are starting to run for various reasons. Many become serious runners. This book will give the reader a basic understanding of the physiological adaptations and problems associated with training and racing.

Written to help you understand the principles of training; this book provides sound information for developing a systematic training program. An understanding of how your body responds and adapts to training is essential for knowing your limitations and establishing your personal goals.

A unique feature of this book is its comprehensive background of scientific findings translated into layman's terms. Each chapter provides information about training from a scientific basis, along with selected comments from some of the top runners in the world. Photographs and a look into the training philosophies of Olympic runners and contenders are included.

This book provides all runners, regardless of level, with a better understanding of training and racing. Common questions concerning the runner will be discussed both scientifically and practically. The beginning runner, as well as the serious competitor, will benefit.

Ken Sparks
Garry Bjorklund

Introduction to Training

What does "getting into shape" mean? Man is a remarkable animal. He can sprint 100 yards in 9 seconds, run a mile in less than 3 minutes and 50 seconds, and run a marathon (26.2 miles) at an average speed of less than 5 minutes per mile. These are astonishing athletic achievements.

What enables certain individuals to perform at such levels? You can see personal variations such as hair color, body build, and facial features, but the internal differences (cellular) are less noticeable, and vary tremendously from person to person. These internal differences determine whether you are a sprinter, middle, or long distance runner. They also make the difference between a great and an also ran runner. Look more closely at the special characteristics of the athlete and see what it takes physiologically to be superior.

Endurance, strength, and efficiency probably, are the major components of a distance runner. Endurance is the ability to keep going for a long period of time at a good rate of speed. In order for the muscles to contract over and over, there must be a constant supply of energy available for fuel, because of the greater energy demands of the working muscle. This increased energy comes from the breakdown of the nutrients in your diet, the most important being carbohydrates (sugars and starches) and fats. (Proteins are used as building blocks for replenishing worn out tissues of the body and are not used for the energy fuel of the body.) The rate at which you can convert fats and carbohydrates into energy will determine how much work you can perform. The most common unit of measurement describing energy production is the calorie. Normally you consume 2,000 to 3,000 calories per day at rest, depending mainly upon your body size and the amount of exercise you are doing.

How does the body change the food you eat into usable energy? Imagine yourself as an oxygen machine. This machine uses oxygen from the air to break down the nutrients, carbohydrates, and fats from your diet into energy. This energy in turn powers the muscles for doing work. The more oxygen your body uses, the more energy you can produce. This is called your aerobic or endurance capacity. The largest amount of oxygen that you can consume per minute is called your maximal oxygen uptake and represents the maximal energy production of the aerobic system.

THE AEROBIC SYSTEM

The aerobic capacity varies widely for basically two reasons: first, your parents provide your genetic makeup, which includes your physical as well as your mental limitations; and second, people differ in the type and amount of physical training they have had.

Many distance runners develop aerobic capacities far beyond those of an average person. They can consume large amounts of oxygen and produce a lot of the energy needed to run long distances at a fast pace. Our ability to consume oxygen is measured in milliliters of oxygen per kilogram (2.2 pounds) of body weight each minute. The maximal oxygen uptake for an untrained person is approximately 40 to 45 milliliters per kilogram of body weight. The aerobic capacity of the elite runner is much higher. Frank Shorter and Bill Rogers reportedly have oxygen uptakes of 70 and 80 milliliters per kilogram of body weight (Figure 1-1). They can run distance races at a very fast pace because they can produce energy very rapidly. The measurement of oxygen consumption provides the precise determination for endurance and energy expenditure. For each liter of oxygen you consume, you can produce about five calories of energy; if you raise your oxygen uptake, you can produce more energy and can do more work.

Training can develop your endurance capacity. When your coach talks about conditioning or getting into shape for distance running, he is referring to an improvement in strength and maximal oxygen uptake. Even though training improves this capacity, there is a genetic limit for its development.

The aerobic or oxygen system in the muscle cell is supported by the circulatory and respiratory systems (heart, lungs, and blood vessels). As the physical stress imposed by training, overload, increases, the body adapts by making more energy available to the working muscles. These adaptations that help to develop your endurance capacity include:

1. An increase in the efficiency of the lungs for processing more air with less effort.
2. The development of more blood vessels for delivery of oxygen.
3. Increased blood volume for carrying the oxygen.
4. Improvement in the muscle's storage capacity for fats and carbohydrates.
5. An increase in the number of sites for energy production (mitochondria) in the muscle cell.
6. An increase in the amounts of compounds called enzymes which speed up the breakdown of nutrients for energy production.

The oxygen system or aerobic system is used predominately during long-term running. As the intensity of running increases, the aerobic system cannot keep up with the energy demands, and an oxygen debt is created. When this happens, energy is supplied anaerobically (without oxygen). This system is inefficient for supplying energy; only short bouts of work, such as sprinting, can be done.

Several factors affect the aerobic capacity. Male distance runners generally have about 20 to 25 percent higher oxygen uptakes than female runners. This is due in part to the differences in body composition (percent of fat and muscle mass). Females may have as much as 2 to 3 times as much stored fat as males have, with only about 75 to 80 percent as much

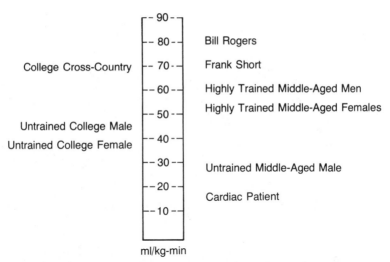

FIGURE 1-1. *Maximal oxygen uptake values for selected groups.*

muscle mass as males. Most of the difference is due to fat storage in the breasts and reproductive system. The difference in muscle mass is due to the male sex hormone testosterone, the hormone responsible for greater muscle growth. These differences lower the oxygen uptake capabilities in women because the muscle uses the oxygen. Females also have smaller hearts, less blood volume, and less cardiac output (blood pumped by the heart per minute) than males have; these factors put the female runner at a slight disadvantage. Even though the aerobic capacity of the female is lower normally, female athletes reportedly have measured as high as 65 to 70 milliliters per kilogram of body weight. Whatever the reasons for the lower oxygen uptakes, better training and coaching have closed the difference between males and females in running performance.

Aging is another factor affecting oxygen uptake. Growing older means different things to every runner. The young runner looks forward to being older and more mature, because running performance begins to improve with additional body size and strength. The older runner is a little less excited about maturity, and fears of decreased performance levels plague his or her thoughts. Shortly after you reach adulthood, your aerobic capacity starts a very gradual decline (Figure 1-2) that does not affect performance for several years. Runners actually perform better with age and often have their best perfor-

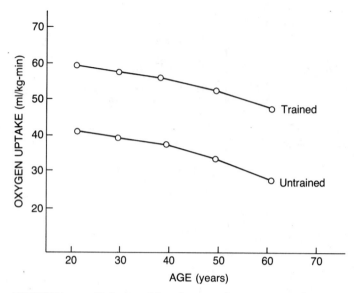

FIGURE 1-2. *Relationship of age and oxygen uptake, trained and untrained men.*

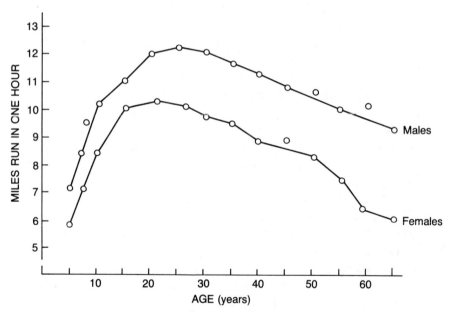

FIGURE 1-3. *American records for the one hour run vs. age and sex.*

mances after age 30 (Figure 1-3). After age 32 there is a considerable decrease in performance times, correlating with a decrease in the maximal aerobic capacity. Although there is a decline, training seems to counteract some of the effects of aging on the endurance capacity. Although degenerative effects are evident, many older runners are very successful in long races. Clarence DeMar won his seventh Boston Marathon at the age of 42 and continued to run very well even after age 60. The effect of aging seems to be of less importance as more and better training techniques become available.

How do you know you're getting into shape? The first noticeable result of training is less fatigue during and after your training sessions. This corresponds to a lower heart rate during your running session. If you obtained a heart rate of 150 beats per minute for running an 8 minute mile pace early in the season, you might expect that after a few weeks of training your heart rate might be 140 beats per minute for that same 8 minute mile. The heart rate is being lowered because more oxygen is being taken from the blood and used by the muscle cells. The heart is capable also of pumping more blood per heartbeat (stroke volume). Therefore, the total amount of blood leaving the heart (cardiac output) is greater per minute. Because of these changes in cardiac dynamics, the heart does not have to work as hard in supplying blood and oxygen to the working muscles. Sometimes the increased efficiency of the heart causes a lowering of your resting heart rate; however, this change is not noticed by everyone.

Your general overall feeling also changes, because exercise helps relieve mental tensions and helps you relax. You sleep better and wake up more refreshed.

Regular exercise helps also in improving digestion. The food you eat is more easily digested, and during training you suffer less from stomach upsets, indigestion, and constipation.

THE ANAEROBIC SYSTEM

Anaerobic running or high intensity running, such as sprinting, can be sustained only for a few seconds or minutes. As the intensity of running increases, so do the energy demands of the muscle. As these energy needs increase, the aerobic system cannot produce energy fast enough to keep the muscles supplied; thus, an oxygen debt is incurred, and energy is being supplied by the anaerobic system.

The anaerobic system is not very efficient in supplying energy; however, it does represent the most rapid source of energy for the muscle. It is involved with the production of energy during high intensity work or during the initial stages of aerobic running. Anaerobic refers to the breakdown of the energy fuel, carbohydrates (glucose), without (or in the absence of) oxygen. This system is used during short bouts of hard work.

The anaerobic system can be developed with proper training. This is called specificity of training when your program is designed to develop the energy system that is providing the energy for competition. Anaerobic running tends to be related to repetitions of faster paced distances, as in interval and fartlek training; however, fast paced continuous running can be equally anaerobic. These all require a large supply of energy that cannot be supplied aerobically, and therefore extend into your anaerobic system.

Anaerobic running produces a substance called lactic acid, an acid that, when accumulated in large quantities, alters muscle contraction. Lactic acid is a byproduct of anaerobic metabolism. It is produced when there is not enough oxygen available for the complete breakdown of carbohydrates (glucose) stored in the muscle. Lactic acid levels are indicators of work intensity. Lactate begins to accumulate when your running pace is hard enough to exceed 60 to 65 percent of your aerobic capacity (Figure 1-4). Many distance runners, however, are characterized by their ability to tolerate high rates of energy expenditure (80 to 90 percent of their aerobic capacity) without accumulating high levels of lactic acid. Frank Shorter, Olympic gold medalist in the marathon, and Derek Clayton, former world record holder in the marathon, run at intensities that normally cause lactic accumulation higher than most runners could tolerate. Normally, runners use about 70 to 75 percent of their aerobic capacity when racing. The exceptional abilities of Shorter and Clayton to run at high intensities without building up a lot of lactic acid probably reflect the high level of intensity training done throughout their programs.

Lactic acid levels have been measured at the end of a marathon and have shown low quantities—only about 2 to 3

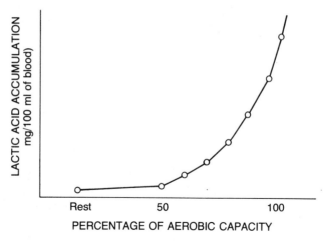

FIGURE 1-4. *Lactic acid accumulation with increased aerobic capacity utilization.*

times the quantities normally found at rest. The fatigue associated with distance running is caused not by a buildup of lactic acid, as in sprinting, but probably by low levels of carbohydrate (glucose) in the muscle.

The muscle soreness that occurs after a distance race is due probably to excessive muscle strain from pounding on the pavement, rather than lactic acid production. If a runner starts a race too fast and goes quickly into anaerobic metabolism, fatigue will come early and cause slower running times. The most efficient way to run a race is a steady pace using the aerobic system for energy production.

Anaerobic training is important to the distance runner as well as to the sprinter. Many races are won or lost during the finishing kick. Aerobic training is the basic foundation for a program, whereas anaerobic training produces the building blocks that are added to the foundation of a sound program. Intensity training, however, has to be a gradual process because of muscle fatigue that can lead to injury.

In general, runners tend to use interrupted work for their anaerobic building and steady work for the aerobic side. However, anaerobic work has its main effect on the heart itself, and aerobic work affects primarily the blood vessels and oxygen supply throughout the body. Anaerobic running increases explosive muscular power; aerobic running increases staying power. The shorter the race, the more significant the anaerobic training (Table 1-1).

TABLE 1-1. *Estimation of the aerobic-anaerobic needs by racing distance*

Race	% Aerobic	% Anaerobic
440 y/400m.	25	75
880 y/800m.	50	50
Mile/1,500m.	70	30
2-Mile/3,000m.	85	15
3-Mile/5,000m.	90	10
6-Mile/10,000m.	95	5
Marathon	99	1

PERCENTAGE OF BODY FAT IN RUNNERS

Runners come in all shapes and sizes. Distance runners are usually characterized as being small and thin, while sprinters are usually taller and more muscular. Both sprinters and distance runners are lean, because the energy needed to carry excess body weight (in the form of fat) decreases running speed and efficiency. The height of runners is less important to successful running than weight. Regardless of body variations, men and women runners possess less body fat than does the average population.

TABLE 1-2. *Body size and percent fat of world class distance runners.*

Athlete	Height (in.)	Weight (lbs.)	% Fat	Fat weight (lbs.)
C. Hattersley	68.25	133.5	4.7	6.6
B. Durden	70.50	145.0	6.6	9.6
R. Wayne	67.72	136.5	7.4	10.1
J. Dimick	68.31	130.7	4.4	5.7
L. Ortega	66.54	132.6	7.5	9.9
T. Sandoval	67.72	119.5	5.7	6.8
R. Mahoney	70.87	141.2	8.1	11.4
F. Shorter	70.00	128.0	3.0	3.8
R. Hodge	67.72	126.0	6.3	7.9
J. Wells	71.46	140.0	7.4	10.4
H. Atkins	71.25	141.5	4.8	6.8
A. Salazar	71.25	148.5	4.6	6.8
B. Rogers	70.00	128.0	6.0	7.7
G. Waitz	66.93	116.2	10.8	12.5

The male distance runner may have as little as three percent of his body weight as fat, far below the average of 13 to 15 percent fat. The female distance runner may have as little as 15 percent of her body weight as fat, compared to 20 to 25 percent for most women of the same age (Table 1-2).

Every cell of the body has to have a certain amount of fat for proper functioning. Fat, therefore, is classified as essential fat and stored fat. The differences between the amount of essential fat in men and women vary according to body size. The average male weighing 150 pounds will have about 3 percent of his body weight as essential fat and the rest in the form of stored fat. The average female weighing 125 pounds has about 12 percent of her body weight as essential fat, and the rest as stored fat. This difference in essential fat between males and females is due to increased fat deposits in the females' breasts and reproductive systems.

Aging reportedly changes the percentage of fat stored on the body. This is true for most people, but is not a result of aging; active men and women engaged in running and exercise in general are usually leaner than other persons their age and may be as lean as the younger runners.

MUSCLE CELL COMPOSITION

Running speed is very important to every sport. Studies suggest that, while training dictates the development for endurance capacity, success in sprint running or distance running is determined partially by the muscle cell (fiber) composition. The human skeletal muscle is basically made up of two types of muscle cells. Some muscle cells have good endurance, while others have poor endurance. The predominance of one or the other of these cell types will determine running speed capability. The physiological properties of these muscle fibers determine the rate at which they can contract.

All muscle cells function basically the same way. When stimulated by the nervous system, the cells develop maximal tension and contract. This tension causes changes in muscle length, producing movement of the skeletal system. Concentric contraction occurs when the muscle contracts and shortens its length at the same time. In order for one set of muscles to contract concentrically, opposing or resisting muscles must lengthen; this lengthening of the muscle when contraction occurs is eccentric contraction.

The rate at which the muscle cell can contract and relax determines the type of muscle fiber. Fibers that contract or develop tension rapidly are called fast twitch or type I muscle cells and provide you with fast running speed. The other major type of muscle fibers found in human muscle develop tension slowly and are called slow twitch or type II muscle fibers.

Scientific advancements have made it possible to take small samples of muscle tissue, using a needle biopsy technique, enabling scientists to examine the physiological properties of muscle fibers and determine the effects of training at the subcellular level.

The microscopic photograph presented in Figure 1-5 shows the two types of muscle fibers found in human skeletal muscle. This muscle sample was taken from Mary Decker, world record holder in the women's mile and 1,000 yard runs. The lightly stained muscle fibers contract fast and recover quickly and are considered fast twitch or type I muscle fibers. The darkly stained muscle fibers are slow contracting and are slow twitch or type II muscle fibers. These two types of muscle fibers have different aerobic and anaerobic capabilities for the production of energy.

FIGURE 1-5. *Muscle fiber composition of Mary Decker.*

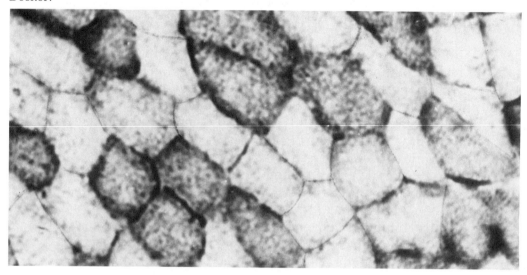

Distance runners possess more slow twitch fibers, as much as 90 percent more than do sprinters. These fibers contract repeatedly, producing the energy needed for distance running. Slow twitch muscle fibers have the ability to produce energy at a constant rate, meaning that their aerobic capabilities are greater than fast twitch fibers. The size or cross sectional area of the slow twitch muscle fibers have been found to be larger than the fast twitch fibers in distance runners, suggesting that training may be responsible for the selective enlargement. The muscle micrograph of Mary Decker bears this out; even though she is primarily fast twitch—65 percent fast twitch and 35 percent slow twitch—at the time this sample was taken, she was doing all endurance training, possibly explaining the larger stained muscle fibers. The actual area distribution between the fast twitch and slow twitch muscle fibers was approximately a 50:50 ratio.

The mixture of fast twitch and slow twitch muscle fibers is predetermined by your genetic makeup and is not changed with training. Endurance training, however, can alter some of the endurance capabilities of some fast twitch muscle fibers. These fibers become more aerobic or able to utilize more oxygen than a true fast twitch fiber. This alteration is strictly an effect of distance training and not a permanent change in the fiber itself.

The chemical adaptations that occur when a muscle undergoes a training effect are very complex. First you have to understand that the production of energy from your dietary nutrients is the important aspect of training. This energy is produced by two types of metabolism (the breakdown of nutrients for energy production): aerobic (oxygen) and anaerobic (without oxygen).

The importance of developing the aerobic and anaerobic systems has already been discussed, but to understand fully what is taking place, you have to look into the subcellular components of the muscle cell (Figure 1-6). Within each muscle cell there are many peanut shaped powerhouses called mitochondria. These powerhouses are responsible for oxidizing fats and carbohydrates during aerobic running. Distance training is responsible for increasing the number of mitochondria, allowing for greater energy production.

In order to provide energy at a faster rate than normal and to provide energy needed to sustain running tempo, special proteins called enzymes are produced to speed up the energy production. Aerobic enzymes are involved in the breakdown of fats and carbohydrates during distance running. Reportedly, distance training is responsible for increasing these oxidative enzymes as much as 3 to 4 times, resulting in greater maximal oxygen uptake capacities. Training increases the oxidative enzymes not only in the slow twitch fibers, but also in the fast twitch fibers, improving their aerobic capacity. This type of fiber is sometimes referred to as an intermediate or type IIa fiber because it has some of the contractile characteristics of a slow twitch fiber.

The fuels for running (fats and carbohydrates) are stored in the liver and in the muscle cell. Carbohydrates are stored in the form of glycogen—many glucose (simple sugar) molecules. Fats are also stored in the muscle cell, as well as in the adipose tissue. Figure 1-6 shows the relationship of the fuels to the mitochondria within the muscle cell. The fuel for the powerhouse is stored next to the mitochondria, allowing for greater efficiency of energy production. As more powerhouses are produced with training, more fuel (fats and carbohydrates) is stored in the muscle cell.

Anaerobic metabolism takes place outside the mitochondria (site for aerobic metabolism) in the fluid portion of

FIGURE 1-6. *Muscle cell and blood capillary.*

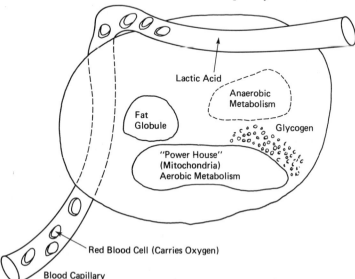

TABLE 1-3. *Chemical and physical properties of different muscle fiber types and the effect of distance training on these properties.*

Muscle Property	Slow Twitch (Type I)	Affect of Training	Fast Twitch (Type II)	Affect of Training
Aerobic Enzyme Activity	High	Increases	Low	Increases
Anaerobic Enzyme Activity	Low	No Change	High	No Change
Contraction Speed	Low	No Change	High	Decreases
Endurance	High	Increases	Low	Increases
Number of Mitochondria	High	Increases	Low	Increases
Number of Blood Capillaries	High	Increases	Low	Increases
Production of Running Speed	Low		High	

the muscle cell (sarcoplasm). Because of the increased amount of oxygen needed to break down a fat molecule, anaerobic work uses only glycogen for its fuel. Therefore, the anaerobic enzymes are referred to as glycolytic enzymes. Anaerobic training, like aerobic training, increases the amount of glycolytic enzymes needed for the production of energy without oxygen. Because of the small amount of anaerobic work performed by distance runners, however, the quantity of glycolytic enzymes is not much greater than that found in untrained people.

Table 1-3 summarizes the chemical and physical properties of the different types of muscle fibers found in human muscle and indicates the training effect on these properties.

REFERENCES

Behnke, A. R., and Royce, J., "Body size, shape, and composition of athletes," *J. Sports Med. and Phys. Fit.*, 6 (1966), 75–88.

Bell, R. D., MacDougall, J. D., Billeter, R., and Howald, H., "Muscle fiber types and morphometric analysis of skeletal muscle in six-year-old children," *Med. Sci. Sport and Exer.*, 12 (1980), 28–31.

Buchthal, F., and Schmalbruch, H., "Contraction times and fiber types in intact human muscle," *Acta Physiol. Scand.*, 79 (1970), 435–452.

Butts, N. K., "Physiological profiles of high school female cross country runners," *Res. Q.*, 53 (1982), 8–14.

Campbell, C. J., Bonen, A., Kirby, R. L., and Belcastro, A. N., "Muscle fiber composition and performance capacities of women," *Med. Sci. Sport and Exer.*, 11 (1979), 260–265.

Costill, D. L., "The relationship between selected physiological variables and distance running," *J. Sports Med. and Phys. Fit.*, 7 (1967), 61–66.

Costill, D. L., "Physiology of marathon running," *JAMA*, 221 (1972), 1024–1029.

Costill, D. L., Bowers, R., and Kammer, W. F., "Skinfold estimates of body fat among marathon runners," *Med. Sci. Sport and Exer.*, 2 (1970), 93–95.

Costill, D. L., Braham, G., Eddy, D., and Sparks, H., "Determinants of marathon running success," *Int: Z. Angew. Physiol.*, 29 (1971), 249–254.

Costill, D. L., Daniels, J., Evans, W., Fink, W., Krahenbuhl, G., and Saltin, B., "Skeletal muscle enzymes and fiber composition in male and female track athletes," *J. Appl. Physiol.*, 40 (1976), 149–154.

Costill, D. L., Fink, W., and Pollick, M., "Muscle fiber composition and enzyme activities of elite distance runners," *Med. Sci. Sport and Exer.*, 8 (1976), 96–100.

Costill, D. L., and Winrow, E., "Maximal oxygen intake among runners," *Arch. Phys. Med. Rehab.*, 51 (1970), 317–320.

Eberstein, D. and Goodgold, J., "Slow and fast twitch fibers in human skeletal muscle," *Amer. J. Physiol.*, 215 (1968), 535–541.

Edstrom, L., and Ekblom, B., "Differences in sizes of red and white muscle fibers in vastus lateralis of musculus quadriceps femoris of normal individuals and athletes, Relation to physical performance," *Scand. J. Clin. Lab. Invest.*, 30 (1972), 175–181.

Essen, B., Jansson, E., Henriksson, J., Taylor, A. W., and Saltin, B., "Metabolic characteristics of fiber types in human skeletal muscle," *Acta Physiol. Scand.*, 95 (1975), 153–165.

Gollnick, P. D., Armstrong, R. B., Saltin, B., Saubert, C. W. IV, Sembrowich, W. L., and Sheppard, R. E., "Effect of training on enzyme activity and fiber composition of human skeletal muscle," *J. Appl. Physiol.*, 34 (1973), 107–111.

Hermansen, L., and Wachtlova, M., "Capillary density of skeletal muscle in well-trained and untrained men," *J. Appl. Physiol.*, 30 (1971), 860–863.

Larsson, L., "Physical training effects on muscle morphology in sedentary males at different ages," *Med. Sci. Sport and Exer.*, 14 (1982), 203–206.

Lindsay, J. E., and others, "Structural and functional assessments on a champion runner—Peter Snell," *Res. Q.*, 38 (1967) 355–365.

Maron, M. B., and Horvath, S. M., "The marathon: A history and review of the literature," *Med. Sci. Sport and Exer.*, 10 (1973), 137–150.

Patton, J. F., and Vogel, N. A., "Cross-sectional and longitudinal evaluations of an endurance training program," *Med. Sci. Sport and Exer.*, 9 (1977), 100–103.

Picci, A. J., and Brooks, G. A., "Effects of training and age on VO_2 maximum in laboratory rats," *Med. Sci. Sport and Exer.*, 14 (1982), 249–252.

Pollock, M. L., Miller, H., and Wilmore, J., "A profile of a champion distance runner: age 60," *Med. Sci. Sport and Exer.*, 6 (1974), 118–121.

Saltin, B., and Astrand, P. O., "Maximal oxygen intakes in athletes," *J. Appl. Physiol.*, 23 (1967), 347–352.

Sparks, K., Wilkerson, J., and Martin, D., "Body composition for elite marathon runners," (unpublished data), 1979.

Thorland, W. G., Johnson, G. O., Fagot, T. G., Tharp, G. D., and Hammer, R. W., "Body composition and somatotype characteristics of Junior Olympic athletes," *Med. Sci. Sport and Exer.*, 13 (1981), 332–338.

Upton, S. J., Hagan, R. D., Rosentswiez, J., and Gettman, L. R., "Comparison of the physiological profiles of middle-aged women distance runners and sedentary women," *Res. Q.*, 54 (1983), 83–87.

Wilmore, J. H., "Body composition in sport and exercise: directions for future research," *Med. Sci. Sport and Exer.* 15 (1983), 21–31.

Wilmore, J. H., and Brown, C. H., "Physiological profiles of women distance runners," *Med. Sci. Sport and Exer.*, 6 (1974), 178–181.

Wilmore, J. H., Miller, H., and Pollock, M., "Body composition and physiological characteristics of active endurance athletes in their eighth decade of life," *Med. Sci. Sport and Exer.*, 6 (1974), 44–48.

Training for Endurance

Anyone who has ever put on a pair of running shoes has his or her own ideas on how to train for performance improvement. Any method of training, providing it does not cause bodily harm, can be successful. The key to training, however, is that your program be built around your personality and physical capabilities. Trying to adopt another runner's program is like wearing another person's hat—it may not fit your style or your personality.

The most important ingredient in anyone's training is desire. The amount of desire will determine the effectiveness of any program; too little or too much can be disasterous. It is essential to keep things in their proper perspectives.

RUNNER'S JARGON

To understand training, you need to develop the runner's language that helps explain the type of training programs outlined.

Aerobic system: The energy producing system that involves the use of oxygen in breaking down nutrients in your diet for supplying a constant energy supply. This system, used during low intensity training, is sometimes referred to as your endurance system, because it maintains high energy levels for long bouts of work.

Anaerobic system: The most rapid source of energy available for the muscle, the anaerobic system provides energy during short bouts of hard work. Anaerobic is defined as being without, or in the absence of, oxygen.

Circuit training: Training that includes various movements of strength, endurance, flexibility, and power. This type of training usually involves jogging, calisthenics, and weight lifting.

Contact: Staying close to the competition so that you are within striking distance of the leader.

Continuous training: Exercise bouts, usually of long duration and high intensity, without rest or relief periods.

Fartlek: A Swedish term that means "speed play." This training, involving both the aerobic and the anaerobic energy producing systems, is performed by running bouts of high intensity spaced with easy and moderate intensities.

In-season: The competitive season; special training should be done to maintain physiological capacities. Sharpness and psychological readiness are major emphases.

Interval training: A system of conditioning consisting of repeated bouts of exercise, usually of high intensity, alternating with periods of rest or relief.

Kick: The spurt or burst of speed at the end of competition. The kick is seldom top speed, such as sprinting.

Lactic Acid: A byproduct of anaerobic metabolism that

can alter the contractile process of the muscle, lactic acid is formed as a result of very high intensity running.

LSD (Long slow distance): A type of training used to improve the capacity for storing nutrients (fats and sugars) in your muscle cells, LSD involves a long duration of energy expenditure with low intensity. This is commonly used by ultra-distance runners or during days of recovery from competition.

Off-season: Easy, relaxing, non-competitive portion of the year when the major emphasis is on building a good physiological base of aerobic capacity.

Over distance: Training at a distance longer than your racing distance.

Oxygen consumption: The maximal rate at which oxygen can be used by the body for the production of energy via the aerobic system.

Pace: Average rate at which a distance is run.

Peaking: Preparing for a mental and physical high point in training for top performance.

Pre-season: The hard training portion of the year when the athlete is preparing for competition. Work intensity and effort increase during this season.

Principle of overload: Applying physical stress on the body to produce adaptation. This is a progressive procedure that increases the intensity and duration of the exercise period that is responsible for a training effect.

Repetition: Number of workout bouts included within a set.

Rest interval: The relief portion of interval training. This could be easy jogging or walking, but never standing.

Set: A group of work bouts interspaced with rest intervals.

Strength training: The lifting of weights to increase the endurance and power of a group of muscles involved in running. The training usually consists of repeatedly lifting light weights.

Time trial: A practice race with simulated racing conditions, used to build confidence and to experiment with pacing.

Training: An active program designed to increase fitness and performance.

GENERAL TRAINING GUIDELINES

Training is a process which makes possible, through a planned, systematic development of your physical capacities, the achievement of better performance without any physical or mental danger.

Every runner needs to think ahead, plan what he or she wants to achieve from a program, and establish a sensible timetable. The beginner needs to keep in mind that athletic performance is the result of many years of training. Thus, the key to the beginner's program is patience.

A long range plan should be the first step in planning a program. This plan should be a 2 year projection with flexibility built in to account for differences in training responses. This long range plan should be followed up by a 1 year program that is divided into shorter phases based on training seasons. Each season can be divided into cycles designed to emphasize specific types of training. Typically these cycles are planned around the competitive season.

The off-season or starting season, if you are just beginning a program, is designed to develop general endurance and strength. This should be a relaxing time of year that allows time for other things in your life. The primary emphasis should be on increasing your aerobic capacity. During this time long enjoyable runs should be taken; pace is not a concern during this time of year. Variety in your runs, however, will help prevent boredom. This variety could mean hill running, tempo running, or running with a companion.

Intensity should build as the pre-season approaches. The pre-season is the time to train hard for the upcoming competitive season. The emphasis is on increased tempo and effort. The early competitive season is sometimes considered a part of this cycle. Competition involves a great deal of hard effort, with less emphasis on performance times. The competitive season should emphasize mental sharpness and physical readiness. The intensity of the training should be increased in order to develop leg speed and neuro-muscular efficiency.

Each training phase should be based on a logical progression, with gradual increases in training stress. The body gradually adapts to increased physical stress, providing sufficient rest is included as a part of your program. It takes about 3 to 4 weeks for the body to respond to training stress; weekly or biweekly training changes may be necessary to allow for recovery from extremely taxing runs.

Warmup

A runner should warm up before exercising. Increasing the muscle temperature will facilitate the exchange of oxygen from the blood to the muscle tissues. Warmup aids nerve transmission and improves both speed and force of muscle contraction. All of this decreases the chance of strain on muscles, ligaments and tendons.

Warmup should be intense enough and long enough to produce a positive effect, but not so intense as to cause fatigue. Intensity and duration will have to be adjusted to the individual. As a rule of thumb, when you begin to break into a sweat, you have raised your internal temperature sufficiently. Weather conditions will obviously alter the duration of warmup. Warmup usually lasts 15 to 30 minutes and includes stretching as well as running; the effects last 30 to 40 minutes. The intensity of warmup should begin to taper off 5 to 10 minutes preceding the event to allow recovery. Warmup also gives the psychological benefit of getting you ready for the task at hand.

Cooldown

The cooldown is an often neglected, but extremely important, part of running. After hard running, you should immediately do some easy running or walking to prevent the light-headed feeling caused by the pooling of blood in the lower legs, and to help in the sustained recovery of heart rate and blood pressure. The continuous movement of the muscle groups in the legs helps in the removal of lactic acid that has accumulated in the muscles due to anaerobic work. The cooldown should last for 5 to 10 minutes, followed by light stretching to minimize muscle soreness and tightness.

TYPES OF TRAINING

Obviously, endurance training is the most important aspect of a distance runner's program. Depending on its intensity, distance training can be divided into two general categories. "Long slow distance" (LSD) and "Fast distance" (tempo running) are the primary programs used by runners to improve endurance or to build a base for other types of training. The major difference in these programs is in the intensity and duration; each has advantages and disadvantages that must be considered.

Long Slow Distance (LSD)

Long slow distance is used primarily as a "base" conditioning program. Long relaxing runs lasting 1 to 2 hours are common practice. This type of training is fun and should not be exhausting; it is not as demanding on the heart and lungs as fast distance. It is demanding on the energy system of the muscles, however. Because this demand on energy utilization via the oxygen system is the purpose of this type of training, many runners who use this system have high maximal oxygen consumption values.

LSD training has several disadvantages. It requires more time than any other type of training system. It also does not provide enough stress on muscle fibers that are primarily speed producing; thus, these muscle fibers are not prepared for the stresses of racing.

Fast Distance (Tempo Running)

Fast distance running or high intensity continuous running involves running at a slightly less than race pace effort for 5 to 10 miles. This places demands on the circulatory and energy systems. The primary advantage of this type of training is that it stimulates racing stresses on the muscle. Because of the added stress, however, runners are more prone to muscle and joint injuries. Almost every runner uses fast distance training in his or her program, either by pushing the tempo while running on the roads or by doing a time trial on the track.

Interval (High Intensity Training)

Interval training is a system of repeated efforts spaced with periods of rest. Usually the efforts are timed or paced, while the rest intervals are usually kept constant in order to make the efforts harder as fatigue sets in.

Interval training involves the development of the anaerobic system as well as of the aerobic system. It enables the runner to do more intense work because of the short rest periods between efforts. Usually the distances covered are from 110 yards to 1 mile, with variations in between. The shorter distances emphasize speed, while the longer distances emphasize stamina. There are several factors to keep in mind while the interval training:

1. Quality refers to the effort of the run. If the intervals are being timed, the quality should remain the same; i.e., if you are running 440 yards in 90 seconds, all repeats should be completed in the same time. If your time starts to drop off, you have misjudged your ability for the quantity chosen.
2. Quantity is the number of repeated efforts that are to be completed without sacrificing quality or changing relief periods.
3. Relief period is the rest taken between efforts; this can be timed or can be a set distance to be jogged between runs.
4. Effort/relief ratio refers to the length of the efforts, either distance or time, and the length of the rest or relief period. Obviously, the closer to a 1:1 ratio, the harder the workout.
5. Variety should always be sought to avoid boredom. Use several distances to make the efforts seem less. A good example of this would be to move down in distance of run, but to increase the effort.
6. Recuperation is very important when training with intervals. Because of the increased stress imposed by the hard efforts, fatigue is greater, and more time is needed by the body to adapt.

Interval running can be adapted to anyone's level of ability. It can be used for the sprinter as well as for the distance runner. There are, however, some disadvantages of interval training. Because of the greater intensity of the runs, interval training often prevents a runner from doing large volumes of work. A second disadvantage is that the runner increases his or her chances of injury, because more stress is placed on the muscles and joints. It is recommended that interval training be used mainly during the pre-season and in-season phases of a training cycle, following a sound "base" conditioning program.

Examples of various types of interval programs:

Speed interval: 6–12 × 100 or 200 m.—very hard effort (in control) walk same distance run or full recovery.
    Purpose: Develop neuro-muscular recruitment of fast muscle fibers.

Repetitions interval: 6–12 × 400 m.—10 seconds off best time short relief period, 1:1 or 1:2 ratio.
    Purpose: Develop pace, stamina and endurance.

Stamina intervals: 4–8 × 800 m. or miles—good pace 30 seconds to one minute off of best pace for mile—short relief interval 1:1 ratio or less.
    Purpose: Develop endurance and stamina.

Speed, stamina: 2–4 × 400 m. or 800 m.—pace near all out effort relief period long—1:4 or 1:5 ratio.
    Purpose: Develop pace, speed and stamina.

Fartlek Training

Many of the runners at the turn of the century used a form of fartlek training; however, it was not until a Swede named Gosta Holmer used it in the 1930s that anyone was credited with this training style. (Fartlek is a Swedish term meaning "speed play.") Fartlek training can be considered a type of unstructured, unregimented form of interval training. Fartlek running involves a blending of continuous tempo running with varying efforts of speed, stamina, and recovery.
    Fartlek training should be done on a cross country course of challenging terrain, although it may be done along a road. It involves a lot of self discipline in order to get the total benefits. A fartlek run usually takes between 45 minutes and 2 hours. The first 10 to 15 minutes should be easy and should serve as a warmup, followed by a hard pace for .75 to 1.5 miles. Easy jogging should follow for 5 to 10 minutes for recovery, then the pace is built into repeated bursts of speed lasting 50 to 75 yards

in length with short easy jogging between each sprint. Fartlek training should include some uphill running of hard efforts with easy striding between each effort. All of the above components should be repeated until the conclusion of the workout period. The demands of fartlek training should not be as demanding as timed interval training, however; the runner will feel taxed, but not exhausted.

Proponents of fartlek training feel that it develops self discipline and helps a runner to mature. It is also mentally stimulating and can be a refreshing break from the usual training regimen. The disadvantage of fartlek running is the freedom it gives, often allowing a young or undisciplined runner to misuse this type of training.

Through the years athletes have struggled and have continually gotten better. The improved performances have been partially due to trial and error, and partially due to scientific findings, but mostly due to hard work on the part of athletes and coaches. The success of any program, however, depends upon the athlete and the confidence he or she has in the program. Besides building confidence, a good program has to be enjoyable and rewarding. For a program to be enjoyable, the training distances, intensities, and terrain have to be as varied as possible within your total training objective. You must feel good about what you're doing and stimulated physically and mentally after working out.

Every runner is different; each responds differently to training; therefore, the mileage and type of program will vary. Each runner has to know his or her strong and weak points, then work accordingly to improve in areas needed. There is nothing magic about running 100 or 150 miles a week, except that not everyone can do it, and not everyone should do it. What everyone else is doing shouldn't govern your program, but serve as a guideline for training ideas. Look at some of the top runner's responses to questions about their training programs and make comparisons in mileage, training systems, and personal strengths or weaknesses during competition.

These athletes are different in their abilities, training beliefs and training systems, but all are successful.

Percentage of training program spent with LSD, continuous, interval, fartlek, and weight training

	LSD	Continuous (tempo running)	Interval	Fartlek	Wt. Training
Frank Shorter	50	34	8	8	0
Bill Rogers	2	90	2	4	2
Benji Durden	75	10	0	10	5
Garry Bjorklund	72	7	7	7	7
Ken Moore	35	20	20	20	5
Alberto Salazar	45	10	25	10	10
Amby Burfoot	80	0	15	5	0
Jeff Wells	85	5	7	3	0
Kirk Pfeffer	50	0	0	50	0
John Dimick	80	5	5	10	seasonal
Greg Meyer	10	80	5	5	0
Stan Mavis	50	10	25	15	0
Tony Staynings	5	60	15	15	0
Doug Brown	80	5	15	5	0
Henry Marsh	25	25	50	0	0
Mike Roche	40	25	20	0	15
Jeff Galloway	90	8	2	0	0
John Anderson	30	45	7	15	3
Don Kardong	85	5	8	2	0
Dick Quax	75	15	8	2	0
Grete Waitz	0	60	22	8	(10% circuit tr)
Lorraine Moller	60	20	13	7	0
Patti Catalano	70	0	10	10	10
Laurie Binder	65	20	5	10	additional
Herb Lindsey	20	30	10	30	10
Ray Flynn	10	50	20	10	10
Tom Fleming	0	85	0	15	0
Marge Rosasco	0	60-80	10	10	1
Ron Tabb	20	50	10	20	0
Bill Anberg	75	15	5	5	0
Marc Nenow	30	50	10	10	0
Nancy Conz	20	50	20	10	0
Charlie Vigil	45	43	13	0	0
Jon Sinclair	15	45	20	10	5
Philip Coppess	15	60	20	5	0
Dick Beardsley	10	50	5	30	5

A week's mileage during little competition and during the peak competitive season

	Mileage During Little Competition	Mileage During Peak Competition
Frank Shorter	100-120	120-140
Bill Rogers	125	125
Benji Durden	85-95	105-110
Garry Bjorklund	60-80	100-125
Ken Moore	70-80	95 if no race/50 if race
Alberto Salazar	120	70
Amby Burfoot	40	60
Jeff Wells	110	60 (wk of marathon)
Kirk Pfeffer	120-140	120-140
John Dimick	95-110	80-85
Greg Meyer	115-125	80-100
Stan Mavis	120-125	90-110
Tony Staynings	100-110	80-90
Doug Brown	30-40	70-80
Henry Marsh	60	40-45
Mike Roche	110-125	80-105
Jeff Galloway	100-140	80-100
John Anderson	110-120	80-90
Don Kardong	70	110
Dick Quax	120-140	75-110
Grete Waitz	80-90	50-55
Lorraine Moller	100-120	80
Patti Catalano	90	140
Laurie Binder	100	120-130
Jon Sinclair	80-100	60-80
Charlie Vigil	80-90	75-80
Nancy Conz	35-45	65-80
Marc Nenow	90-115	90-115
Bill Andberg	40	40
Ron Tabb	110-120	90
Mary Decker	60-70	30-50
Tom Fleming	140	115-120
Herb Lindsey	70-90	60-80
Ray Flynn	90	40
Marge Rosasco	60-80	50-70
Philip Coppess	100-140	85-120
Dick Beardsley	120-130	115-125

Length of time running before first marathon; age at first marathon

	Years Running Before First Marathon	Age	Best Marathon Time
Frank Shorter	7	22	2:10:30
Bill Rogers	10	25	2:09:27
Benji Durden	11	24	2:10:41
Garry Bjorklund	14	25	2:10:20
Ken Moore	4	19	2:11:36
Alberto Salazar	9	22	2:08 World Record
Amby Burfoot	2	18	2:14:28
Jeff Wells	6	18	2:10:15
Kirk Pfeffer	3	15½	2:11:50
John Dimick	5	19	2:11:52
Greg Meyer	10	25	2:13:07
Jeff Galloway	4	18	2:16:35
John Anderson	5	22	2:12:03
Don Kardong	7	23	2:11:16
Dick Quax	16	34	2:10:47
Grete Waitz	10	25	2:25:41
Lorraine Moller	11	24	2:31:42
Patti Catalano	5 months	23	2:30:57
Laurie Binder	2	30	2:38:09
Marge Rosasco	3	24	2:56:29
Tom Fleming	13 months	18	2:12:05
Ron Tabb	6	22	2:11:00
Bill Andberg	1	56	2:51:44
Nancy Conz	4	23	2:33:23
Charlie Vigil	2	19	2:15:19
Jon Sinclair	7	21	2:13:29
Philip Coppess	3 months	21	2:13:27
Dick Beardsley	3	21	2:08:53

Number of races per year; greatest tactical strength; problem racing conditions

	Number of Races Per Year	Greatest Tactical Strength	Problem Racing Conditions
Frank Shorter	25	pace	rain, cold
Bill Rogers	30	following and down hill running	heat, humidity, altitude
Benji Durden	30	down hill running	altitude
Garry Bjorklund	20	pace	humidity
Tony Staynings	35-40	kicking	none
Doug Brown	20	pace	humidity

Henry Marsh	15-20	kicking, pace, following	heat, humidity, altitude
Mike Roche	15-20	leading	rain, cold, altitude
Jeff Galloway	20	pace, following	none
John Anderson	10-15	pace	altitude, humidity
Don Kardong	15-20	pace	cold (occasionally), humidity, heat
Dick Quax	20-30	kicking, leading, hill running	cold, altitude
Grete Waitz	30	pace, leading	rain, cold
Lorraine Moller	20-25	pace	humidity
Patti Catalano	30-35	ability to surge	cold
Laurie Binder	35-40	ability to surge, hill running	altitude, humidity
Ken Moore	8	kicking, down hill running	cold, humidity
Alberto Salazar	20	pace, ability to surge, leading	none
Amby Burfoot	30	ability to surge, mental relaxation	heat, humidity
Jeff Wells	15-20	pace, kicking	heat, humidity, altitude
Kirk Pfeffer	15-20	leading, hill running	none
John Dimick	15	pace	heat, humidity
Greg Meyer	18-25 (10 hard efforts)	kicking, pace, ability to surge, hills	altitude
Stan Mavis	20-30	kicking	humidity
Jon Sinclair	20	hill running, kicking, ability to surge	rain, cold
Ray Flynn	50	pace, ability to surge	altitude
Tom Fleming	15	leading, hill running	heat, humidity
Herb Lindsey	20-25	kicking, different terrain, pace	heat, humidity
Charlie Vigil	12-18	pace, hill running, leading	rain, humidity, wind
Nancy Conz	20	pace, mental attitude	none
Marc Nenow	12	ability to surge, following, hill running	heat, humidity
Mary Decker	15-20	kicking, leading	cold
Philip Coppess	32	pace	humidity, altitude
Dick Beardsley	20-25	leading, pace, ability to surge	cold, altitude

The Magic of a Marathon Race

There seems to be some kind of intriguing mystery about running 26 miles, 385 yards. The challenge is the ultimate for a distance runner and gives a feeling of success to all who try and succeed regardless of their finish time. Marathon running requires a special dedication and should involve many months of preparation. There is no shortcut to successfully completing a marathon run. Competing at long distances without proper training usually results in discouragement or injury. Most marathon runners have been training and racing at shorter distances for many years before attempting the 26 mile distance.

How long does it take to prepare for a beginning runner to successfully complete a marathon? Several factors, such as age, previous physical training, physical capacity, and running technique, have to be considered. We questioned some of the best runners in the world, and they responded as follows:

Bill Rogers: A beginning runner should allow 1 year for preparation before running a marathon.

Benji Durden: 9-12 months of training should be the shortest time for getting ready for a marathon.

Frank Shorter: I feel a runner should build up to 70 miles per week and then cover the mileage for 3 months before attempting a marathon.

Alberto Salazar: My guess for the shortest preparation time would be 1 year.

Grete Waitz: 1 year would be the shortest time for a beginning runner.

Lorraine Moller: I believe it depends on the person, age, and level of fitness. At least a year, but preferably 4 to 5 years. The longer the better, and the more enjoyable marathoning will be. Beginning runners should shoot for shorter races first and get good at those, then move up. I think it's easier to try to go further and a little slower than faster and shorter (unless you are Shorter).

Patti Catalano: 6 months would be the minimum time for a beginner.

Laurie Binder: 3 months of proper training, including gradual building of mileage, long runs every week, etc.

It seems that most runners feel that the longer the training period, the better the results. Running for survival is not the proper way to approach a long race.

Amby Burfoot: A year from absolute scratch and 3 months from running 20 miles a week.

John Dimick: 1 year of preparation and then run the first one just to finish. You should be able to average 50 miles per week for 10 weeks prior to race.

Stan Mavis: To finish comfortably, for a sedentary person, 1 year. For an already active person, six months.

Mike Roche: To survive without damage, 2 to 7.5 years; to finish and die 1 year; to die and not finish, less than 1 year.

Jon Anderson: From zero, I suggest at least 1 year and discourage that. I believe 2 years would result in the likelihood of a positive experience.

Don Kardong: It could be done in 6 months.

Ron Tabb: It would depend on what physical condition the individual is in. I feel that 6 months would be fine.

Marge Rosasco: Of course, this depends on the person, age, weight, and natural ability. Even for a good natural athlete, I would say a minimum of 1 year.

Herb Lindsey: There are many variables to consider such as age, level of fitness at start, etc. There should be an internship through shorter races for all runners.

Tom Fleming: 1 year or 50-60 miles a week, at least.

Mary Decker: At least 1 year of running.

Nancy Conz: It depends on so many different factors, such as a person's running ability, talent, and goals. Maybe a year, but I would not advise it, even after a year. I would like to see someone prepared for a marathon; it takes a lot out of a person.

Dick Beardsley: A beginning runner should allow at least 6 months for training before running a marathon.

TRAINING THE YOUNG RUNNER

Now that there are more road races and more opportunities for younger runners to compete, training has been adapted to the young runner. There is much controversy about the hard training programs that some coaches are using with their young athletes. The endurance training of young athletes must be supervised. Training and biological development should be in a balance whereby physical stress does not alter the emotional or physical growth of the child.

Some researchers feel that hard early training may result in early successes, but seldom results in later world-class performances. Several physiological differences exist between the young and the mature runner. Particular attention should be taken in planning an endurance program for young runners because children, compared to adults, have:

- Smaller stroke volumes (amount of blood pumped by the heart per beat)
- Less stability in endurance
- Slower adaptation rate to anaerobic work
- Longer recovery rate for maximum workloads
- Less muscle, ligament, and tendon strength

The response of a young athlete to training loads, however, is similar to that of an adult—stroke volume increases, oxygen consumption increases, breathing rate decreases, heart rate stabilizes, and metabolism becomes more efficient. The early years should therefore be used as a base for later training. The intensity should be less, and the importance of competitive performances should not be overemphasized. Longer periods of rest should be used following maximal stress; the recovery period should not be shorter than 36 to 48 hours. Group training may prove to be too hard for the young runner who is at a different biological age than other runners of the same chronological age. Experiments with 10- to 17-year-old students running at 75 percent of maximum speed to exhaustion, showed that running pace increased in proportion to the age, indicating that speed, not distance, was the limiting factor. Studies show that young runners train best with longer steady runs, not with shorter, high intensity training; therefore, a limited amount of fast tempo running is recommended.

Training performances should be evaluated regularly and adjustments made if technique and running pace drop off or if tightness becomes obvious.

Careful planning and observation are the key to training young runners. The program should always include variety, rest, and challenge. The early developmental years are very important for later great performances.

OVERTRAINING (SIGNS AND SYMPTOMS)

Exhaustion and overtraining are always concerns of the competitive runner. Even though the human body is a durable instrument, it can break down from overstress. Many runners don't realize that in order to adapt to training, the body needs time to rest and rebuild tissues. The desire to succeed can make runners try too hard. Proper amounts of psychological and physical stress make your body stronger; however, too much stress makes it weaker and could produce breakdown or injury.

The signs and symptoms of overtraining need to be known in order to adjust training programs.

Symptoms of Overstress

- Persistent soreness and stiffness in muscles, tendons, and joints
- Lowered general resistance (frequent colds, sniffles, and fever blisters)
- Loss of appetite (causing weight loss and stomachaches)
- Diarrhea or constipation
- Constant tired feeling, but inability to rest comfortably
- Depression, headaches, and irritability
- Drops in performance
- Acne
- Sore lymph glands
- Desire to quit during races

Overstress can cause a number of these symptoms to occur, and the only cure is rest. There are early warning signs of overfatigue before the problem is actually experienced.

These signs include:

- Higher than normal resting pulse rate
- Slightly higher resting lactic acid levels
- Sluggish, heavy feeling during runs
- Staleness

These early signs are less serious, but should be taken seriously. The best thing to do is ease your training, make sure you are getting at least eight hours of sleep a night, and eat a well balanced diet. High intensity or anaerobic training should be eliminated until signs or symptoms subside. Use your head, listen to your body, and be fair with yourself.

THE PSYCHOLOGICAL ASPECTS OF TRAINING

The mental aspects of running are very important; runners need to develop mental toughness in order to succeed in competition. Every runner who has ever stepped on a starting line feels the anxiety and experiences the emotions of competition. Running, like no other sport, allows the novice runner to feel the excitement of being in the same race as the superstars.

Relaxation

One of the most important aspects of running is relaxation. Learning to relax does not mean shutting out or not paying attention to running, but just the opposite. Runners should concentrate on what they are doing and should consciously stay in tune with their bodies. Norman Vincent Peal's book, *The Power of Positive Thinking*, uses positive thoughts to prevent negative thoughts from entering the mind; this positive approach can be applied to running.

You can do many things to relieve tensions while running. Dropping your arms momentarily or placing your thumb and middle finger together helps in relieving the tension in the arms and shoulders. Concentrating on knee lift and visualizing in your mind the smooth mechanics of striding helps in producing positive relaxation.

Learning to relax when not running is also important. Running should not be the all encompassing aspect of your life. All work and no play causes added pressures when training. Worrying about your training or competition takes the enjoyment out of running. Although you want to do your best, training and competition always should be kept in the proper perspective.

The following comments were made by some of the athletes surveyed, concerning their relaxation when not running:

Amby Burfoot: I like to read, write, go for walks, or go to movies or plays. I also like to play with children, including my 3 year old son.

Frank Shorter: I like to read, go skiing, or work when I need to relax while not running.

Ken Moore: I relax with reading, music, gardening, or cooking.

Alberto Salazar: When I'm not running, I like to go out with friends, have dates, listen to music—normal activities.

Jon Anderson: I enjoy family activities such as skiing, camping, swimming, and playing with my two children.

Jeff Galloway: I relax by reading, watching movies on TV, or taking walks.

Dick Quax: When I'm not running or training hard, I like to play golf, cross country ski, camp, read, or take in a movie.

Don Kardong: I enjoy reading, watching TV, playing golf, or skiing when not running.

Laurie Binder: I like to relax by sitting in our hot tub in the backyard when not running.

Sue Strickland: I enjoy lying around, reading, painting, or writing. When not running, I also like to bike, cross country ski, and practice ballet.

Patti Lions Catalano: I like to entertain my husband, cook, and read if time permits.

Benji Durden: I enjoy reading science fiction and working crossword puzzles.

Bill Rogers: I read a lot—fiction, newspapers, and magazines. I also enjoy all types of music—blues, folk, rock and roll, and classical.

Jon Sinclair: I like to backpack, train, drink beer, and sleep.

Charlie Vigil: I read, play the guitar, listen to music, and plan ahead.

Nancy Conz: Don't have much time to relax because I work 40 hours and run. I like to ride a bike, read, and visit friends and family.

Marc Nenow: I listen to music, read, and hit the town with friends.

Bill Andberg: I like to fish and work around the house.

Mary Decker: I like to relax by shopping, writing, gardening, sewing, cooking, and having lunch with the girls.

Tom Fleming: I work in my store with other runners, read books, listen to music, and watch TV.

Herb Lindsey: I like to read, bike, take a hot tub or sauna, and go to the movies.

Dick Beardsley: I do things around the farm—hunt, fish, walk, and read.

A major part of the mental preparation for a race is making sure that all the pre-race details have been taken care of. You should make a list of all the things that have to be done; the following checklist can serve as a guideline:

1. Make sure of the entry deadline; don't miss a race because you didn't get your entry in on time.
2. Make all of your travel arrangements in advance.
3. Be sure to know the check-in time and where to report.
4. Check the starting time and place. Allow plenty of time to get there without having to rush.
5. Familiarize yourself with the course; either go over or study a map of the course.
6. Be sure to have the proper running gear with you.

If you take care of all of these things, you avoid some of the hassle and worry of the race and you have more time to relax and prepare yourself mentally for the competition.

Preparing for a Race

Many races are won or lost because of self confidence. If your training has been going well and you feel fit, it should be easy to convince yourself that you are ready for the task at hand. Don't let the opposition scare you. A successful performance doesn't have to mean winning or running a great time, but just doing your best for the conditions and your training level. Don't be discouraged; remember, it's only a race and not life or death.

Most athletes find getting "psyched-up" before a race adds to their confidence. When asked what they do to prepare for a race, some top runners gave the following answers:

Bill Rogers: I concentrate on major events, train through lesser races. I believe you should prepare your training and racing programs carefully within your general lifestyle.

John Dimick: I "psych-up" for important races by doing tougher workouts. I do mental race simulation and try to focus on positive aspects of training.

Laurie Binder: I try to vision myself as running strong, smooth and relaxed.

Henry Marsh: I try to relax and not dwell on an important race until the day of it. The atmosphere at important races, such as the crowd and the competition, gets me psyched.

Mike Roche: I think of the people I'm running against. I picture myself in various routines and predicaments during the race. I think about the splits and how I might feel. I try to assure myself by having confidence in my training.

Lorraine Moller: I follow a routine that I am comfortable with and know works for me, from training throughout the week to breakfast the morning before the race. I spend time reviewing my previous races and training, dwelling on my successes in particular to feel confident, and then developing my strategy to attain my goals for that race.

Patti Lions Catalano: I mentally prepare myself for racing by wanting to beat a particular person or wanting to win.

Greg Meyer: I do a few blow out intervals to give me confidence. I tend to get a little more withdrawn socially.

Alberto Salazar: I psych myself up by going over the race in my head. I think about it months before the race.

Amby Burfoot: The mental and physical go together. As I taper off for the race, I begin to mentally rehearse all the things I would like to do in the race and to review the preparations I have made that should make those results possible.

Gary Fanelli: I psych up by sitting down, looking at my training book, and seeing how hard I trained. I visualize myself winning and tell myself I can do it.

John Lodwick: I get excited about races; however, I anticipate big ones and get nervous before them. Mentally I try to maintain a positive attitude and a workable strategy. I try to do the best I can and leave the results to the Lord.

Alex Kasich: I prepare myself the same way for all races. Each race is a test to see what I can do time and place wise. I try to know the course and whom I will be racing against.

Doug Brown: I get psyched up by thinking about the race for months.

John Flora: I psych up by sitting quietly and listening to Dark Side of the Moon, an album by Pink Floyd, two or three nights before the race.

Jeff Wells: I pray and talk about a race, and become more and more motivated. I think it is very important that one does not get up too much for a race.

Benji Durden: Six to eight weeks before a major effort, I begin to think about the race during training runs and visualize various scenarios with my overcoming all challenges.

Don Kardong: I "psych-up" by "psyching-down" and trying to stay relaxed.

Sue Strickland: I try not to get "psyched." I still don't have the real hang of it. I try to stay loose, but run the race over in my mind. I listen to Beethoven's Sixth for relaxation. I think good psyching comes with familiarity of racing and confidence in training and ability.

Ray Flynn: I realize the importance of the race, respect and not underestimate opposition. The size of the race has a way of making the adrenaline flow, and when I sense these occasions, I become serious and concentrate, thinking about the race and being positive before and during it.

Herb Lindsey: I developed my own personal mental game plan to maximize my athletic potential through reading *Peak Performance* by David Kauss.

Tom Fleming: Be positive. I only think to myself about how well I'm going to do in that race. Visualization method is great; daydream, but be positive on the results.

Mary Decker: Think positive thoughts; think of reasons why I should win or run fast.

Dick Beardsley: I try to picture the race in my mind, find out my opponents' weaknesses, and try to get ready for the unexpected.

The wise competitor always plans his or her training and racing strategically. Some races should just be a part of the training. More important races are planned ahead of time to allow for peaking. Peaking is when the mental and physical preparations are at their highest point and should mean a top performance.

When peaking for a race, it is essential to cut back on training and concentrate on racing. A well planned, smooth, even paced race should result if everything is ready. The race strategy is based on a goal, which may be winning, bettering a previous time, or just finishing, if this is your first experience at a new distance. The excitement of competition should not alter the plan or cause a tactical blunder. Keep in mind that in racing and training the body only does what the mind will let it.

Common questions always come up about the training programs of good runners. Some of these questions deal with training frequency, peaking, dividing programs into seasons, and even about training with a companion. The following section helps you get a feeling for the answers to these questions.

	Training Sessions Per Week	Training With a Companion	Peaking How Often Per Year	Maintain Training Diary	Divide Program Into Training Seasons
Mary Decker	13	as often as possible approx. 70% of time	1	Yes	Yes
Ron Tabb	12-14	very little until I was married	4	Yes	No
Jon Sinclair	14	12-14	2-3	Yes	Yes
Charlie Vigil	7	2-3	never physically; mentally I concentrate on some races more.	Yes	No
Nancy Conz	10	0	None	Yes	No
Marc Nenow	0	0	0	Yes	No
Tom Fleming	13-14	3	2	Yes	No
Herb Lindsay	Run 13, Bike 2 Swim 3, Weight 3	maybe 1	2	Yes	Yes
Ray Flynn	13	13	3	Yes	No
Jon Anderson	13	1-2	2-4	Yes	Yes
Mike Roche	12-14	7	whenever possible	just starting	No
Henry Marsh	12, Rest on Sunday	2	1	Yes	Yes
Greg Meyer	13	6	2-3	Yes	No
Tony Staynings	14	10	2-3	Yes	Just mentally
Kirk Pfeffer	5 days twice daily; 2 days once 20 miles a day	0	never	Yes	No
Amby Burfoot	7	2-3	3	Yes	Yes
Dave Smith	12	0	2-3	Yes	No
Chuck Smead	14	3-6	1-3	Yes	No
Don Kardong	10	3	2	Yes	No
Sue Strickland	10-12	5-7	2 for marathon	Yes	No
Kevin McCarey	13	2	3	Yes	No
Benji Durden	10	1	2	No	No
Frank Shorter	13	2	2	Yes	No
Ken Moore	13	0	1	No	Yes

	Training Sessions Per Week	Training With a Companion	Peaking How Often Per Year	Maintain Training Diary	Divide Program Into Training Seasons
Lionel Ortega	11	1	2	Yes	Yes
Ted Castanada	6	0	3	No	Yes
Jim Crawford	5	0	3	Yes	Yes
Steve Flannagan	13	7	2-3	Yes	No
Steve Plasencia	13	4-5	1-2	No	Yes
Lee Fiddler	14	1	2	Yes	Yes
Laurie Binder	12-14	3	3	Yes	No
Jeff Galloway	10-14	3-5	1	Yes	No
Doug Brown	12	2-3	1	Yes	No
Jeff Wells	11-13	2	4	Yes	No
Mike Penochi	15	5-6	2-4	Yes	No
Gary Fanelli	14	0	2	Yes	Yes
Dick Quax	12-14	12-14	2	Yes	Yes
Grete Waitz	12-14	5-7	3-4	Yes	Yes
Paul Geis	7	2	1	No	No
Patti Lions Catalano	14	14	0	Yes	Yes
Lorraine Moller	12	6	2	Yes	Yes
Donna Burge	12	10	3	Yes	No
Bill Rogers	14	7	2	Yes	Yes
Garry Bjorklund	13	3-4	2	Yes	Yes
Alberto Salazar	13	7	2	Yes	No
Dick Beardsley	13-14	0	1-2	Yes	No

TRAINING TIPS

Dave Babriacki: I've always worked on a hard-easy program no matter what time of the year.

John Flora: I think keeping a mental attitude totally independent of this world, yet being highly sensitive to your own physical space on earth, compared to everyone else's space, helps.

Ken Moore: Crucial to my success was the intelligent application of hard-easy training forced on me by Bill Bowerman. It takes me 2 to 3 days to recover completely from one long and hard workout. Without the easy 5 miles of jogging days, I'd just have declined into sickness, injury, and bitterness.

Frank Shorter: I believe the success of any training program is consistency.

Benji Durden: I use heat stress to supplement my training. I wear sweats in the summer on my easy days if the temperature is less than 80 and wear sweats everyday in the winter. I hesitate to guess what advantages this gives me, but it seems like I run stronger when doing this kind of training.

Kevin McCarey: The problem that many runners face is lack of speed and pace awareness. I think many runners place too high a priority on high mileage, instead of running faster pace work and low mileage.

Sue Strickland: I ran for 3.5 years before I felt that I could really begin to train right and hard enough. It is too easy to get burned out. I did that and quit running for over a year. I think there is a lot of pressure to perform well before one is ready, and you pay for it.

Alex Kasich: I usually train in a way that you could call "racing my way into shape." Ideally, I like to get at a certain fitness level, maintain a plateau, and race as long as I can.

John Lodwick: I have found that I always run better when my priorities are in line, when running does not take a dominant place in my life. My relationships with God, my wife, family, and friends must come before running, and when they do, running becomes a lot more enjoyable.

Hank Pfeifle: Rest is important; easy days must be built into a training schedule along with enough sleep at night. Regimentation is important; let your body get into a rhythm. Reevaluate your program; don't let yourself get stale.

Don Kardong: I am constantly changing my approach. I currently do almost no runs shorter than 9 to 10 miles. This allows several days a week of single workouts with a total mileage of about 110. I feel this allows for better recovery.

Chuck Smead: I seem to have most success with a mixture of long runs, fast running, interval, and hill running, as long as I don't overdo any one phase. I take 1 day off (30 minutes of slow running) per week. I also recommend taking the day off after any race, whether you feel tired or not.

Dave Smith: I feel the most important thing to do is to be adaptable to race conditions, as well as racing and training circumstances. Patience and understanding are two of the most important factors to keep in mind.

Amby Burfoot: My training has changed dramatically in the past few years, from 7 days a week (100 miles) to 4 days (50 miles). I have been amazed to find that I still run reasonably well on this kind of schedule; I'm less tired, never injured, and enjoying running more. I have taken out a lot of "empty miles" and replaced them with specific workouts, i.e., hills, track, fartlek, and over distance.

Kirk Pfeffer: No substitution for hard work.

John Dimick: I find that it is very important to keep some balance in your lifestyle. If running is the only interest you have, you will find injuries particularly devastating.

Stan Mavis: Training is like anything else: you have to plan and stick to the plan and workload.

Tony Staynings: I feel the most important aspect of both racing and training is to maintain a moderate sense of enjoyment. Too much stress and tension can prevent one from reaching his potential.

Henry Marsh: Listen to your body and obey it.

Jon Anderson: I believe the long Sunday run is most important to my training week. I usually do two other hard workouts in a week, one interval, one fartlek, and the other four days are easy.

Ray Flynn: It is very hard to quantify what an athlete does in a training session. It is not the number of miles, but how you do them. Also, types of training differ between mile and marathon training. It is much easier for a middle distance runner to compete often and use racing as part of training.

Herb Lindsay: To reduce stress to the body, I am now utilizing biking (long spins to 90–100 RPM's for 1 to 2 hours). I also swim repeat 440s and take long swims frequently. I like to run in 4 to 5 feet of water as a resistive workout.

Tom Fleming: If I were to do it all over again, I would have stayed with the shorter races and track longer before going to the marathon. I have run 51 marathons, 22 faster than 2:20 pace; it has taken a physical toll on my body.

Nancy Conz: I run as much as possible on soft surfaces to reduce chances for injuries, plus it's more enjoyable to run on trails or dirt roads. I take a fairly low-key approach to running and I enjoy it very much. I train hard, but I think that for myself it's important to have easy days as well. I've never had a coach, so I just do what I think is best and what I enjoy doing. I like running alone, because I must do my own workouts, not someone else's.

Marge Rosasco: I think quality miles in training are more important than quantity. In the past 3 years I've reduced my average pace per mile from 7:30 to 6:30 by pushing in my pace runs. Eventually the body adjusts—I just finished an 18 mile run (solo) in a 6:29 pace—starting with 6:40's and finishing with 6:15's. I'll never run sub 6's in training like Grete Waitz.

REFERENCES

Astrand, P. O., "Human physical fitness with special reference to sex and age," *Physiol. Rev.*, 36 (1956), 307–335.

Astrand, P. O. and K. Rodahl, *Testbook of work physiology* (New York: McGraw-Hill Book Company, 1970).

Bresnahan, George T., and Tuttle, W. W., *Track and field athletics* (St. Louis: The C. V. Mosby Company, 1937).

Conley, D. L., and Krahenbuhl, G. S., "Running economy and distance running performance of highly trained athletes," *Med. Sci. Sport and Exer.*, 12 (1980), 357–360.

Costill, D. L., *Prerequisites for successful distance running: A symposium on the medical and scientific aspects of distance running* (Muncie, Indiana:

Midwest Chapter of American College Sports Med., Ball State University, Nov., 1973).

Costill, D. L., and Fox, E. L., "Energetics of marathon running," *Med. Sci. Sport and Exer.*, 1 (1969), 81–86.

Costill, D., Thomason, H., and Roberts, E., "Fractional utilization of the aerobic capacity during distance running," *Med. Sci. Sport and Exer.*, 5 (1973), 248–252.

Costill, D. L., and Winroy, E., "Maximal oxygen intake among marathon runners," *Arch. Phys. Med. Rehab.*, 51 (1970), 317–320.

Daniels, J., "Physiological characteristics of champion male athletes," *Res. Q.*, 45 (1974), 342–348.

Daniels, J. T., "A five-year look at Jim Ryun: some physiological attributes of a champion miler," *The Physician and Sports Medicine* (In press).

Daniels, J. T., and Oldridge, N., "The effects of alternate exposure to altitude and sea level on world-class middle-distance runners," *Med. Sci. Sport and Exer.*, 2 (1970), 107–112.

Davies, C. T. M., and Thompson, M. W., "Aerobic performance of female marathon and male ultramarathon athletes," *Eur. J. Appl. Physiol.*, 41 (1979), 233–245.

Doherty, Ken, Ph.d., *Track and field omnibook* (Swarthmore, Pennsylvania: Tafmop Publishers, 1971).

Editors of *Sports Illustrated*, and Dunawaway, James O., *Sports Illustrated Book of Track and Field Running Events* (Philadelphia and New York: J. B. Lippincott Company, 1968).

Ekblom, B., and Hermansen, L., "Cardiac output in athletes," *J. Appl. Physiol.* 25 (1968), 619–625.

Ekblom, B., Astrnad, P. O., Saltin, B., Stenberg, J., and Wallstrom, B., "Effect of training on circulatory response to exercise," *J. Appl. Physiol.*, 24 (1968), 518–528.

Foster, C., Daniels, J. T., and Yarbrough, R. A., "Physiological training correlates of marathon running performance," *Aust. J. Sports Med.*, 9 (1977), 58–61.

Fox, E., and Mathews, D, *Interval Training* (Philadelphia: W. B. Saunders Co., 1974).

Hickson, R. C., and Rosenkoetter, M. A., "Reduced training frequencies and maintenance of increased aerobic power," *Med. Sci. Sport and Exer.*, 13 (1981), 13–16.

Hogan, R. D., Smith, M. G., and Gettman, L. R., "Marathon performance in relation to maximal aerobic power and training indices," *Med. Sci. Sport and Exer.*, 13 (1981), 185–189.

Homola, Samuel, *Muscle training for athletes* (West Nyack, New York: Parker Publishing Company, Inc., 1968).

Luke, Brother Gideon, *Coaching high school track and field* (Englewood Cliffs, New Jersey: Prentice-Hall, Inc., 1958).

O'Conner, Harold W., *Motivation and racing tactics in track and field.* (West Nyack, New York: Parker Publishing Company, Inc., 1970).

Saltin, B. and Astrand, P. O., "Maximal oxygen uptake in athletes," *J. Appl. Physiol.*, 23 (1967), 353–358.

Saltin, B., Blomquist, B., Mitchell, J. H., Johnson, Jr., R. L., Wildenthal, K., and Chapman, C. B., "Response to submaximal and maximal exercise after bed rest and training," *Circulation*, 38, Suppl. 7 (1968).

Start, J. B., and Himes, J., "The effect of warming-up on the incidence of muscle injury during activities involving maximal strength, speed and endurance," *J. of Sport Med.*, 3 (1963), 208–209.

Virw, A. A., Urgenstein, Y. U., and Pisuke, A. P., "Influence of training methods on endurance," *Track Technique*, 47 (1972), 1494–1495.

Wilt, F. with H. Falls, ed., *Training for competitive running, Exercise Physiology* (New York: Academic Press, 1968).

Wilt, Fred, and Ecker, Tom, *International track and field coaching encyclopedia* (West Nyack, New York: Parker Publishing Company, Inc., 1970).

The Development
of Strength

Improvements in muscle strength can aid athletic perform-ance. For optimal performance you should choose a type of strength training program that matches the type of athletic event. (Strength is defined as the force that a muscle group can exert in one maximal contraction.) Researchers have shown that by increasing strength, you will improve muscle en-durance and power. Muscle endurance, ability of the muscle to contract repeatedly with little fatigue, is very important for the distance runner in maintaining running pace, kicking at the end of a race, or running hills. Muscle power, the ability of the muscle to exert a great force in a very short time, is more important in sprint running or events that require a great ef-fort in a few seconds.

To illustrate the relationship between strength, power, and endurance and the specificity of training on performance, a recent study was conducted at the Olympic Training Center in Colorado Springs. In this study world class sprinters and distance runners were evaluated, using CYBEX isokinetic testing equipment, for leg strength, power, and endurance.

The runners consisted of three groups of athletes. All athletes were top U.S. runners in the marathon, 400 meters, and 100 meter distances. Maximal strength and power were measured at 6 different muscle contraction speeds. As you

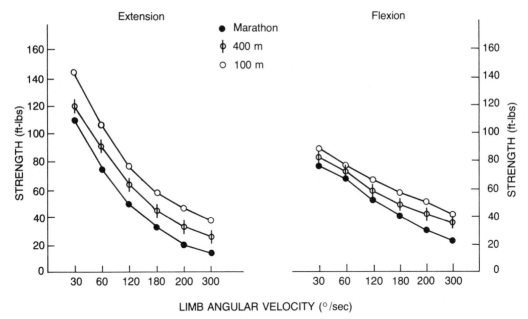

FIGURE 3-1. *Maximal strength comparison—flexion and extension.*

might expect, the 100 meter runners were considerably stronger at all contraction speeds (Figure 3-1) than were the 400 meter and marathon runners. This difference in strength was closely associated with higher power production by the sprinters (Figure 3-2). It is interesting to note the decrease in power by the marathon runners at the faster contraction speeds. This is probably due to the difference in the number of fast contracting muscle fibers and helps explain why marathon runners do not have explosive speed. However, when strength was measured for endurance, the marathon runners showed only an 11 percent decrease in strength while the sprinters had as much as 40 percent loss in maximal strength (Figure 3-3). This indicates that the greater strength and power of the sprinters are specifically for short term running, and that when maximal strength is needed for endurance, sprinters just don't have it.

This study is a good example of why strength training programs should be specifically for the development of muscular endurance and power. It is obvious that a distance runner would not train the same as a shotputter or sprint runner. Training specificity is very important, the major difference being in the intensity of lifting and the repetitions.

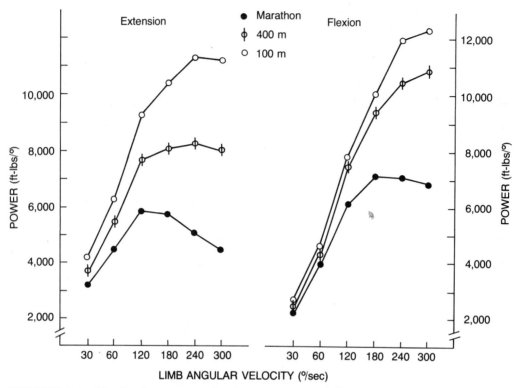

FIGURE 3-2. *Maximal power production comparison—flexion and extension.*

FIGURE 3-3. *Fatigue curve for marathon, 400 m., 100 m. runners.*

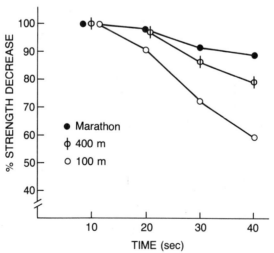

MUSCLE STRUCTURE

There are approximately 434 muscles in the human body, accounting for 40 to 45 percent of your body weight. Of these muscles, only 75 pairs are involved in general body movement. The development of strength for these muscles is specific for their particular function. To better understand muscle function and how strength can be improved, you need to know some of the basic anatomy of a skeletal muscle.

The smallest unit of a muscle is the muscle cell or fiber (Figure 3-4). Muscle cells are composed of fine thread-like filaments of contractile elements (myofibrils) that cause the muscle to change in length when the fiber is stimulated by the nervous system. Muscle cells are innervated by motor nerves from the spinal cord, making up the motor unit which is the functional aspect of muscle contraction. The number of muscle cells innervated by the motor nerves varies from only a few to over 1,000. The muscle fibers that are included in a motor unit will determine the gradation of movement. An example of this would be the fine control of the eye muscles which have only about 5 muscle fibers included in a motor unit, whereas the large muscles of the legs, which require less fine control,

FIGURE 3-4. *Levels of organization in the structure of skeletal muscle.*

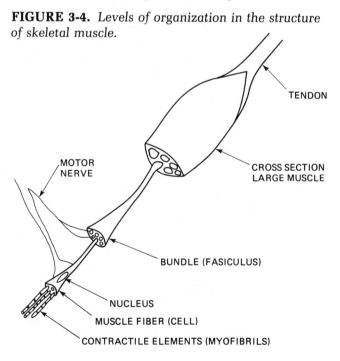

TENDON

MOTOR NERVE

CROSS SECTION LARGE MUSCLE

BUNDLE (FASICULUS)

NUCLEUS

MUSCLE FIBER (CELL)

CONTRACTILE ELEMENTS (MYOFIBRILS)

may have several hundred muscle cells included in a motor unit.

Many motor units make up the total muscle, and only when maximal strength is needed do all fire at the same time. There are different kinds of motor units. Motor units that contain slow contracting fibers (slow twitch) are more resistant to fatigue than the fast contracting motor units which are made up of fast twitch muscle fibers. The fast contracting motor units are responsible for power production, but they tire very rapidly. The kind of motor unit determines the type of strength training program needed for endurance or power.

The nucleus or "brain" of the muscle cell controls the subcellular processes that occur within the muscle cell. One of these processes is that of adaptation to physical training. The type of training imposed on the body will determine specific changes within the muscle cell. During growth and weight training, protein synthesis is controlled by the nucleus of the cell, building new tissue for greater strength.

The muscle cells are arranged into bundles (fasiculus) that make up the larger muscle. This cable-like structure of the muscle provides for the greater strength necessary in producing movement. The large muscle is attached to the body levers of the skeletal system by muscle tendons. Muscle tendons should not be confused with cartilage or ligaments which bind bones together at a joint. This gross structure of skeletal muscle is important to fully understand strength development and muscle contraction.

IMPROVING STRENGTH

Many people confuse weight training with weight lifting. Weight lifting is an international competitive sport, while weight training is a method of improving muscle strength.

The overload principle is the basis of all weight training programs. This principle contends that by applying a greater than normal stress on the body, it will respond by adjusting or adapting to that stress. Muscle size, strength, and endurance increase as a result of repeated overload. Because these changes are slow in happening, a gradual program of progressive resistance should be used. This program will depend upon three major variables—resistance placed on the muscles (overload), duration of stress, and frequency of the training sessions.

Strength training programs can basically be the same for men and women. Women gain in strength just as men do; however, due to hormonal differences, women usually don't gain in strength to the same degree as men and are usually lower in initial strength. Increases in muscle strength are often attributed to increases in muscle size. The cross sectional area of a muscle is proportional to the strength of that muscle. The maximal force that a muscle can exert is approximately 3 to 4 kilograms per cubic centimeter of muscle. The increase in muscle size is due to a greater number of contractile elements (myofibrils) contained in each muscle fiber. Weight training stimulates the production of these contractile elements, increasing muscle size and strength. Because of the hormonal differences, women don't have to worry about developing large bulging muscles; although not all is known about the role of hormones in stimulating muscle growth, it is known that the male hormone testosterone is important for developing muscle size and strength.

Muscle strength can be developed in other ways without increasing the size of the muscle. Distance runners do not possess large bulky muscles, but their muscles are strong for the function they perform. Muscle strength can be developed by neuro-muscular adaptation. This means that a muscle can develop more strength by activating more muscle fibers or motor units per contraction or by increasing the frequency of the impulses coming from the nervous system. Weight training can increase the number of fibers recruited, bringing about a more synchronous firing of motor units. Some of these adaptations may be learned, accounting for the rapid gains in strength during the early stages of weight training.

Improvement in strength varies from individual to individual. Differences in body type, age, sex, and genetic makeup cause rates of improvement to vary. Today there are several types of programs that will increase muscular strength, power, and endurance. Everyone has to evaluate the benefits of each program and match it to his or her personality and objective for weight training.

There are three types of muscle contraction; each type has been used as the basis for a type of training method.

Isotonic exercises are designed to work the entire range of motion of a joint in one contraction. Isotonic movement includes two types of muscle contraction, concentric and eccentric. When the muscle shortens causing movement, it is called concentric muscle contraction or positive work. When the muscle lengthens during isotonic contraction, it is called eccentric or negative work. The third kind of muscle contraction is called isometric. During an isometric contraction the muscle is working against a great resistance in which no movement is accomplished. Isometric or static contractions technically perform no work, even though the muscle is subjected to a great stress.

All types of muscle contractions when done repeatedly under greater than normal resistance will develop strength. However, in order to be specific for the correct kind of development, different programs should be used to meet the needs of the athlete.

Isometric Programs

The oldest and most simple exercise program involves the isometric principle. This type of program is accomplished by applying as much muscle strength as possible to an immovable object. As muscle tension is increased and maintained for short periods of time (5 to 8 seconds), muscles are strengthened. The advantages of this program are that no equipment is needed and it can be done almost anywhere. The disadvantage of isometric programs is that the greatest strength is only at one angle of the total range of motion. Since strength training for endurance involves total range of movement, isometrics are of little value for the runner.

Isotonic Programs

Isotonic exercises are performed through a range of motion. This form of exercise involves physically lifting or pulling a resistance or object to a predetermined position and then returning it to its original position. Strength gained will be developed throughout the total range of movement.

Before starting a program, you should carefully plan out your strategy. Strength programs for development of bulk, endurance, and power are different even though there may be some overlap. Weight lifting terminology should be understood and used when planning your program.

- *Repetition Maximum* (RM)—This term indicates the maximum resistance that can be lifted for the indicated number of repetitions.
- *Repetition*—The total number of contractions of executions of a particular exercise.
- *Set*—One set is the number of repetitions done consecutively, without resting.

Athletes use strength training as a supplement to their entire training program and should be concerned only about developing those muscles that will help in improving performance in their event. Muscular strength for greater power production is best achieved when the resistance is high and the number of repetitions is low; this type of program sometimes results in greater muscle hypertrophy. An example of a power program would involve a resistance that could only be lifted 6 to 10 times maximally. This would be repeated 2 to 3 times (sets) with rest intervals between each set. As a general rule, about 1 to 2 minutes of rest are taken between each set of exercises and 2 to 3 minutes between each different exercise.

Muscular endurance is best developed when the resistance is relatively low and the number of repetitions high. With this kind of program you would use lighter weights and lift them 15 to 20 times RM per set. The same number of sets may be performed as in the program for power production.

Isotonic programs have several advantages. The exercises can be planned to cover the specific muscle groups that need to be strengthened. It is also easy to adjust to the specific kind of program for power or endurance development.

SPECIFIC MUSCLE GROUPS NEED IMPROVEMENT IN RUNNERS

Many runners ignore the fact that upper body strength is important in running. The muscles of the shoulders, back, abdomen, and arms are important in maintaining running posture and balance (Figure 3-5). You should know some of the anatomy that is associated with running, in order to better plan an effective strength training program.

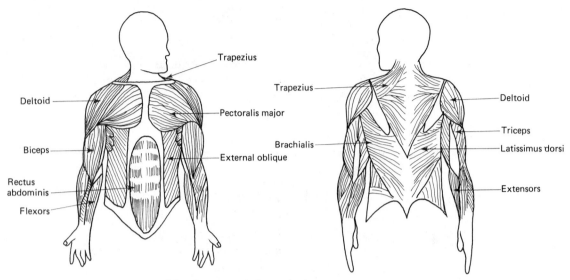

FIGURE 3-5. *Front and back view of the muscles of the upper body.*

The latissimus dorsi muscle is a triangular muscle that covers the lower part of the back, sweeps upward, and attaches to the upper arm bone. It's responsible for pulling the arm and shoulder backward and rotating the arm inward. This muscle and the pectoralis major muscles covering the upper front part of the chest are important for the arm swing during running.

The deltoid muscles of the shoulders and the trapezius muscle of the upper back are important in shoulder movement and help in maintaining running posture. Other muscles that are important in maintaining balance and arm movement are the biceps and triceps of the upper arm.

The muscles of the abdomen aid breathing, help in maintaining posture, and support the internal organs of the body. Because runners sometimes overlook abdominal muscles, they may develop low back pain. The muscles of the lower back may overdevelop in relation to the abdominal muscles, resulting in a disalignment of the spine and the pelvis and causing irritation to nerves coming from the spinal cord.

Development of these major muscles of the upper body will help in sustaining running form and posture, important during hill running and kicking at the end of a race. The following weight lifting exercises, using freeweights, are designed for greater strength development of the upper body.

Two-Arm Front Curl

Starting Position

Ending Position

PURPOSE
To develop arm flexors, biceps, and muscles of the forearm.

STARTING
POSITION
Hold the bar in front of your thighs with the palms facing outward. Your hands should be approximately shoulder width apart.

MOVEMENT
With your elbows close to your sides, bring the weight up to your chest by flexing your arms at the elbow. The tendency for the elbows to move backward should be avoided. Do not jerk or heave the bar; it should be a continuous movement. Slowly return the bar to the starting position. This exercise can be done with barbells or dumbells.

Triceps Extension (lying on a bench)

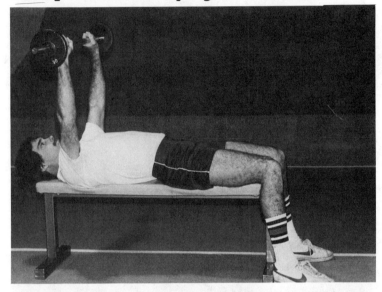

Starting Position

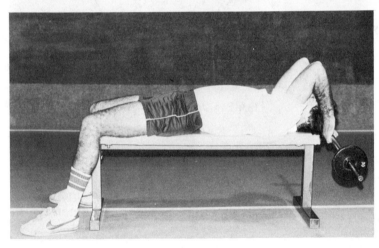

Ending Position

PURPOSE   To develop the triceps and muscles of the forearm.

STARTING   While lying on your back, fully extend your arms upward, sup-
POSITION   porting the weight with elbows locked.

MOVEMENT   Slowly lower the bar down to the bench over your head and
return to starting position.

Triceps Extension (standing)

Starting Position   Ending Position

PURPOSE   To develop the triceps and muscles of the forearm.

STARTING   While standing, fully extend your arms upward, supporting
POSITION   the weight with elbows locked.

MOVEMENT   Slowly lower the bar down behind your head and return to
starting position.

Two Arm Standing Press (barbell press)

Starting Position

Ending Position

PURPOSE	To strengthen shoulders, deltoids, triceps, and upper back muscles.
STARTING POSITION	Hold the barbell to your chest with your palms forward and hands shoulder width apart. Your feet should be shoulder width apart and knees locked to provide balance and support.
MOVEMENT	Slowly push the bar over your head; your arms should be fully extended. Slowly lower the bar back to the starting position.

Arm Pullover

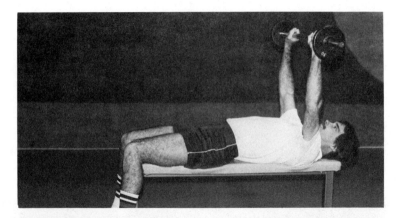

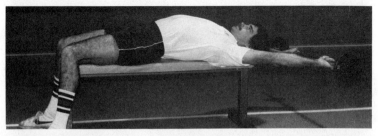

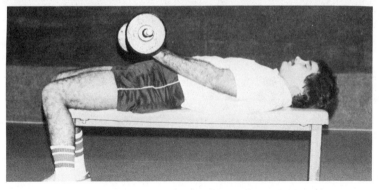

PURPOSE	To strengthen the muscles of the chest and shoulders.
STARTING POSITION	While lying on your back, support the weight at arms length over your head; your hands should be 10 to 12 inches apart.
MOVEMENT	Keeping your arms straight, lower the weight over your head, slowly bring it back to the starting position, and lower the weight to your thighs, keeping your arms straight. Return to starting position. You should inhale deeply when lowering the bar.

High Pull-Ups

Starting Position

Ending Position

PURPOSE
To strengthen the shoulders, upper back muscles, biceps, and forearm muscles.

STARTING POSITION
Hold the bar with your hands together and palms facing inward; rest the bar on the front of your thighs with your arms extended.

MOVEMENT
Pull the bar up to your chin; your elbows should be raised as high as possible. Slowly return the bar to the starting position.

Lateral Arm Raise

Starting Position

Ending Position

PURPOSE
To strengthen the deltoids and other muscles of the shoulders.

STARTING POSITION
Hold a dumbell in each hand with your palms facing inward and your arms hanging down at your sides.

MOVEMENT
Raise your arms out to the side until the weight is slightly above the level of your shoulders. Return the weight to the starting position.

Bench Press

Starting Position

Ending Position

PURPOSE
To strengthen the extensors of the arms, and muscles of the shoulders and chest (triceps, deltoids, pectoralis major).

STARTING POSITION
While lying on your back, rest the weight over your chest. Your arms should be a little more than shoulder width apart and the palms of your hands should be facing your feet.

MOVEMENT
Push the bar to arms length over your chest, and lower it slowly to the starting position. You should take certain precautions to avoid dropping the weight when you are fatigued. Lift with a spotter present to help in controlling the weight.

The muscles of the legs and buttocks are of major importance for the driving force needed to push the body forward when running. Greater strength in the muscles of the upper and lower legs (Figure 3-6) will help in maintaining a smooth, even stride length and knee lift during the later stages of endurance running as fatigue increases.

The large gluteus muscles of the buttocks help in maintaining an erect posture during running and walking. The quadricep muscles on the front of the thigh are made up of four parts, hence the name "quad," meaning four. The quadriceps are responsible for extension of the lower leg during the running stride.

The muscles located on the back of the upper leg are called the hamstring muscles. The hamstrings are composed of the biceps femoris, the semitendinosus, and the semimembranosus. These muscles are responsible for bending the leg at the knee; therefore, the hamstrings are important in producing a driving force in running.

The gastrocnemius and soleus muscles of the lower leg make up the calf muscle. These muscles are very important in running, because they enable the runner to rise on the balls of the feet, providing for much of the push-off during the running stride. The gastrocnemius is attached to the heel of the foot by the Achilles tendon, the largest tendon of the body. Because of the continuous driving force needed in running, the Achilles tendon is many times injured or inflamed. It is very important to increase the strength of the calf muscles and the Achilles tendon to help in avoiding injury.

FIGURE 3-6. *Front and back view of the muscles of the legs.*

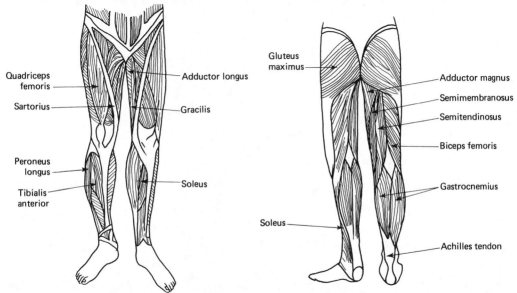

Half Squat

Starting Position   **Ending Position**

PURPOSE
To strengthen the quadricep and knee extensor muscles of the thigh.

STARTING POSITION
Rest the barbell on your shoulders behind your head. Your feet should be spread slightly for balance.

MOVEMENT
Slowly squat down until your thighs are parallel to the floor. Slowly rise to the starting position. Be sure to keep your back straight to avoid possible injury.

Starting Position

Ending Position

PURPOSE   To strengthen the calf muscles.

STARTING   Rest the barbell on your shoulders behind the head, just as in
POSITION   the half squat.

MOVEMENT   Raise up on your toes as high as possible, then return slowly to
the starting position. To increase the range through which the
calf muscles work, stand on a board with your heels lower
than your toes.

Knee Extension (Extension, Flexion Machine)

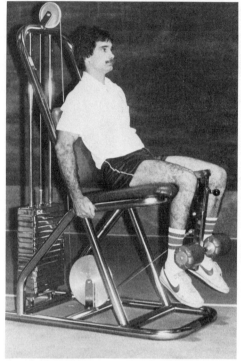

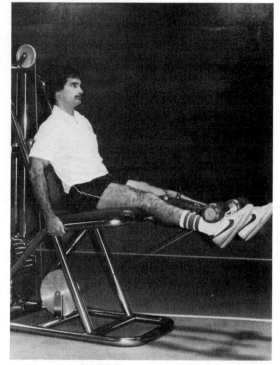

Starting Position   **Ending Position**

PURPOSE   To strengthen the quadricep muscles of the thigh.

STARTING   Sit on the end of the bench with the padded resistance bar
POSITION   resting on the front of your lower shins at the ankles. Your
           hands should be gripping the bench behind your hips.

MOVEMENT   Extend your legs out straight, raising the resistance bar. Slow-
           ly return to the starting position. This exercise can be done
           with both legs at the same time or one leg at a time.

Knee Flexion (Flexion, Extension Machine)

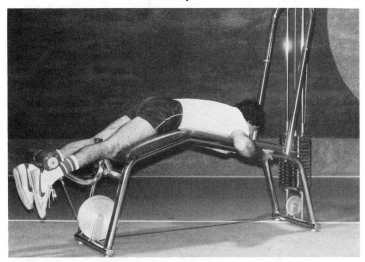

Starting Position

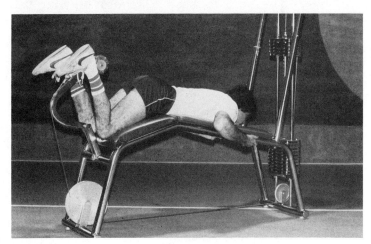

Ending Position

PURPOSE

To strengthen the hamstring muscles of the upper leg.

STARTING
POSITION

While lying on your stomach on the bench, hook your heels under the padded lever bar. Grip the sides of the bench with your hands to avoid sliding.

MOVEMENT

Flex the legs at the knees, raising the weight. Slowly return to the starting position. This exercise can be done with both legs or one leg at a time.

It is very important to follow a planned routine when lifting weights for strength development. Athletes need to train scientifically in order to achieve maximum results. The following hints should be considered when planning and conducting a program for distance runners.

Helpful Hints

1. The number of workouts for general strength training should be 2 to 3 days per week, with at least 1 day of rest between each workout session.

2. A good warmup of jogging, bending, and stretching should precede each workout.

3. Select 8 to 10 exercises that are specific for your needs.

4. Be sure to keep a record of your exercises with the number of repetitions, sets, and poundage used.

5. Your first workout should only include 1 set of each exercise selected. You should build up to 3 sets per exercise by the end of the second or third week.

6. Assuming you are performing 3 sets of an exercise, you should increase the weight, from the first set to the second set and from the second set to the third set, in a gradual manner. Example: set, 50 pounds; 2nd set, 55 pounds; 3rd set, 60 pounds. The muscle will build into the stress of the exercise.

7. As a general rule, about 1 to 2 minutes of rest are taken between sets and approximately 3 to 4 minutes between each exercise.

8. When performing each exercise, breathe properly. *DO NOT* hold your breath for several repetitions, but breathe between each repetition. A general rule for all exercises is that the breath is taken before the exertion part of the exercise.

9. The number of repetitions should be 15 to 20 per set for greater endurance development, and 6 to 10 repetitions per set for power development.

10. Always do the movement to the full range of emotion.

11. Change your poundage *only* when it gets easy. *DO NOT* try to lift heavy weights.

12. Do all sets of 1 exercise before moving on to the next exercise.

13. Remember, weight training is only a supplement to your total program and should not be substituted for your running.

14. Choose the program to meet your needs and make up your mind to stick to it. Don't waste your time by lifting only when you feel like it.

To achieve top performance levels you have to train regularly and in the correct way. You can expect best results from your training program if it is progressive and properly proportioned, taking into account age, physical capabilities, and personal objectives. Your weekly and monthly training should lead to your overall aim of performance. The following program for strength for better endurance is an example of a systematic approach to a 6 week program. Determining what weight resistance to start with will require some experimentation on your part (see Table 3-1).

When the poundage increases, the number of sets decreases. This type of progressive resistance program is important in avoiding injury to muscles and joints. Injury caused by a weight training program will cause a setback in your running. Be patient and do not try to lift heavy weights before you are ready.

TABLE 3-1. *Suggested starting weights for a beginning endurance lifting program for runners.*

Exercise	Reps	Sets	Suggested Weight
Two Arm Front Curl	20	3	25 lbs.
Triceps Extension (standing)	20	3	10 lbs.
Triceps Extension (lying)	20	3	10 lbs.
Two Arm Standing Press	20	3	30 lbs.
Arm Pullover	15-20	3	10 lbs.
High Pull-ups	20	3	20 lbs.
Lateral Arm Raise	15-20	3	5 lbs.
Bench Press	20	3	40 lbs.
Half Squat	20	3	45 lbs.
Heel Raise	20	3	45 lbs.
Knee Extension	15-20	3	20 lbs.
Knee Flexion	15-20	3	15 lbs.

Six week strength endurance program for distance runners

WEEK #1 (Monday, Wednesday, Friday)

Selected Exercise	Reps	Sets	Poundage
Two Arm Front Curl	20	1	25 lbs.
Triceps Extension (standing)	20	1	10 lbs.
Half Squat	20	1	45 lbs.
Heel Raise	20	1	45 lbs.
Bench Press	20	1	40 lbs.
Arm Pullover	15	1	10 lbs.
Knee Extension	15	1	20 lbs.
Knee Flexion	15	1	15 lbs.
High Pull-ups	20	1	20 lbs.

WEEK #2 (Monday, Wednesday, Friday)

Selected Exercise	Reps	Sets	Poundage
Two Arm Front Curl	20	2	25 lbs.
Triceps Extension (standing)	20	2	10 lbs.
Half Squat	20	2	45 lbs.
Heel Raise	20	2	45 lbs.
Bench Press	20	2	40 lbs.
Arm Pullover	18	2	10 lbs.
Knee Extension	18	2	20 lbs.
Knee Flexion	18	2	15 lbs.
High Pull-ups	20	2	20 lbs.

WEEK #3 (Monday, Wednesday, Friday)

Selected Exercise	Reps	Sets	Poundage
Two Arm Front Curl	20	3	25 lbs.
Triceps Extension (standing)	20	3	10 lbs.
Half Squat	20	3	45 lbs.
Heel Raise	20	3	45 lbs.
Bench Press	20	3	40 lbs.
Arm Pullover	20	3	10 lbs.
Knee Extension	20	3	20 lbs.
Knee Flexion	20	3	15 lbs.
High Pull-ups	20	3	20 lbs.

WEEK #4 (Monday, Wednesday, Friday)

Selected Exercise	Reps	Sets	Poundage
Two Arm Front Curl	20	2	30 lbs.
Triceps Extension (standing)	20	2	15 lbs.
Half Squat	20	2	50 lbs.
Heel Raise	20	2	50 lbs.
Bench Press	20	2	45 lbs.
Arm Pullover	15	2	15 lbs.
Knee Extension	15	2	25 lbs.
Knee Flexion	15	2	20 lbs.
High Pull-ups	20	2	25 lbs.

WEEK #5 (Monday, Wednesday, Friday)

Selected Exercise	Reps	Sets	Poundage
Two Arm Front Curl	20	3	30 lbs.
Triceps Extension (standing)	20	3	15 lbs.
Half Squat	20	3	50 lbs.
Heel Raise	20	3	50 lbs.
Bench Press	20	3	45 lbs.
Arm Pullover	18	3	15 lbs.
Knee Extension	18	3	25 lbs.
Knee Flexion	18	3	20 lbs.
High Pull-ups	20	3	25 lbs.

WEEK #6 (Monday, Wednesday, Friday)

Selected Exercise	Reps	Sets	Poundage
Two Arm Front Curl	20	3	30 lbs.
Triceps Extension (standing)	20	3	15 lbs.
Half Squat	20	3	50 lbs.
Heel Raise	20	3	50 lbs.
Bench Press	20	3	45 lbs.
Arm Pullover	20	3	15 lbs.
Knee Extension	20	3	25 lbs.
Knee Flexion	20	3	20 lbs.
High Pull-ups	20	3	25 lbs.

Isokinetic Programs

A third type of training, isokinetic training, combines the good from both isometric and isotonic programs. This method uses the resistance as a function of the force applied. In order to understand this principle, we have to look at the mechanical analysis of body movement.

The long bones of the skeletal system serve as levers for movement, and the muscular system provides the means for applying force to these levers, resulting in motion. The amount of effort required by the muscle depends on the length of the levers, muscle attachment, and angle of the joint. As the angle of the joint changes during flexion and extension, the mechanical advantage also changes, requiring more or less muscle tension throughout the full range of movement.

Isokinetic methods use specially designed equipment that retards the speed at which the user can move through the range of motion. The user applies maximum effort and the resistance automatically varies to accommodate to the muscles' change in mechanical advantage. The muscle is working optimally at every angle or point in the full range of movement. Most of the isokinetic equipment, such as the CYBEX machine, is very expensive and would be prohibitive for most people to buy.

Nautilus, Universals, mini-gyms and the exer-geni are other examples of equipment that accommodate to the resistance change through a range of motion. These machines use various sizes of cams that will develop tension differences as the angle of the joint changes its mechanical advantage. These machines combine the isotonic principle and the isokinetic principle in improving strength and endurance. The major problem with these machines is that there is no way to tell accurately how much force is being applied to the muscle with the plates lifted. This equipment, too, is very expensive, and the less expensive machines make it very hard to evaluate progress.

In determining the best kind of program for strength development, you have to evaluate each program and the availability of equipment. Compare the kinds of programs and equipment in order to make your decision.

Isometrics

Advantage: Little or no equipment needed; little time involved for the workout.

Disadvantage: Boring, hard to evaluate progress, and because of isometric or static contraction, does not develop strength through the entire range of movement.

Isotonic

Advantage: The equipment (free weights) is inexpensive and is generally available. Specific muscle groups may be strengthened through various designed exercises. Strength is gained throughout the range of motion.

Disadvantage: Resistance is nonaccommodating to changes in mechanical advantage. Workout time is increased because of changing weights for different exercises.

Isokinetic

Advantage: The lever system allows the resistance to change throughout the full range of motion. There is also less chance for muscle soreness and injury.

Disadvantage: Equipment is expensive and the exercise movements are limited.

There are alternatives to these basic kinds of training programs. Calisthenics are useful in developing greater flexibility and strength. For instance, sit-ups, pull-ups, push-ups and arm circles are a few examples of exercises that require no equipment and that aid in development of muscle tone and flexibility. However, most calisthenic exercises are limited to the upper body and do not provide the degree of strength development that the progressive resistance programs do.

Circuit Weight Training

Circuit weight training is a relatively new concept in training. The general purpose of circuit training is to develop muscular strength, muscular endurance and cardiovascular endurance all at the same time. Circuit training has several advantages and can be used with any of the methods of training— isometric, isotonic, and isokinetics. It can be done with little or no equipment and can accommodate large numbers of athletes at the same time.

Circuit training uses the element of time for each exercise, instead of a set number of repetitions. In circuit weight training an individual performs the exercise as many times as possible in a defined period of time, and the rest interval between each exercise is very short in order to keep the heart rate elevated.

The following steps are used in planning a circuit weight training program:

1. Select 8 to 10 exercise stations that are specific for your training needs.
2. The exercises should be arranged in the circuit so that the same muscle groups are not exercised in succession.
3. Determine a designated time period for execution of each exercise.
4. Record the total number of repetitions completed for each exercise and the total time elapsed during the entire circuit. This serves as an evaluation of your progress; you should strive for more repetitions as you get stronger.
5. Repeat the circuit several times as you advance into the program.

On the next page is an example of a circuit weight training program using the five steps.

Exercise time: 30 seconds, 10 exercise stations, 15 seconds rest interval between each station.

Circuit training is very vigorous and is an excellent type of training program for off-season training where the emphasis is not only on strength development but also on aerobic conditioning. Research has shown that circuit training is effective for both men and women and is ideal for the coach when training the entire team at the same time.

In summary, various weight training programs have been developed over the years to improve athletic performance. A program of progessive resistance causes alterations in the

Station	Exercise	Muscle Groups
#1	Sit-ups	Abdominal muscles
#2	Half Squat	Quadriceps and muscles of the thigh
#3	Two Arm Front Curl	Biceps and muscles of the forearm
#4	Heel Raise	Calf muscles
#5	Bench Press	Triceps, deltoids and muscles of the chest
#6	Knee Flexion	Hamstring muscles
#7	Triceps Extension (standing)	Triceps and forearm muscles
#8	Knee Extension	Quadricep muscle of thigh
#9	High Pull-ups	Shoulder, upper back and arms
#10	Leg Press	Muscles of the thigh

muscle's contractile elements and neuromuscular recruitment, resulting in greater strength production. Greater strength is positively correlated with improvement in muscular endurance and power. Men and women both gain in strength when subjected to weight training; however, due to hormonal differences, women usually don't gain in muscle bulk as much as men.

Isotonic and isokinetic programs have been found to be more effective than isometric or calisthenic programs for strength development. Circuit training is advocated for those sports that require high levels of strength, power, and muscular endurance. The use of strength training can aid athletic performance and should be used as a supplement to running, but not as a substitute.

Retention of Strength and Muscular Endurance - There has been some concern in the past about the loss of strength gains after a weight training program has been stopped. Research indicates that once strength has been developed, the rate of decline is slower than was the rate of development. This is very important because many runners do not like to continue lifting weights during the competitive season.

In a study conducted by Berger, it was found that strength gained during a 3 week program of 3 times per week was not lost after training had been stopped. The retention of the strength gained was still evident even after 6 weeks of no training.

Muscular endurance is also lost at a slower rate than was the development time (Figure 3-7). Retention of endurance after an 8 week program of 3 days per week using high repetitions was not lost even after 12 weeks of no training; 70 percent of the gained endurance was still maintained. Most of the loss was noticed during the first few weeks after training stopped.

The retention of strength and endurance after training may be maintained using as little as 1 workout per week. However, even a slight amount of decline may reduce performance of some events. The training specificity is very important for strength retention.

Athletes were surveyed to see whether or not they use weight training as a part of their training program. The responses showed that about half did use some kind of strength training program. Most athletes use light weights and train for upper body strength more than lower body strength. Most of the athletes who weight train use some kind of specialized lifting equipment, such as Nautilus or Universal Gyms.

Although the sample size was small, the female runners surveyed all use some form of strength training as a part of their running program.

FIGURE 3-7. Weeks of training & no training

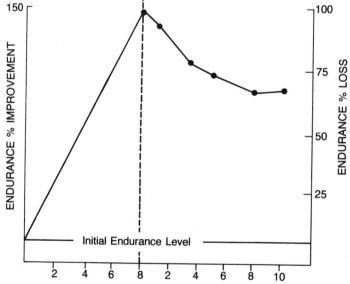

Summary of athletes' responses to weight training

Athlete	Weight Train	Times/Week	Time of Year	Major Emphasis	Type of Lifting	Equipment
John Anderson	Yes	1–2	During build-up	Upper body	Light weights	Free weights & Universal Gym
Alex Kasich	No					
Alberto Salazar	Yes	2	Just started	Lower body	Light weights	Nautilus
Lee Fiddler	No					
Paul Geis	Yes	3	Fall, winter early spring	2/3 Upper 1/3 Lower	Heavy weights	Free weights
Henry Marsh	No					
Ken Moore	Yes	2	Almost all year stopping 10 days before major race	Upper body	Light weights	Free weights & Pull-up bar
Jeff Wells	No					
Frank Shorter	Yes	3	1–2 months in fall & winter	Upper body	Light weights	Free weights & Nautilus
Don Kardong	No					
Amby Burfoot	Yes	3	Whenever I have time. Running training not considered.	Upper body	Light weights	Free weights & Universal Gym
Dick Quax	No					
Chuck Smead	No					
Ellison Goodall	Yes	every day ½ hour	Build-up phase & coming off injuries	Upper body	Light weights	Free weights & Universal Gym
Kirk Pfeffer	No					
Gary Fanelli	Yes	3	Off-season & build-up phase	Upper & lower body	Heavy weights Pull-ups & abdominal exercises	10% Free weights 90% Universal Gym
Tony Staynings	No					
Hank Pfeifle	Yes	3	Build-up phase	Upper body	Light weights Sit-ups (incline board) push-ups	Inner tube tacked or hung from wall or low branch

Summary of athletes' responses to weight training (continued)

Athlete	Weight Train	Times/Week	Time of Year	Major Emphasis	Type of Lifting	Equipment
Dave Babriacki	Yes	2	Build-up phase only	Upper body	Light weights	Free weights & Nautilus
Bill Rogers	Yes	2	From November to March, cool weather months	Upper body	Light weights	Free weights, occasional sit-ups & push-ups
Jon Sinclair	Yes	3	Off-season	Upper body	8–12 reps maximum	Nautilus
Charlie Vigil	Yes	every other day	All year	Lower body	2–3 sets of 12–15 reps maximum	Free weights
Robert Hodge	Yes	every other day	During build-up period, not at all near races.	Upper body	Light weights	Free weights & Universal Gym
Steve Flanagan	No					
Lionel Ortega	Yes	2	Pre-season & off-season	Upper body	Light weights	Free weights
Jeff Galloway	No					
Steve Plasencia	Yes		Usually in streaks	Upper body	Light weights	Universal Gym & Nautilus
Mike Roche	Yes	2	All year when possible	Upper & lower body	Medium weight 10 RM	Free weights & Universal Gym
John Flora	No					
Kevin McCarey	Yes	3	Lift right up to competitive season	Upper body	Light weights	Free weights
Doug Brown	No					
Benji Durden	Yes	2	Year-round except 1 week before & after marathons or key road races	Upper body	Light weights	Universal Gym & Nautilus
John Lodwick	Very little			Upper body	Push-ups after morning run	
Nancy Conz	No					
Marc Nenow	No					
Mary Decker	Yes	2–3		Upper body	Light	Nautilus
Tom Fleming	No					

Name	Weight train	Times/week	When	Body area	Weight	Equipment
Herb Lindsey	Yes	2–3	on noninterval days	Both, more aggressive with upper body	Light (20 reps)	Nautilus
Ray Flynn	Yes	3	During build-up Fall, little during competitive season	Upper body	Light	Free weights
Marge Rosasco	Yes	2–3	When racing a lot but only when not tired	Upper body	Light	Free weights
Laurie Binder	Yes	3	Every week	Upper body	Light weights	Free weights chin-ups on curl bar.
Patti Catalona	Yes	3	12 months	Upper & lower	Heavy weights	Nautilus
Sue Strickland	Yes		Sporadically I need to be more consistant	Upper	Light weights	Nautilus
Dave Smith	Yes	2	During times of little competition	Upper body	Light weights	Free weights & Universal Gym
Garry Bjorklund	Yes	3	Through fall and winter months	Upper body	Light weights	Free weights & Universal Gym
Mike Slack	Yes	3	During times when there is very little racing	Upper body	Light weights	Free weights
Grete Waitz	No					
Greg Meyer	Yes	2–3	No change unless big race coming	Upper & lower	Light weights	Universal Gym & Nautilus
Stan Mavis	No					
Jim Crawford	Yes	2–3	Fall and winter months	Upper body	Light weights	Free weights or Universal Gym
Donna Burge	Yes	3	All year except when tapering for race	Upper & lower	Light weights	Free weights & Universal Gym
Lorraine Moller	No		I swim a mile or so twice a week to develop upper body strength			
Dick Beardsley	Yes, just started Nov.	Every other day	Nov. 1 to heavy racing schedule	Upper & lower	Light weights	Free weights & Universal Gym

REFERENCES

Berger, R., "Effect of varied weight training programs on strength," *Res. Q.*, 33 (1962), 168–181.

Brown, C. K., and Wilmore, J. H., "The effects of maximal resistance training on strength and body composition of women athletes," *Med. Sci. Sport and Exer.*, 6 (1974), 174–177.

Clark, D. H., "Adaptations in strength and muscular endurance resulting from exercise," *Exercise and Sport Revew*, 1 (1973), 73–102.

Fahey, T. D., and Brown, D. H., "The effects of an anabolic steroid on the strength, body composition, and endurance of college males when accompanied by a weight training program," *Med. Sci. Sport and Exer.*, 5 (1973), 272–276.

Fahey, T. D., Rolph, R., Moungmee, P., Nagel, J., and Mortara, S., "Serum testosterone, body composition, and strength of young adults," *Med. Sci. Sport and Exer.*, 8 (1976), 31–34.

Gettman, L. R., Ayres, J. J., Pollock, M. L., and Jackson, A., "The effect of circuit weight training on strength, cardiorespiratory function, and body composition of adult men," *Med. Sci. Sport and Exer.*, 10 (1978), 75–78.

Gettman, L. R., Ward, P., and Hogan, R. D., "A comparison of combined running and weight training with circuit weight training," *Med. Sci. Sport and Exer.*, 14 (1982), 229–234.

Goldberg, A. L., "Mechanisms of growth and atrophy of skeletal muscle," *Muscle Biology* (P. Cassens, ed.) (New York: Dekker, 1972), 89–115.

Hislop, H. and Perrine, J., "The isokinetic concept of exercise," *Phys. Therm.* 47 (1967), 114–117.

Johnson, B. L., "Eccentric vs. concentric muscle training for strength development," *Med. Sci. Sport and Exer.*, 4 (1972), 111–115.

Johnson, B. L., Adamczyk, J. W., Tennoe, K. O., and Stromme, S. B., "A comparison of concentric and eccentric muscle training," *Med. Sci. Sport and Exer.*, 8 (1976), 35–38.

Lamb, D. R., *Physiology of Exercise, Responses and Adaptations* (New York: Macmillan, 1978).

Larsson, L., "Physical training effects on muscle morphology in sedentary males at different ages," *Med. Sci. Sports and Exer.*, 14 (1982), 203–206.

Lesmes, G. R., Costill, D. L., Coyle, E. F., and Fink, W. J., "Muscle strength and power changes during maximal isokinetic training," *Med. Sci. Sport and Exer.*, 10 (1978), 266–269.

Moffroid, M., Whipple, R., Hofkosh, H., Lowman, E., and Thistle, H., "A study of isokinetic exercise," *Phys. Ther.*, 49 (1969), 735–746.

Pipes, T. V. and Wilmore, J., "Isokinetics vs. isotonic strength training in adult men," *Med. Sci. Sport and Exer.*, 7 (1975), 262–274.

Rasch, P. J., *Weight Training*, (Dubuque, Iowa; Wm. C. Brown, 1966).

Syster, B., and Stull, G., "Muscular endurance retention as a function of length of detraining," *Res. Q.*, 41 (1970), 105–109.

Thorstensson, A., "Muscle strength, fiber type and enzyme activities in men," *Acta. Physiol. Scand. Suppl.*, (1976).

Thorstensson, A., Larson, L., Tesch, P., and Karlsson, J., "Muscle strength and fiber composition in athletes and sedentary men," *Med. Sci. Sport and Exer.*, 9 (1977), 26–30.

Waldman, R., and Stull, G., "Effects of various periods of inactivities on retention of newly acquired levels of muscular endurance," *Res. Q.*, 40 (1969), 396–401.

Wilmore, J. H., Parr, R. B., Girandola, R. N., et al, "Physiological alterations consequent to circuit weight training," *Med. Sci. Sport and Exer.*, 10 (1978), 79–84.

Wilmore, J. H., Parr, R. B., Ward, P., et al, "Energy cost of circuit weight training," *Med. Sci. Sport and Exer.*, 10 (1978), 75–78.

4

Stretching

Running is brought about by a combination of coordinated forces produced by the muscles of the legs, buttocks, and back. The arms, shoulders, chest and abdominal muscles are also important for running posture and balance. Because of the great number of muscles involved in running, it is no wonder that all kinds of aches and pains may crop up during your training. The constant pounding that comes with running can cause muscles to become tight and inflexible. When this happens, injuries are more likely to occur.

Muscle and tendon strains are less likely to be a problem if properly stretched before your training session. Stretching helps to increase blood circulation, flexibility, and range of motion in a joint. Stretching reduces the muscle tension and helps the muscle to relax. Many injuries or cases of muscle soreness can be eliminated if proper warmup and stretching are a part of your running program.

Stretching should not be taken lightly as a part of your daily program. Proper technique is essential for full benefit. 10 to 15 minutes of stretching each day could save you days of recovery time from a muscle or tendon injury.

Flexibility is simply defined as the range of possible movement in a joint. The need for greater flexibility for the athlete is essential. Greater flexibility helps to guard against muscle and tendon injury. The limiting factors in the range of motion are the muscles and the fascial sheaths that surround them, the joint capsule, ligaments, and the tendons which attach the muscle to the bone.

The loss of flexibility leads to shortened muscles and tendons, resulting in an imbalance of strength between opposing pairs of muscles. This imbalance can lead to injury if a sudden stretch, such as sprinting, is done by the distance runner. Distance runners are not known for their flexibility. Endurance training tends to decrease flexibility because of the shorter stride length and less use of the full range of movement during the slower running speeds. Stretching is therefore imperative and should be used to compensate for this lack of movement in the joint.

Other factors that effect flexibility are age, sex, and muscle temperature. As you grow older, you tend to lose some of your range of movement. Older runners should stretch more to help prevent the possibility of injury. Although women are more flexible than men, stretching is still important for the women runners.

Flexibility can be improved as much as 20 percent if the temperature of the muscle is increased. This is important when warming up. Light exercise of easy jogging or walking should precede muscle stretching.

STATIC STRETCHING VERSUS BALLISTIC STRETCHING

There are basically two methods of stretching: (1) passive or static stretching, and (2) active or ballistic stretching. Static stretching places a constant stretch on a muscle without bobbing or forcing the stretch. During static stretching the final position should be held for several seconds before returning to the starting position. In static stretching you should feel a stretch in the muscle, but should not feel pain. Relaxation during the stretch is essential. You should never have anyone hold or push any part of your body in order to achieve more stretch. This could result in injury to the muscle or joint.

Ballistic or active stretching involves bobbing to achieve a stretching effect. During ballistic stretching the final position is not held. Both types of stretching will improve flexibility; however, the use of ballistic stretching can cause tissue damage and is not recommended. If you stretch too far, the body has a protective mechanism called the stretch reflex. This reflex responds to stretch, especially to greater than normal stretch, such as forcing a stretch. It responds by causing the muscle to contract to avoid hyperextension. Overstretching, passive or ballistic, can activate this reflex; therefore, it works in opposition to its intended use.

Flexibility should be developed over several weeks without forcing movements. The following rules should be applied when conducting a stretching program for improved flexibility.

1. Slowly work into a stretching routine.
2. Use static stretching methods and hold each stretch for several seconds.
3. Easy warmup should precede stretching for best results.
4. Do not force a stretch.
5. Do not hold your breath while stretching. Your breathing should be slow and under control.
6. Be relaxed when stretching.
7. Make stretching a part of your warmup.
8. Make light stretching a part of your cooldown.
9. Regular stretching will help improve flexibility.
10. Design your program to be specific for your activity.
11. Be sure to do all stretches correctly.

STRETCHING PROGRAM FOR RUNNERS

Everyday training should include stretching. Stretching is important in preparing the body, muscles, tendons, ligaments, and joints for running. Prior to stretching, you should do some brisk walking or easy jogging to increase muscle temperature. Stretching helps to elevate your heart rate and blood pressure gradually, thus avoiding the sudden shock of exercise on the body. Stretching should be a part of the warmup phase. Stretching can help in guarding you against soreness and possible injury. You should do from six to ten stretching exercises that involve the major muscles for running. The following exercises are suggested for runners. Choose the ones that meet your needs and do them correctly.

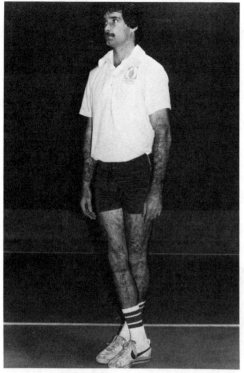

Starting Position

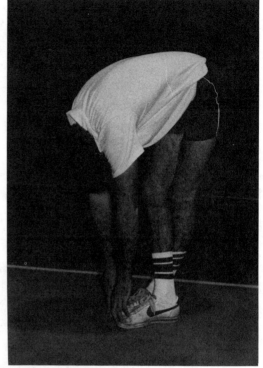

Ending Position

PURPOSE: To stretch the back of the legs and muscles of the back.

STARTING POSITION: Cross the right leg over the left leg, which is held straight. Rest the foot at the outside border of the left foot. (This will stretch the left side.)

MOVEMENT: Bend down toward the toes using the weight of your upper body for resistance. Caution! Do not bounce. Hold for 5 seconds, repeat 3 times, then cross left leg over the right leg and repeat.

Hurdle Stretch

Ending Position

Starting Position

PURPOSE: To stretch the low back, hamstrings, and adductor muscles of the legs.

STARTING POSITION: Sit with the right leg bent back and to the side, with the left leg extended out straight.

MOVEMENT: Gently reach forward touching the left toe, then gradually lean back keeping the right knee on the floor. Hold each position 5 seconds. Alternate legs and repeat.

Starting Position   **Ending Position**   **Variation Position "B"**

PURPOSE: To stretch the calf muscles and Achilles tendon.

STARTING   Stand facing the wall at arms' length. Keeping your knees
POSITION: straight, lean forward, placing your palms on the wall with
            your fingers pointing upward, your arms straight and your feet
            pointing towards the wall.

MOVEMENT: Slowly lower yourself to the wall. Be sure to keep your heels
            flat on the floor. Hold for 5 to 10 seconds. You should feel a
            stretch in the lower leg, but not pain. A variation to this is posi-
            tion "B." Place one foot slightly in front of the other and lean
            forward as before, being sure to keep your heels flat on the
            floor.

Stride Stretcher

Starting Position

Ending Position

PURPOSE: To stretch the leg muscles, hip flexors, and the muscles of the lower back.

STARTING POSITION: Lean forward with your hands on the floor and your leg flexed under your chest. The other leg should be stretched out behind.

MOVEMENT: Keeping your arms straight, lean forward, pushing your hips downward and straighten the trailing leg. Hold for 10 seconds, then return to starting position.

Quadricep or Thigh Stretcher

Starting Position

Ending Position

PURPOSE: To stretch the muscles of the thigh.

STARTING POSITION: While sitting on your heels, place your hands behind you, resting on the floor for balance and control.

MOVEMENT: Move your hips upward until you feel a stretch in the front of your thighs. Hold for 5 seconds. Return to starting position.

Low Back and Hamstring Stretcher

Starting Position

Ending Position

PURPOSE: To stretch the hamstring and low back muscles.

STARTING POSITION: While lying on the floor with your knees bent, grasp one leg with your hands around the shin.

MOVEMENT: Gently pull and straighten the leg in toward the chest. Let the opposite leg hang in a bent position. Hold for 10 seconds. Return to starting position. Do this 3 to 4 times for each leg.

Heel Cord Stretcher

Starting Position

Ending Position

PURPOSE: To stretch the hamstrings and muscles of the lower leg and to stretch the Achilles tendon.

STARTING POSITION: Bend at the knees and grasp the front of the toes of both feet.

MOVEMENT: Straighten your knees keeping hold of your toes. Maintain the stretch for 10 seconds, then return to starting position.

Side Stretcher

2nd Position   **Starting Position**   **3rd Position**

PURPOSE: To stretch the muscles of the sides and shoulders.

STARTING POSITION: Stand with your feet shoulder width apart and your hands clasped overhead.

MOVEMENT: Bend from side to side holding 5 to 10 seconds for each side. Repeat 3 times each side.

Starting Position

Ending Position

PURPOSE: To stretch the lower back and hamstring muscles.

STARTING
POSITION: Lie on your back with your arms extended out from your sides.

MOVEMENT: With your legs straight, bring your legs over your head, bending at the waist. Roll back until you feel a stretch in the low back area. Hold for 10 seconds and return to starting position.

Lower Leg Stretch

Starting Position

Ending Position

PURPOSE: To stretch the front and back muscles of the lower leg.

STARTING POSITION: Stand with your feet 6 to 8 inches apart and parallel to each other.

MOVEMENT: Bend your knees and lower yourself downward until you feel a stretch in the back and front of the lower leg. Be sure to keep your heels flat on the floor and your back straight. Hold for 5 to 10 seconds and repeat.

Shoulder and Upper Back Stretcher

Starting Position

Ending Position

PURPOSE: To stretch the muscles of the shoulders and upper back.

STARTING POSITION: Place your hands on the wall at shoulder height. Walk backward three to four feet, keeping your feet about one foot apart and parallel to each other.

MOVEMENT: Straighten your arms while bringing your spine towards the floor and rotate your pelvis to place a sag in the low back. Hold for 20 to 30 seconds.

Groin Stretcher

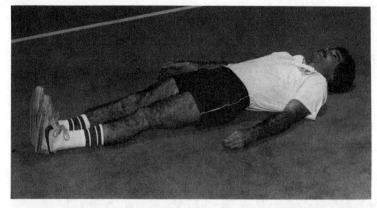

Starting Position

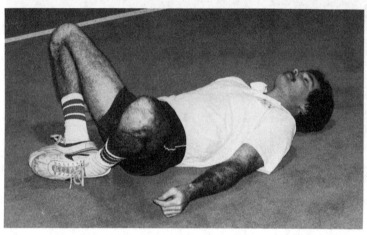

Ending Position

PURPOSE: To stretch the muscles of the upper leg and groin area.

STARTING POSITION: Lie on your back with your legs extended and relaxed.

MOVEMENT: Bend your knees and put the soles of your feet together. Move to a position that promotes stretch and hold for 30 seconds, then return to starting position.

STRENGTHENING EXERCISES

Some exercises that are good for stretching one group of muscles can be excellent for developing strength in another area. Some of these exercises include push-ups, bent knee sit-ups, alternating prone lifts, pull-ups and half curl-ups. If you are not familiar with these strengthening exercises, the following explanations will help you.

Bent-Knee Sit-ups

Starting Position

Ending Position

PURPOSE: To develop strength of the abdominal muscles.

STARTING POSITION: Lie on your back with your hands behind your head. Your knees should be bent with your feet flat on the floor. You may need something to hold your feet down. A partner or a weighted object will suffice for this.

MOVEMENT: Curl your back and raise your trunk until your elbows pass your knees. Then slowly return to the starting position. Perform this movement slowly and avoid pulling on the back of your head.

Half Curl-up

Starting Position

Ending Position

PURPOSE: To strengthen the abdominal muscles.

STARTING POSITION: Lie on your back with your knees bent and your feet flat on the floor. Place your hands on your abdomen.

MOVEMENT: Curl your back and raise your trunk and shoulders toward your knees. When you feel your abdominal muscles tighten, hold for 5 seconds and return to the starting position. Do not hold your breath. Do several repetitions, relaxing 2 to 3 seconds between each repetition.

Push-Ups

Starting Position

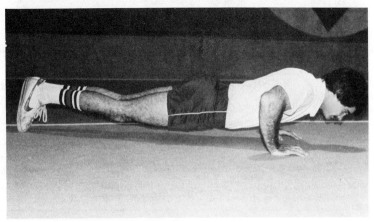

Ending Position

PURPOSE: To develop strength in the triceps, chest, and shoulder muscles.

STARTING POSITION: While keeping your back and knees straight, support your body on your hands and toes.

MOVEMENT: Lower your body downward by bending at the elbows. Your chest should touch the floor, and your back should be straight. Return to starting position.

Pull-Ups

Starting Position

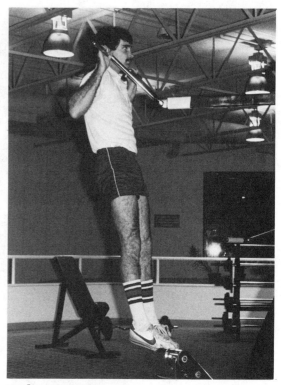

Ending Position

PURPOSE: To develop strength in the arms, shoulders, and upper back.

STARTING POSITION: Grasp an overhead bar with your palms facing outward. Your arms and legs should be fully extended.

MOVEMENT: Bend your arms at the elbows and pull yourself upward until your chin clears the top of the bar. Slowly lower yourself back to the starting position.

Alternating Prone-Lifts

Starting Position

2nd Position

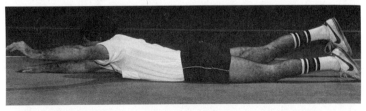

3rd Position

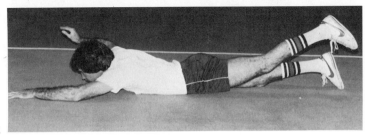

PURPOSE: To strengthen the muscles of the lower back and hip.

STARTING POSITION: Lie face down on the floor with your arms and legs extended.

MOVEMENT: Raise your right arm and left leg simultaneously and hold for 5 seconds, then return to starting position. Alternate from right to left side of the body.

Choose the exercises that meet your needs, and do them correctly. Relaxation is the key to performing the stretching exercises. Be faithful to the stretching routine that you have chosen. Remember that preventing injuries is always best, and greater flexibility helps protect you against muscle strains and pulls. Not all athletes stretch on a regular basis, even though they realize they should. The following table gives you an idea of how many runners stretch and what their major emphases are when stretching.

Athlete	Stretch Daily	Stretch Before Run	Stretch After Run	Total Time Per Day	Muscles Emphasized For Stretching
Tony Staynings	Yes	Yes	Yes	15 minutes twice	Lower and upper leg, arms, neck, back, shoulders
Gary Fanelli	Yes	Very little	Yes	5–15 min.	Lower and upper leg, back
Kirk Pfeffer	Never				
Ellison Goodall	Yes	Yes	Yes	10–15 min.	Lower and upper legs
Chuck Smead	Yes	No	Yes	15–30 min.	Lower and upper leg, back
John Lodwick	Yes	Yes	Very little	Approximately 12 minutes	Upper and lower leg, back
Steve Plasencia	Yes	No	Yes	15 minutes	Upper leg
Lionel Ortega	Yes	No	Yes	10 minutes	Lower and upper leg
Robert Hodge	Yes	Very little	Yes	10 minutes	Lower and upper leg, back
Amby Burfoot	No	No	Yes	Very little	Lower leg, back, neck, shoulders
Frank Shorter	No	No	Yes		Upper leg and back
Ken Moore	Yes	No	Yes	10–15 min.	Upper and lower leg, back
Alex Kasich	Yes	Yes	No	10–15 min.	Upper and lower leg, arms, back, neck, and shoulders
Alberto Salazar	Yes	Yes	Yes	40 minutes	Upper and lower leg
Paul Geis	No				
Jon Anderson	Yes	Yes	Yes	20–30 min. in evening 3–5 times/week and 5 min. before & after run	Upper and lower leg, back
John Dimick	Yes	Yes	Yes	5 min before 10–20 min after frequently during run	Upper and lower leg, back
Bill Rogers	Yes	Seldom	Usually	15–20 min.	Lower and upper leg, back, neck and shoulders
David Babriacki	Yes	Sometimes	Yes	10 minutes	Lower and upper leg, back, arms, neck and shoulders

Athlete	Stretch Daily	Stretch Before Run	Stretch After Run	Total Time Per Day	Muscles Emphasized For Stretching
Doug Brown	Yes	Yes	Seldom	5–10 min.	Upper leg
John Flora	Yes	Yes	Sometimes	10–20 min.	Lower and upper leg, arms, back, neck, shoulders
Jeff Galloway	Yes	Throughout the day		10 minutes	Lower and upper leg, back
Steve Flanagan	Yes	Yes	Yes	20 minutes	Upper and lower leg
Dick Quax	Yes	Yes	Yes	10 minutes	Lower and upper leg, back
Don Kardong	Most of the time	Yes	Yes	10 minutes	Upper and lower leg
Jeff Wells	Yes	Yes	Yes	5 minutes	Upper leg
Henry Marsh	Yes	Yes	No	5–10 min.	Upper leg
Lee Fidler	Yes	Yes	Yes	35 min. total	Upper and lower leg, back
Laurie Binder	Yes	Yes	Yes	5–10 min.	Upper and lower leg
Sue Strickland	Yes	Yes	Later after run	30 minutes	Upper and lower leg, arms, back, neck and shoulders
Patti Lions Catalona	Not daily	When I do it's before & after run		10 minutes	Upper leg, back
Hank Pfeifle	Yes	Yes	Yes	15 min. before & after run	Upper leg and back
Mike Roche	Usually	Yes	Yes	20–30 min.	Lower and upper leg, arms, back, neck, shoulders
Charlie Vigil	Yes	Yes	Seldom	15 minutes	Legs, arms, back, neck, and shoulders
Philip Coppess	Yes	Yes	No		Upper legs, back
Jon Sinclair	No	Sometimes	Sometimes		Legs, arms, back and shoulders
Ron Tabb	Yes	Yes	Yes	5 minutes	Legs, arms, back and shoulders
Ray Flynn	Yes	Yes	Yes	20 minutes	Legs, arms, back and shoulders
Herb Lindsey	Not always	Yes	Yes	20 minutes	Legs, arms, back and shoulders
Tom Fleming	3 times per wk	No	Yes		Lower and upper legs

Athlete	Stretch Daily	Stretch Before Run	Stretch After Run	Total Time Per Day	Muscles Emphasized For Stretching
Mary Decker	Yes	Yes	Yes	20–30 min.	Lower and upper legs, back and shoulders
Bill Andberg	Yes	Yes	Yes	20 minutes	Lower and upper legs, back
Nancy Conz	Yes	No	Yes		Lower and upper legs, back
Marge Rosasco	Yes	Yes	Yes	5–15 min.	Legs, arms, back
Kevin McCarey	Yes	Yes	Yes	25 minutes	Upper leg and back
Benji Durden	Yes	Yes	Yes	20–30 min.	Upper & lower leg, back
Dave Smith	Yes	Yes	Yes	15–20 min.	Upper and lower leg, back
Jim Crawford	No	No	No	Before racing	Arms, neck & shoulders
Stan Mavis	No	I stretch only when I feel tight or stressed, infrequently.			
Donna Burge	No	I stretch if I am doing intervals or racing.			
Ted Castanada	Yes	Yes	Yes	10–15 min. before & after	Upper & lower legs
Grete Waitz	Yes	No	Yes	10 min. after each workout	Upper & lower legs
Lorraine Moller	Yes	No	Yes	20 min. daily	Legs, arms, back, neck and shoulders
Dick Beardsley	Yes	No	Yes	20 minutes	Legs, arms, back

REFERENCES

Anderson, R., *Stretching* (California: Shelter Publications, Random House, 1980).

Anderson, R., "The perfect pre-run stretching routine," *Runner's World*, 13 (May 1978), 56–61.

Devries, H., "Evaluation of static stretching procedures for improvement of flexibility," *Res. Q.*, 33 (1962), 222–229.

Getchell, L., *Physical Fitness A Way of Life*, 2nd ed. (New York: Wiley, 1979).

Holland, G., "The physiology of flexibility: A review of the literature," *Kinesiology Review*, (1968), 49–62.

Mathews, D. K., and Fox, E. L., *The Physiological Basis of Physical Education and Athletics*, 2nd ed. (Philadelphia: W. B. Saunders, 1976).

Sheehan, G., "Six steps toward painless running," *Runner's World* (Dec. 10, 1975), 41.

Weber, S., and Kraus, H., "Passive and active stretching of muscles," *Phys. Ther. Rev.*, 29 (1949), 407–410.

5

Altitude Training

The effects of altitude on performance have been of concern ever since the 1968 Olympic Games, held in Mexico City. Since that time runners have used altitude training as a means of increasing their performances at lower altitudes. However, the rationale for improved performance after returning from high altitude is obscure, and contradictory evidence exists. Many athletes attribute some of their success to training at altitude, while others believe that the gain is more psychological than physiological when competing at a lower altitude. To better understand altitude training, let's look at the physiology of going to high altitude.

As you travel from sea level to high altitude, you experience decreases in performance times, especially in those events of long duration. These decreases in performance are associated with your ability to use oxygen, or your aerobic capacity. Even though the percent of oxygen is the same (20.3 percent) at sea level and at altitude, the barometric pressure is less. This means that the pressure surrounding the body is less help in filling the lungs and saturating the blood with oxygen. At sea level the barometric pressure is 760 mm. Hg., but at an altitude of 7,400 feet, such as in Mexico City, the barometric pressure is reduced to 580 mm. Hg. Consequently, this reduced air pressure makes breathing difficult.

The oxygen in the lungs may decrease as much as 25 percent when moving to an altitude of 7,400 feet. To help compensate for this decrease in oxygen to the lungs, ventilation increases significantly; however, the exchange of oxygen is less adequate, and the limits of oxygen consumption are reduced. The overall inefficiency of the heart and lungs in delivering oxygen to the tissues at altitude results in decreased performance. Maximal oxygen consumption decreases about 3 to 3.5 percent for each 1,000 feet you travel above 5,000 feet (Figure 5-1). Below 5,000 feet there is a less noticeable effect on the endurance capacity of runners.

Results of competition requiring intense efforts of one minute or less are not affected by altitude, and in events such as sprinting, the reduction of the air resistance may enhance performance. In Mexico City during the 1968 Olympic Games, running distances up to 400 meters were actually better than performances at sea level. Impairment in the 1,500 meters was about 3 percent, or 7 seconds, and about 8 percent in the 5,000 and 10,000 meter races. This amounts to about one minute in the 5,000 meters and about 2.5 minutes in the 10,000 meter races.

Runners who live and train in altitude are probably better accustomed to racing at altitude. This was evident in the 1968 Olympics, where many of the athletes from high altitude countries were successful in the endurance events. Since that time,

FIGURE 5-1. *Influence of altitude on aerobic capacity*

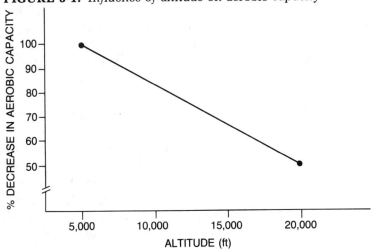

many runners have included training as a part of their preparation for performances, not only at altitude, but at sea level as well.

When moving to altitude from sea level for training, the intensity and duration of training runs are usually less for the first few days until the body becomes better accustomed to the thinner air. Efforts should be made to put the quality back into training sessions as soon as possible, because reducing quality can sometimes cause changes in muscular power and normal competitive rhythm. Initial training at altitude also produces more fatigue, meaning more sleep is needed. A quality diet should be maintained during early training at altitude.

Runners should train at least three weeks at altitude to have any acclimatization, and even longer periods are necessary for complete adaptation. Training at altitudes of less than 6,500 feet is less beneficial in producing positive effects from altitude training. Because of the time needed to produce altitude adaptation and the expense involved in going to high altitude, many athletes cannot afford to include this in their training. Therefore, we need to look at the benefits of training at altitude and see if the time and expense can be justified.

ADAPTATION TO ALTITUDE

As you ascend above sea level, the air becomes thinner, making oxygen available to the tissues less adequate. High altitudes alter the saturation of the blood with oxygen. The saturation of the blood with oxygen at sea level is approximately 97 percent. As you move into altitude, this saturation drops, resulting in less oxygenated blood for tissue use. However, it must be recognized that for a substantial drop in oxygen saturation, you would have to climb to altitudes of 10,000 feet or more. Very few athletes ever train at these altitudes.

The primary reason for decreased performance at altitude is a lowered oxygen pressure in the lungs, causing a lack of adequate oxygen for diffusion into muscle tissue. The inadequate oxygen stimulates mechanisms in the body to adapt to the stress imposed by altitude. Several factors such as height of altitude and duration of stay are important to how much adaptation will result.

The immediate response to altitude is increased ventilation. This increase is more evident during the first few days of working at altitude; it stabilizes after about a week. Hyperventilation (overbreathing) helps flush the lungs with more oxygen, aiding the oxygen saturation of the blood. Hyperventilation also causes an increased amount of carbon dioxide to be exhaled, leading to the feeling of lightheadedness or nausea. This loss of carbon dioxide changes the acid-base balance of the body, resulting in a higher pH level in the blood. To compensate for the change in pH, the kidneys eliminate bicarbonate in the urine, reducing the alkaline reserve in the blood. This reduced alkaline reserve may effect the anaerobic capacity in the acclimatized athlete, resulting in a reduction of anaerobic power.

The reduced pressure of oxygen causes the body to produce more red blood cells and hemoglobin, which carries most of the oxygen in the blood, providing more chance for greater oxygen saturation of the blood.

Several adaptations that aid oxygen utilization happen in the muscle cell itself. These include an increased amount of myoglobin which, like hemoglobin in the blood, combines with oxygen to enhance oxygen stores; and an increase in the number of mitochondria. The mitochondria are responsible for producing energy with the use of oxygen (Chapter 2). Increased mitochondrial density is associated with increased amounts of the oxidative enzymes needed in the rapid production of energy.

Exposure to altitude also increases the blood capillaries feeding the muscle, making more blood available for the exchange of oxygen. These adaptations at the tissue level require longer exposure to altitude and are mainly found in residents of high altitude and not in athletes spending a few weeks training at altitude.

At greater altitudes the air becomes thinner, allowing more exposure to radiation from the sun and causing sunburn. The air is also dryer, meaning that heat loss is greater and evaporation is more efficient. However, because of the dryness, many runners lose weight initially because the sweat loss is less noticeable. It is a good idea to make an effort to drink more fluids when moving to altitude.

The physiological adaptations to altitude training are basically the same as those changes achieved through training at sea level. Some research has shown that the better conditioned athletes moving to altitude do not show as much adaptation as more poorly conditioned runners. This is probably due to near optimal development of the circulatory and respiratory systems during sea level training, reducing the amount of possible adaptation due to genetic limitations. Highly trained runners returning to sea level from altitude training are no better off physically than they were before going to altitude. However, training at altitude probably enhances sea level performance in the unconditioned runner. If any adaptations have occurred as a result from training at altitude, they are lost within 2 to 3 weeks after returning to sea level.

In summary, let's look at the physical adaptations that occur as a result of training for an extended period of time at altitude.

1. Increased breathing will be noticed because of the thinner air.
2. A reduction in anaerobic power may result from over-breathing and bicarbonate loss in the urine.
3. Increased myoglobin content in the muscle will provide for greater oxygen storage.
4. Mitochondrial density increases due to greater need for oxygen.
5. Oxidative enzymes increase for better oxygen utilization.
6. The number of blood capillaries feeding the muscle increases, providing for greater oxygen transport.
7. The number of red blood cells and amount of hemoglobin increase, allowing for greater oxygen transport.

All of the adaptations that occur at altitude are similar to training adaptations that occur at sea level training. Many runners, however, still like to do some altitude training in case there might be some other edge that cannot be measured by the physiologist. If you wish to train at altitude, the following recommendations should be helpful:

1. Training should take place at moderate altitudes of 6,500 to 7,500 feet.

2. The quality of training should be the same as that at sea level to assure maintenance of muscular power and normal competitive rhythm.

3. More rest and sleep will be needed during the first couple of weeks at altitude.

4. Efforts should be made to drink plenty of fluids while exposed to the drier environment.

5. The duration of stay for training at altitude should be at least 3 weeks.

6. After returning to sea level, you should schedule important competition within 2 weeks.

7. Altitude training is probably most important if competing at altitudes over 5,000 feet.

Ever since the Olympic Games in Mexico City, athletes have experimented with altitude training. Much controversy exists about the benefits of altitude upon return to sea level running.

Athletes were asked what they felt were the advantages or disadvantages of altitude training.

Frank Shorter: Altitude training places more stress on the body. Altitude training may be more psychological; I like to view the scenery. You train best where you're most comfortable.

Chuck Smeed: The advantage is better cardiovascular fitness. The disadvantage is that it is hard to run fast. Altitude training is very significant if racing at altitude. It helps me feel like I am fit if I can run well at altitude.

Doug Kardong: The advantage is that all of the other stars are there; disadvantage—no surfing. There is a physiological boost if used correctly and a psychological boost in those who have faith.

Dick Quax: Yes, I believe that altitude training has some advantages.

Jeff Galloway: You can push yourself harder, get closer to your limits. If prolonged, you get a greater oxygen carrying capacity. The disadvantage of altitude training is that you can't get quality speed work.

Gary Fanelli: I have seen results from watching born foreigners, especially Kenyans, and Americans training at altitude. I believe it makes a difference. I have tried it myself, and it truly felt great. I could run with less effort, and when I returned to sea level, it was easier for me to train and race. I believe you have better oxygen uptake and utilization adaption. Psychologically, it can be a boost because you feel good and it's easier to run upon returning to sea level.

Steve Plasencia: You can train less and get more aerobic development. Or if you train the same (volume), you'll be more fit than at sea level. Psychologically, interval training is more difficult at altitude. You hurt much more doing quality work. Mentally, this expectation of pain keeps many athletes away from interval or fartlek work. Boulder, Colorado produces more road runners than track runners. My experience was that I raced successfully while based at altitude. Some of this was because I got more hill training in, strengthening my legs and making me a stronger runner.

Amby Burfoot: I'm not sure about physiological advantages, but they seem likely for those who train at altitude for long periods. I suspect there are significant psychological advantages. I believe the psychological side of running performance is extremely important, and training at altitude may be one more way of creating a self-fulfilling prophecy.

Mike Roche: Training at altitude increases oxygen intake; however, if not timed properly (through experimentation), the advantages may not be fully utilized. Perhaps coming down from altitude psychologically aids the athlete when training well. If so, this is a significant factor.

Robert Hodge: Personally, I believe the advantages are mostly psychological. Some people swear by it and other people do very well without it. If you read about it and train at altitude and do well with it, you'll believe in it whether you could have done without it or not.

Hank Pfeifle: I have never done it, but I think it would have positive psychological effects because if you know you can handle the work load at altitude, then you know you've built yourself up. Your body is at a higher level of fitness. Physiologically it increases lung capacity and oxygen uptake in the blood.

Lionel Ortega: If you believe that training at altitude will help you, then it will. Altitude training is a big psychological boost.

Kevin McCarey: I trained at altitude two different times, in Los Alamos (7,300 feet) and Pueblo, Mexico. It definitely improved my marathon times. All I know is that when it came time to race at sea level, I felt better physically and mentally.

Paul Geis: I think you do more work for less effort. It seems easier to breathe at sea level upon return from altitude.

Steve Flanagan: If I train at 100 miles per week in Boulder, Colorado, I enjoy a cardiovascular stress level of approximately 120 to 130 miles per week at sea level without the concurrent skeletal-muscular stresses of pounding the pavement those additional 20 to 30 miles. When I need to sharpen before short race efforts (1,500 to 5,000 meters), the necessary leg rate is difficult to attain at altitude. I'm psychologically better equipped to handle an immediate and extreme oxygen debt as a result of my altitude training. It's not that physiologically I enjoy any advantage racing at sea level, but I feel this gives me a psychological edge.

John Lodwick: I think there are objective physical benefits from altitude training. They relate to being able to run more efficiently at sea level after altitude training. Altitude also increases red blood cell count, hemoglobin, and hematocrit. Running at altitude also builds one's confidence in his training and helps him anticipate races. The only disadvantage to altitude training relates to priorities; time away from family and work can be hard on a guy and may demotivate him.

Doug Brown: There is no question in my mind that after three training experiences at altitude, there is a significant advantage, but I still don't know how long it helps. I think it depends greatly on the amount of time spent there and repetition. I have had great results immediately following altitude training. I'm no rookie; I feel I know when I've been helped. Altitude works, but it's temporary.

Kenny Moore: The assorted adaptations that altitude training affects (blood, lungs, chemistry) prove that it definitely makes one a more efficient runner at sea level. How much it helps is probably different for everybody. For me, it's worth 30 seconds in a 10,000.

Henry Marsh: Effects of altitude training are very individual. It is difficult to do quality intervals shortly before big competitions (intervals 800 meters or longer). However, it builds your base capacity. It think best results are within two weeks after returning to sea level.

Tony Staynings: I don't know enough to make any viable comment on the advantages or disadvantages of altitude training. However, I believe there are tremendous physiological and psychological benefits.

Benji Durden: Altitude increases cardiovascular stress at lower training speeds. Psychologically, you believe you are working harder, giving a positive self-image. The disadvantage is that because of the lack of humidity, acclimation can be a problem in race situations.

Lee Fiddler: I feel that training at altitude for an extended period of time can be beneficial because of the additional stress added to one's training. Physiologically, it improves the body's oxygen transport system. I think altitude training gives one a great boost of confidence.

Alberto Salazar: I believe there are both physiological and psychological benefits to altitude training. It gives you extra endurance and cardiovascular development.

Alex Kasich: Are there any real advantages? Many do very well without the aid of altitude. It's hard for me to give an opinion, since I haven't trained much at altitude. Advantages may be psychological in that you can't train as hard, so there is less chance of injury. Altitude can help if you believe it will, the placebo effect, since the mental aspect of running is highly significant.

Sue Strickland: There are advantages to altitude training only if a person has lived at altitude for an extended period of time, preferably from birth, in order to develop greater cardiovascular and respiratory systems. Altitude also raises your hemoglobin. Four weeks does nothing except make you tired.

Patti Lions Catalano: Although I have never trained at altitude, I plan to do so in the future. I believe that added stress on your respiratory and circulatory system would be beneficial. Physically, it helps the body become more efficient with less oxygen; therefore, it would give you a mental boost.

Laurie Binder: I have never done any altitude training, but I have raced at altitude, and it is definitely more difficult to breathe. Once you adapt to it, though, I imagine you could run much more easily.

Dave Babriacki: I feel the only advantage is if you have to race at altitude. After living two years in Utah, I found no real advantage in coming down to low altitude. I think it depends on the athlete.

Kirk Pfeffer: The only benefit from training at altitude is if you race at altitude. It's 99 percent psychological."

Jeff Wells: I am skeptical about altitude training, although I've done it. Obviously there would be the psychological advantage of confidence, if one believes in it.

John Flora: I think doing 140 to 150 miles a week makes up for the benefits of what you can obtain at higher altitude, because you're doing much more than your opponents, regardless of their environmental conditions. I don't think there are any physical or mental benefits.

Jon Anderson: I haven't had much experience with it, but have read and talked with athletes, coaches, and physiologists who believe it can be an advantage. I believe the documented effects on blood cell counts and that these effects are beneficial. Athletes who go to altitude often submerge themselves in training, so the effects are often not only from altitude. Psychological benefits are obvious since athletes who train at altitude usually believe the altitude is beneficial. Runners who believe in their training techniques are usually tough when they're fit.

Bill Rogers: Altitude is another form of stress you can work on to improve yourself within a controlled manner. Cardiorespiratory improvement should result. It is psychologically beneficial because it conquers a form of stress.

Stan Mavis: I believe you have to have generations behind you at altitude in order to benefit, i.e., Henry Rono, Tony Sandoval. The disadvantage of altitude training is the slower leg rate that the percent of oxen forces you into.

Donna Burge: Altitude training causes increases in red blood cell production to transport greater amounts of oxygen. After the initial adaptation, I feel that I would have an advantage over sea-level opponents without doing any extra training.

Lorraine Moller: I have never trained or raced at altitude. However, I believe training at altitude would be of value in competing at altitude.

Greg Myer: Altitude training has a physiological advantage bacause we have been led to believe it is beneficial. Physically, it is more resistant and taxes our cardiovascular system much more. The disadvantage is that you can't do the same quality in your speed workouts; you can't run fast enough for a long enough time due to the lack of oxygen.

Grete Waitz: I have had no experience with altitude training.

Marge Rosasco: An obvious disadvantage of altitude training is that it makes training much harder until your body adjusts.

Marc Nenow: I think it is beneficial if you're racing at altitude. Otherwise, I don't feel any disadvantage by not being at altitude. Psychologically, it may give a runner a sense of advantage.

Tom Fleming: The added stress can only help if used in the correct manner of training. The stress of altitude combined with interval and hill training is very effective for me (minimum stay at least two months). Psychologically, if you think it will work, it will!

Ray Flynn: There is an advantage to altitude training, particularly for the longer distances. My girlfriend lives in Cheyenne, Wyoming (6,200 feet). I've raced immediately after training there; I've bombed out, but have run excellently about ten days later. For distances up to 5,000 meters, I personally believe I do not need altitude training.

Jon Sinclair: For some people who are adapted to it, altitude can increase efficiency (cardiopulmonary), but it also limits speed training (intervals).

Charlie Vigil: In essence, training at altitude is great for racing at altitude, but not really conducive to racing well at sea level. It is very hard to simulate leg speed and weather conditions of sea level while living and training at altitude, and most world class races are run at sea level. I feel it is very important to become as knowledgeable as possible as to what to do to get fit and race well at sea level and altitude while training at altitude, such as simulating the right intervals, recovery, etc. Otherwise a runner after altitude training will race at sea level and breathe well, but his legs won't churn over as well as he expects.

Philip Coppess: I believe there is an advantage; however, the disadvantage of training at altitude is living at sea level.

Dick Beardsley: I am in the process of using the PO_2 Aerobic Exercises, which simulate an altitude of 7,500 feet. I definitely think they will help my racing. I believe altitude training helps increase red blood cells, and having a positive attitude that it will help is worth much more than most people think.

The question of altitude training is a tough one to answer. The consensus is that there is an advantage, but maybe not as much as some think, especially for racing at sea level.

REFERENCES

Adams, W. C., Bernauer, E. M., Dill, D. B., and Bomar, J. B., "Effects of equivalent sea level and altitude training on VO_2 max and running performance," *J. Appl. Physiol.*, 39 (1975), 262–266.

Alexander, J. K., Hartley, L. H., Modelski, M., and Grover, R. F., "Reduction of stroke volume during exercise in man following ascent to 3,100 m. altitude," *J. Appl. Physiol.*, 23 (1967), 849–858.

Astrand, P. O., and Rodahl, K., *Textbook of Work Physiology*, 2nd ed. (New York: McGraw-Hill, 1977).

Billings, C., Bason, R., Mathews, D., and Fox, E., "Cost of submaximal and maximal work during chronic exposure at 3,800 m.," *J. Appl. Physiol.*, 30 (1971), 406–408.

Buskirk, E., Kollias, J., Akers, R., Prokop, E., and Picon-Reategue, E., "Maximal performance at altitude and on return from altitude in conditioned runners," *J. Appl. Physiol*, 23 (1967), 259–266.

Buskirk, E., Kollias, J., Picon-Reategue, E., Akers, R., Prokop, E., and Baker, P., "Physiology and performance of track athletes at various altitudes in the United States and Peru," The International Symposium on the Effects of Altitude on Physical Performance, ed. R. F. Goddard, (Chicago: The Athletic Institute, 1967), pp. 65–72.

Cerretelli, P., and Margaria, R., "Oxygen consumption at altitude," *Intern. Z. Angew. Physiol.*, 18 (1961), 460–464.

Consolazio, C. F., Submaximal and maximal performance at high altitude, The International Symposium on the Effects of Altitude on Physical Performance, ed. R. F. Goddard, (Chicago: The Athletic Institute, 1967), p. 91.

Costill, D. L., "A Scientific Approach to Distance Running," *Track and Field News*, Los Altos, California, 1979.

Craig, A. B., "Olympics, 1968: A postmortem," *Med. Sci. Sport and Exer.*, 1 (1969), 177–180.

Daniels, J., "Effects of altitude on athlete accomplishment," *Mod. Med.*, (June 1972), 73–76.

Daniels, J., and Oldridge, N., "The effects of alternate exposure to altitude and sea level on world-class middle-distance runners," *Med. Sci. Sport and Exer.*, 2 (1970), 107–112.

Dejours, P., Kellogg, R. H., Pace, N., "Regulation of respiration and heart rate response in exercise during altitude acclimatization," *J. Appl. Physiol.*, 18 (1963), 10–18.

Faulkner, J. A., Daniels, J. T., and Balke, B., "Effects of training at moderate altitude on physical performance capacity," *J. Appl. Physiol.*, 23 (1967), 85–89.

Faulkner, E. R., Killias, J., Favour, C. B., Buskirk, E. R., and Balke, B., "Maximum aerobic capacity and running performance at altitude," *J. Appl. Physiol.*, 24 (1968), 685–691.

Grover, R. F., and Reeves, J. T., Exercise performance of athletes at sea level and 3,100 meters altitude, The International Symposium on the Effects of Altitude on Physical Performance, ed. R. F. Goddard, (Chicago: The Athletic Institute, 1967), 80–87.

Grover, R. G., Reeves, J. T., Grover, E., and Leathers, J., "Muscular exercise in young men native to 3,100 m. altitude," *J. Appl. Physiol.*, 22 (1967), 555–564.

Hansen, J. E., Stelter, G. P., and Vogel, J. A., "Arterial pyruvate, lactate, pH, and PCO_2 during work at sea level and high altitude," *J. Appl. Physiol*, 23 (1967), 523–526.

Hansen, J. E., Vogel, J. A. Stelter, G. P., and Consolazo, C. F., "Oxygen uptake in man during exhaustive work at sea level and high altitude," *J. Appl. Physiol.*, 23 (1967), 511–522.

Hultman, H. N., Kelly, J., and Miller, P., "Pulmonary circulation in acclimatized man at high altitude," *J. Appl. Physiol.*, 20 (1965), 233–238.

Kollias, J., Buskirk, E. R., Akers, R. F., Prokop, E. K., Baker, P. T., Picon-Reategue, E., "Work capacity of long time residents and newcomers to altitude," *J. Appl. Physiol.*, 24 (1968), 792–799.

Leary, W. P., and Wyndham, C. H., "The possible effect on athletic performance of Mexico City's altitude," *S. Afr. Med. J.*, 40 (1966), 984–985.

Mathews, D. K., and Fox, E. L., *The Physiological Basis of Physical Education and Athletics*, 2nd ed., (Philadelphia: W. B. Saunders, 1976).

Pugh, L., "Athletics at altitude," *J. Physiol.*, 192 (1967), 619–747.

Saltin, B., "Aerobic and anaerobic work capacity at altitude on physical performance," The International Symposium on the Effects of Altitude on Physical Performance, ed. R. F. Goddard, (Chicago: The Athletic Institute), pp. 97–102.

Vogel, J. A., Hansen, J. E., and Harris, C. W., "Cardiovascular response in man during exhaustive work at sea level and high altitude," *J. Appl. Physiol.*, 23 (1967), 531–539.

Vogel, J. A., Hartley, L. H., Cruz, J. C., and Hogan, R. P., "Cardiac output during exercise in sea level residents at sea level and high altitude," *J. Appl. Physiol.*, 36 (1974), 169–172.

Vogel, J. A., Hartley, L. G., and Cruz, J. C., "Cardiac output during exercise in altitude natives at sea level and high altitude," *J. Appl. Physiol.*, 36 (1974), 173–176.

West, J. B., Lahiri, S., Gill, M. B., Milledge, J. S., Pugh, L. G., and Ward, M. P., "Arterial oxygen saturation during exercise at high altitude," *J. Appl. Physiol.*, 17 (1962), 617–621.

Wyndham, C. H., and Leary, W. P., "Physiological problems expected at Mexico City Olympic Games," *S. Afr. Med. J.*, 40 (1966), 985–987.

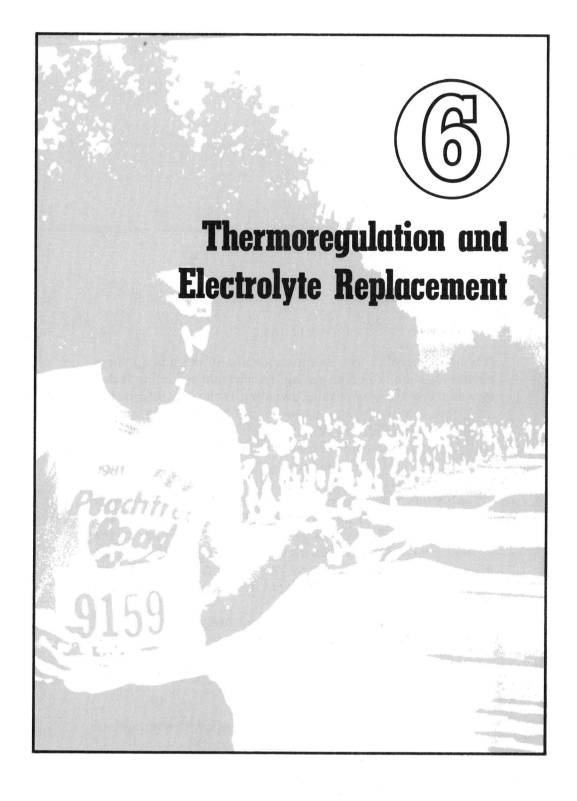

Thermoregulation and Electrolyte Replacement

It is not unusual to lose as much as 5 to 10 pounds during a training session or during racing. This weight reduction is due to water loss from sweating. Sweating is needed in order to cool down the body and to avoid overheating. The human body can only tolerate a few degrees change in temperature, and even under mild weather conditions the risk of overheating is probably the greatest threat to the distance runner (Figure 6–1).

Most of the energy produced by the body is lost by heat production. The body is only about 20 to 30 percent efficient in its energy utilization; the other 70 to 80 percent is lost in the form of heat. As the energy demands increase with running, more heat is produced, causing your temperature to rise. The body must be cooled down to avoid damaging brain cells as a result of heat injury or heatstroke.

The hypothalamus, located in the brain, acts as a thermostat for the body. If your body temperature changes, up or down, the hypothalamus senses this and signals mechanisms in the body to either turn up heat production (if you're shivering) or cool down the body (in the case of increased temperature).

The primary method for reducing body temperature during exercise is by producing changes in the circulation of

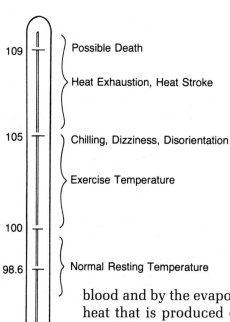

109 — Possible Death

Heat Exhaustion, Heat Stroke

105 — Chilling, Dizziness, Disorientation

Exercise Temperature

100 —

98.6 — Normal Resting Temperature

FIGURE 6-1. *Range of body temperature for heat disorders.*

blood and by the evaporation of sweat from the skin. The body heat that is produced during the metabolism of fats and carbohydrates is transported from the muscles by the circulatory system. The increased temperature of the blood causes the body's thermostat (the hypothalamus) to respond by sending signals through the nervous system to all parts of the body. The result is more blood flow to the surface of the skin. The blood is cooled as it flows near the skin's surface, allowing heat to be dissipated from the body.

Sweat glands are also stimulated to start pouring out perspiration for evaporation, helping to facilitate blood cooling. During running the amount of heat lost by evaporation depends upon the amount of sweat produced by the body and environmental conditions, such as temperature, humidity, and air movement over the skin. Water loss through sweating may be as much as two to three liters (one liter equals approximately one quart) per hour during heavy exercise. This water loss can lead to dehydration of the body, decreasing your ability to tolerate exercise.

WATER LOSS AND DEHYDRATION

Water is the largest single constituent of the body, representing 45 to 75 percent of the total body weight, varying according to age and body fat content. Body water consists of two types, intracellular and extracellular water. The water within each cell (intracellular water) may make up as much as 30 to 40 percent of your body weight. The rest of the water, classified as extracellular water, includes blood plasma, lymph, and water between the cells of the body (interstitial fluid).

With the onset of sweating there are shifts in body water from the various compartments, causing some circulatory problems. Water from the extracellular compartment is reduced during dehydration, causing a smaller blood volume. As dehydration increases (3 to 5 percent of body weight), the blood supply to the skin is reduced to protect the vital organs within the body. This places a stress on the circulatory system resulting in higher heart rates and body temperature (Figure 6–2). If dehydration is allowed to continue, sweating will stop and the skin will become dry. At this point chilling, dizziness, and possible unconsciousness may occur unless you receive immediate treatment for lowering body temperature and replenishing body fluids.

Heatstroke doesn't just happen without warning; your vision may become blurred, your breathing becomes irregular,

FIGURE 6-2. *Relationship between changes in body weight and heart rate (A) and rectal temperature (B).*

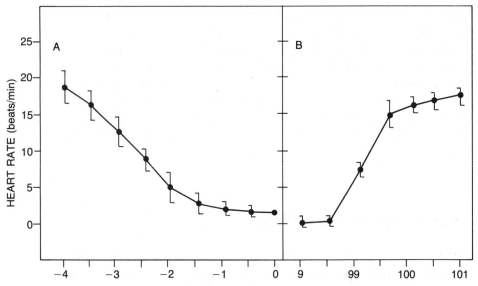

Adapted from Costill, D. L., Kammer, W. F., Fisher, A., Fluid ingestion during distance running, *Arch. Environ. Health,* 1971.

and you may become disoriented and start to weave back and forth across the road as you try to continue to run. At this point, the safe thing to do is to slow the pace to reduce heat production, or maybe even discontinue the run.

FLUID INGESTION

The administering of fluids can help in preventing heat injury. However, the type of fluid ingested is important for greater effectiveness against dehydration and temperature regulation.

Most long distance runners agree that drinking fluids is very important during a long training run or long race. However, there is no consistancy among runners as to what, how much, and how often to drink along the way. During a hot day or hard running, you may be losing body water at the rate of one to two quarts per hour. This makes it impossible to ingest enough fluid to avoid dehydration. Even during laboratory experiments in which fluid was ingested every ten minutes throughout the run, subjects still had weight losses of 4 to 6 pounds. Further investigation of these runners showed that much of the fluid ingested was still in the stomach. Fluid can only be effective if it gets into the system quickly and out of the stomach. The amounts of fluid left in the stomach vary for basically one reason, the concentration of dissolved substances in the solution (osmolality). Solutions can be classified according to their osmolality when compared with the body fluids. Solutions that have a higher concentration of substances dissolved in them (greater osmolality) than in body fluids are called hypertonic, and solutions that have a lower concentration (low osmolality) are hypotonic solutions.

Some commercial drinks are very concentrated (hypertonic), slowing down their absorption from the stomach. The major dissolved substances that make these solutions hypertonic are electrolytes and sugar. A good fluid to ingest while running should contain low concentrations of these substances to be effective. However, athletes need more of these substances because of the high energy usage and sweat loss. Does this mean you have to choose between being dehydrated and depleting your sugar and electrolyte stores? The answer to this question is not simple, but there are facts about the amount of sugar and electrolytes that need to be contained in a solution to be consumed during running.

During long races, such as marathons, many runners "hit the wall" during the later portion of the race. Hitting the wall, or running out of gas, has been correlated with drops in blood sugar and low glycogen (sugar) levels found in the muscle cell. It stands to reason that administering sugar solutions during the race could be beneficial in offsetting dehydration and counteracting fatigue at the same time. However, additions of sugar even in small amounts can drastically impair the rate of stomach emptying. Some commercial drinks, designed for the purpose of replenishing body fluids, contain as much as 5 percent sugar, making the drink more concentrated than the body fluids (hypertonic). This slows down its effectiveness in combating dehydration, the major reason for drinking fluids. A drink consumed during running should not be more than a 2.5 percent solution (about one tablespoon of sugar per quart) in order to empty from the stomach quickly.

Carbohydrate supplementation during marathon running is of secondary importance and would probably be too slow and take too long getting into the system to help in supplying sugar for additional energy.

Electrolyte Solutions

Electrolytes, as the name implies, are concerned with the conduction of electrical charges responsible for muscle contraction within the body. Sodium, potassium, chloride, magnesium, and calcium are some of the electrolytes needed by the body for proper muscle contraction, temperature regulation, and fluid balance. You have more than adequate supplies of these electrolytes stored in your body, and only under extreme conditions would their loss during running be significant.

The body makes adjustments to conserve electrolytes and water during successive days of profuse sweating by limiting the amounts being lost in sweat and urine. One of the major functions of the kidneys is to regulate the amount of fluid and electrolyte loss by the body. During exercise the kidneys retain more water and electrolytes in the body. This regulation by the kidneys is controlled by secretion of an antidiuretic hormone

(ADH) that acts on the specialized cells in the kidney to reabsorb water and electrolytes that would normally be excreted in urine. This hormone (ADH) is secreted in response to the body's need for water. The result is concentrated urine which is dark yellow in color. A change in the color of your urine is a good indicator of your state of rehydration. This response by the kidneys is just one way the body responds to keep the fluid environment of the cells relatively unchanged.

Since salt (sodium chloride) is the common electrolyte lost in sweat, some coaches advise their athletes to take salt tablets to help replace the lost salt. This can actually be detrimental and can cause further dehydration. This practice should only be used when proper supervision is provided. Moreover, after evaporation takes place, salt remains on the surface of the skin, building in concentration as more sweat secretions take place. This high concentration of salt slows down evaporation. To avoid this salt buildup, race officials often provide sponges to the runners for wiping off the excess salt that has collected on the skin's surface.

During exercise you are losing more water than electrolytes; therefore, the addition of electrolytes to solutions for rehydration is not necessary. To help in selecting a good drink for rehydrating the body during running, the following guidelines should be considered:

(1) The drink should empty out of the stomach quickly.
(2) The drink should be hypotonic in relation to body fluids. (approximately 200mOsm/liter)
(3) The drink should contain less than 2.5 percent sugar.
(4) The drink should contain very few, if any, electrolytes.
(5) The drink should be consumed cold for greater absorption and cooling effect.

Fluid Replacement

Is there a perfect drink? Nature has provided us with probably the best product, and the cost is right for everyone—water. Water meets all of the guidelines for a good drink for fluid replacement during racing or training.

Drinking while running presents a big problem because of

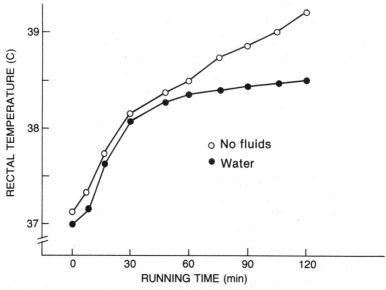

FIGURE 6-3. *Mean rectal temperature responses during 120 minutes of running.*

Adapted from Costill, D. L., Kammer, W. F., and Fisher, A. "Fluid ingestion during distance running," *Arch. Environ. Health*, 1970.

the spilling that occurs when you are trying to drink out of a cup and run at the same time. Although you will find it difficult to drink and run at the same time, taking even a couple of swallows will do more good than taking nothing at all. Costill has reported that partial fluid replacement helps in reducing the severity of dehydration and the effects of overheating (Figure 6-3). It is probably wise for the beginning marathoner to slow down the pace and drink as much fluid as possible, because the first marathon is grueling enough without compounding the problem by overheating.

Fluid intake during shorter races (less than 45 minutes) is usually not needed because of the time it takes for the fluid to empty out of the stomach and enter the system. However, races of longer duration should provide frequent aid stations to help in avoiding overheating. It is the wise runner who takes advantage of all the aid stations. It is too late to start drinking when you begin to feel the need to drink and the symptoms of heat exhaustion. Even if you don't feel like drinking early in the race, it is a good idea to do it anyway; remember, prevention is the best treatment for heat injury.

Running In The Heat

The body is continually producing heat in the working muscles during the high energy demands of running. In order to maintain a relatively stable body temperature, the body must dissipate this heat. The amount of heat that can be lost by the body and the rate at which the heat can be lost depend largely upon weather conditions. High environmental temperature, high humidity, and bright sunlight can add to the problem of distance running. Even on cool days the body can overheat if humidity and bright sunlight are present. The body actually gains heat that is radiating from the sun. This heat transfer from the sun is even a greater problem if both temperature and humidity are high.

Since we cannot turn down the sun, we must use common sense in dealing with it. Dark colors absorb more heat than light colors. Light colors actually reflect some of the heat from the sun. The wise competitor will dress accordingly.

Most of the heat loss from the body is facilitated by evaporation. If sweat is not evaporated, the cooling effect is reduced, and overheating may occur. Air movement and humidity greatly affect evaporation. In order for evaporation to occur, the air surrounding the body must be dryer than the surface of the skin. If high humidity exists, evaporation is less, and most of the sweat produced drips off the body without helping to cool it. Clothing may also hinder evaporation by holding heat and moisture next to the body, not allowing for heat transfer. Lightweight material such as nylon mesh should be worn to allow air to move through it, increasing the chances for evaporation and cooling.

The high humidity that is apparent during a rain has a minor effect on body temperature because of the cooler raindrops striking the surface of the body and cooling it. Even though running in the rain may not be desirable, it is better for heat dissipation than running in very high humidity without rain.

Naturally, performances are better if ideal weather conditions exist (Figure 6-4). An ideal day for running would be a dry (low humidity), cool (45 to 50 degrees F), cloudy day. This might not be the day for a picnic, but it would be welcomed by the distance runner.

The American College of Sports Medicine has a position

Bright Sunlight

High Humidity &
High Enviornmental Temperature

"Ideal Weather Conditions"

Cloudly, Overcast, Moderate Temperature,
Low Humidity

FIGURE 6-4. *Weather conditions and performance.*

statement on the prevention of heat injuries during distance running. The college has established seven major guidelines for the runner and race promoter dealing with racing in the heat.

1. Distance Races (16 kilometers or 10 miles) should *not* be conducted when the wet bulb temperature/wind temperature* exceeds 28°C (82.4°F).

2. During the periods of the year when the daylight dry bulb temperature often exceeds 27°C (80°F), distance races should be conducted before 9:00 A.M. or after 4:00 P.M.

3. It is the responsibility of the race sponsors to provide fluids which contain small amounts of sugar (less than 2.5 g glucose per 100 cc. of water) and electrolytes (less than 10 mEq sodium and 5 mEq potassium per liter of solution).

4. Runners should be encouraged to ingest fluids frequently during competition and to consume 2 glasses of fluid 10 to 15 minutes before competition.

5. Rules prohibiting the administration of fluids during the first 10 kilometers (6.2 miles) of a marathon race should be amended to permit fluid ingestion at frequent intervals along the race course. In light of runners' high sweat rates and body temperatures during distance running in the heat, race sponsors should provide "water stations" at 3 to 4 kilometer (2 to 2.5 mile) intervals for all races of 16 kilometers (10 miles) or more.

6. Runners should be taught how to recognize the early warning symptoms that precede heat injury. Recognition of symptoms, cessation of running, and proper treatment can prevent heat injury. Early warning symptoms include the following: piloerection on chest and upper arms, chills, throbbing pressure in head, unsteadiness, nausea, and dry skin.

7. Race sponsors should make prior arrangements with medical personnel for the care of cases of heat injury. Responsible and informed personnel should supervise each "feeding station." Organizational personnel should reserve the right to stop runners who exhibit clear signs of heatstroke or heat exhaustion.

*Adapted from Minard, D., "Prevention of heat casualties in Marine Corps Recruits," *Milit. Med.*, 126 (1961), 261.

Acclimatization to Running in the Heat

The body goes through a gradual change when subjected to repeated days of running in the heat. Heat adaptation improves the circulatory and sweating responses which facilitate body cooling, minimizing chances for overheating (Table 6-1). Acclimatization can be accomplished within 1 to 2 weeks by training in higher than normal temperatures or by daily elevating the body temperature. Thus, some heat acclimatization can occur even in winter months, if training on a daily basis causes body temperature to raise.

While heat adaptation is taking place, runners should not let themselves become dehydrated and possibly suffer from heat injury. Running in the heat also requires greater energy demands that may result in more fatigue, making the legs feel heavy and sluggish. Acclimatization should, therefore, be a progressive process in which the training intensity and duration are gradually increased over several days to avoid possible injury.

The circulatory system responds to acclimatization by providing greater blood flow to the surface of the skin for greater cooling. The responses to changes in blood flow are also quicker after adaptation has taken place. These changes allow for earlier and more heat transfer from the working muscles.

As the body temperature rises, sweat glands are stimulated. Acclimatization increases the number of functioning sweat glands, providing for better distribution of the sweat over the body's surface, maximizing evaporative processes,

TABLE 6-1. *Physiological adaptations to training in the heat*

Physiological Mechanism	Physiological Adaptation	Result of Acclimatization
CIRCULATION	Increased blood flow to the skin	Decreased body temperature
	Quicker response to blood flow changes	Lower heart rate, better regulation of blood pressure
SWEAT	Increased sweat rate	Greater cooling
	Quicker onset of sweating	Earlier cooling effect
	Better sweat distribution	Increased evaporation
	Less salt content in sweat	Less electrolyte loss

and avoiding sweat loss in the form of water droplets dripping off of the skin. Other sweat adaptations include a quicker onset of sweating and a more dilute sweat. You will notice less salt left on your skin and clothes after exercise, because the salt content (sodium and chloride) is conserved, allowing for less electrolyte loss and greater evaporation during running.

Performance in the heat will be better tolerated after acclimatization takes place. However, the possibility of heat injury still exists, and the early signs of heat exhaustion should be recognized by every runner in order to make appropriate adjustments in running strategy and pace.

Fluid loss is a problem while running events lasting an hour or more. The following observations were made after several of the world's best marathoners (times in parentheses) were asked what they drank during a race, how much, and when they started to drink:

Bill Rogers: (2:09:27) Bill felt that dehydration was a problem not only while racing, but also during his training. After his training runs he drinks Pepsi, water, coffee, tea, ERG, or fruit juices. During a race, however, he drinks water or ERG. The amount of fluid consumed during a race depends on the conditions; for example, in hot weather he may drink as often as 3 to 15 times or approximately 1 quart of fluid; in cold weather he drinks 3 to 4 times or about 1 pint of water or ERG.

Greg Meyer: (2:13:01) During a race, Greg drinks as often and as early as possible. He actually starts to drink before the race to assure proper hydration. He drinks approximately 10 to 20 ounces of water and Squincher.

Don Kardong: (2:11:16) During training dehydration is not usually a problem with Don. He replaces this fluid loss with water or diluted Tang. During a marathon he starts to take fluid as early as possible, if at all, depending on the temperature. When taking any fluids during a race, he drinks water or diluted ERG.

Benji Duden: (2:10:41) Benji starts to consume fluids during a marathon race by 5 kilometers and drinks every 15 to 20 minutes thereafter, depending on temperature. Even drinking this often, he only gets about 16 to 20 ounces of slightly dilute lemon Koolaid sweetened with saccharin.

Donna Burge: (2:44:46) Donna consumes about 8 ounces of water and ERG at 6 stations, starting at 2.5 miles into the race.

Lorraine Moller: (2:31:42) Lorraine takes fluids (water) as soon as possible during a marathon. She drinks at every stop if it is hot and humid, probably drinking about 1 pint total.

Grete Waitz: (2:25:41) Grete begins drinking fluid during a marathon at about 4 to 5 miles. She drinks very little during a race, but tries to drink Gatorade, water, or ERG when she does take fluid.

Ellison Goodall: (2:42:23) Ellison has run one and only one marathon. She had never gone anywhere near that distance before while training, so it was difficult for her to answer with authority based on experience. However, Boston 1980 was a deceptively hot, dry day, and dehydration took its tolls. What she did learn was the need to take sips of water all the way to the starting time and to drink as early and as much as possible for prevention of later dehydration.

Laurie Binder: (2:38:23) Laurie drinks during a marathon only if it is hot, whereupon she starts to drink water at about 10 kilometers. If the weather is below 50°, she doesn't take fluid.

Sue Strickland: (2:58:23) Dehydration is not a problem during her training because she lives in a cool climate. However, she is very aware of the problems that can exist because she started running in Hawaii. She starts to consume fluids well before the start of a race and drinks through 18 miles if the weather is warm. She prefers to drink water when racing.

Patti Lions Catalano: (2:30:57) Patti drinks 8 ounces of fluid just before the start of a race and then drinks as often and as much as she can during a marathon, totalling about 32 ounces. She prefers water and ERG as fluid replacements.

John Dimick: (2:11:52) In order to help prevent dehydration, John drinks early in the race and continues until 23 miles or so. He drinks a couple of ounces of water at each station.

Jon Anderson: (2:12:03) Jon consumes 16 to 20 ounces throughout a race. He starts drinking as soon as available, even right before the start if possible. He drinks his own mix of Coke, ERG, and fruit juice.

Dick Quax: (2:10:47) Dehydration can be a problem for Dick during training and racing. He starts to take fluids as early as possible and drinks as much as he can. He estimates drinking about 200 cc of fluid every 15 minutes during a marathon.

Jeff Galloway: (2:16:35) Jeff takes only a few sips of water during a race. However, he pours water on himself at every station for cooling.

Alberto Salazar: (2:09:41) Alberto starts drinking water at four miles into the race and continues to consume 1 quart over 8 stations.

Ken Moore: (2:11:36) As a veteran runner, Ken feels dehydration is a problem in both racing and training. During a race he starts to drink water as early as offered or at 5 miles maximum; he then continues to take fluids every 5 miles.

Frank Shorter: (2:10:30) Frank drinks his own brew of Coke and water during a race. He starts taking fluids at the first station and continues at every station, totaling about 25 ounces.

Amby Burfoot: (2:14:28) Temperature determines when Amby starts to take fluids; the hotter the day, the earlier he drinks. Amby guesses he consumes about 12 ounces of water and ERG during a race.

John Lodwick: (2:10:54) John drinks water and ERG during a marathon. He starts drinking at the first station and proceeds to drink 5 to 6 times throughout the race. He doesn't consume more than just a few swallows.

Lionel Ortega: (2:14:24) Dehydration doesn't seem to be much of a problem for Lionel. He drinks very little fluid during a race, starting at 13 miles.

Robert Hodge: (2:10:59) Bob feels that dehydration is a problem both in training and racing. Therefore, he drinks as soon as possible and as often as he can during a race. He drinks mostly water and ERG for fluid replacement.

Dave Babriacki: (2:16:45) Dave drinks water during a marathon race, starting at 3 to 6 miles out, and continues to drink throughout the race (approximately 10 times).

Jeff Wells: (2:10:15) Jeff starts to drink fluids at the first station or about 3 miles into the race. He then drinks some fluid every 3 miles, totalling about 7 to 8 ounces. He likes an ERG and water mixture.

Garry Bjorklund: (2:10:20) Garry seems to have a problem with dehydration during training and racing. He drinks water as often as he can, or about every 3 miles. He consumes 2 to 3 ounces at each station.

Charlie Vigil: (2:15:19) "Sometimes dehydration can be a problem; during my training I usually drink water and tea for fluid replacement. During a marathon I drink either water or ERG. I start drinking at the first station and drink as often as I can after that until around 23 miles. I guess I consume about 1 quart during a marathon race and drink plenty of fluids before a race, up to 15 minutes before the race."

Herb Lindsey: "Sometimes dehydration is a problem during my training; however, it depends on the weather and on the length of training sessions. I rehydrate with nothing special, just water."

Tom Fleming: (2:12:05) The weather determines when Tom starts drinking; during hot days he starts consuming water, ERG, or Coke as early as he can.

Nancy Conz: (2:33:23) "Dehydration can be a problem when training. I drink plenty of water and maybe a little ERG during the summer. During a marathon race I drink water at all aid stations; however, I have difficulty drinking without stopping."

Dick Beardsley: (2:08:53) "I really don't know how much I drink during a marathon, but I take as much as I can get and drink as often as I can. I usually drink water or Gatorade during a marathon."

Marathon running presents a unique problem for most runners. Almost all runners try to consume some fluid during a race. The quantities of fluid taken in are only a fraction of the fluid lost; however, most athletes feel that every little bit helps.

REFERENCES

Allen, T. E., Smith, D. P., and Miller, D. K., "Hemodynamic response to submaximal exercise after dehydration and rehydration in high school wrestlers," *Med. Sci. Sport and Exer.*, 9 (1977), 137–142.

American College of Sports Medicine, "Position statement on prevention of heat injuries during distance running," *Med. Sci. Sport and Exer.*, 7 (1975), 7–9.

Astrand, P. O., and Rodahl, K., *Textbook of Work Physiology*, 2nd ed. (New York: McGraw-Hill, 1977).

Costil, D. L., Bennett, A., Branam, G. et al, "Glucose ingestion at rest and during prolonged exercise," *J. Appl. Physiol.*, 34 (1973), 764–769.

Costil, D. L., Kammer, W. F., and Fisher, A., "Fluid ingestion during distance running," *Arch. Environ. Health*, 21 (1970), 520–525.

Costil, D. L., and Saltin, B., "Factors limiting gastric emptying at rest and during prolonged severe exercise," *Acta. Scand. Physiol.*, 71 (1967), 129–139.

Costil, D. L., and Sparks, K. E., "Rapid fluid replacement following thermal dehydration," *J. Appl. Physiol.*, 34 (1973), 299–303.

Dill, D. B., Soholt, L. F., McLean, D. C. et al, "Capacity of young males and females for running in desert heat," *Med. Sci. Sport and Exer.*, 9 (1977), 137–142.

Eddy, D. O., Sparks, K. E., and Turner, C. L., "The adipokinetic effect of hyperthermic stress in man," *Europ. J. Appl. Physiol.*, 35 (1976), 103–110.

Edington, D. K., Edgerton, V. R., *The Biology of Physical Activity* (Boston: Houghton Mifflin, 1976).

Kozlowski, D., and Saltin, B., "Effect of sweat loss on body fluids," *J. Appl. Physiol.*, 19 (1964), 1119–1124.

Lamb, D. R., *Physiology of Exercise, Responses and Adaptations* (New York: Macmillan, 1978).

Mathews, D. K., and Fox, E. L., *The Physiological Basis of Physical Education and Athletics*, 2nd ed. (Philadelphia: W. B. Saunders, 1976).

Nadel, E. R., "Control of sweating rate while exercising in the heat," *Med. Sci. Sport and Exer.*, 11 (1979), 31–35.

Pugh, L. G. C., Corbett, J. I., and Johnson, R. H., "Rectal temperature, weight loss, and sweat rates in marathon running," *J. Appl. Physiol.*, 23 (1967), 347–352.

Roberts, M. F., Wenger, C. B., "Control of skin circulation during exercise and heat stress," *Med. Sci. Sport and Exer.*, 11 (1979), 36–41.

Robinson, S., "Temperature regulation in exercise," *Pediat.*, 32, *Supplement* (1963), 691–702.

Rowell, L. B., Kraning, K. K., Kennedy, J. W., and Evans, T. O., "Central circulatory responses to work in dry heat before and after acclimatization," *J. Appl. Physiol.*, 22 (1967), 509–518.

Rowell, L. B., Marx, H. J., Bruch, R. A., Conn, R., and Kusumi, F., "Reductions in cardiac output, central blood volume with thermal stress in normal men during exercise," *J. Clin. Invest.*, 45 (1966), 1801–1816.

Saltin, B., "Aerobic work capacity and circulation at exercise in man: With special reference to the effect of prolonged exercise and/or heat exposure," *Acta Physiol. Scand.*, 62, *Supplement* 230 (1964), 1–52.

Senay, L. C., "Effects of exercise in the heat on body fluid distribution," *Med. Sci. Sport and Exer.*, 11 (1979, 42–48.

Shvartz, E., Shapiro, Y., Birnfeld, H., and Magazanik, A., "Maximal oxygen uptake, heat tolerance and rectal temperature," *Med. Sci. Sport and Exer.*, 10 (1978), 256–260.

Sparks, K. E., Dickinsin, A., Haymes, E., and Chambers, H., "Effects of caffeine on gastric emptying during distance running" (unpublished data).

Strydom, N. B. et al, "Acclimatization to humid heat and the role of physical conditioning," *J. Appl. Physiol.*, 21 (1966), 636–642.

Wells, C. L., "Responses of physically active and acclimatized men and women to exercise in a desert environment," *Med. Sci. Sport and Exer.*, 12 (1980), 9–13.

Wyndham, C. H., and Strydon, N. B., "The danger of an inadequate water intake during marathon running," *S. Afr. Med. J.*, 43 (1969), 893–896.

7

Nutrition

The amount of food intake needed by people depends on the amount of energy expended during the day. The energy needs of the body are dependent on age, body size, and amount of physical activity (Table 7-1). Most people need 1700 to 3000 calories per day in order to maintain their body weight. Runners need more calories because of the additional energy used while training. Running requires from 10 to 16 calories per minute, depending on the intensity of the run and the efficiency of the runner. The young athlete expands more energy

TABLE 7-1. *Recommended daily dietary allowances.*

	Age (yrs.)	Weight	Height	Calories	Calories per lb.
BOYS	10-12	77	55	2,500	33
	12-14	95	59	2,700	28
	14-18	130	67	3,000	23
	18-22	147	69	2,800	19
GIRLS	10-12	77	56	2,250	29
	12-14	97	61	2,300	24
	14-16	114	62	2,400	21
	16-18	119	63	2,300	19
	18-22	128	64	2,000	18

From Nutrition for the Athlete, American Association for Health, Physical Education and Recreation, Washington, D.C., p. 9.

because during the growing years, 12 to 22, the body requires more nutrients for the building of new tissues. After the growing years the caloric needs of the body are less. It is at this time that many people begin to put on extra pounds because of eating habits formed in earlier years.

The energy nutrients essential in your diet are fats, proteins, and carbohydrates. These nutrients along with vitamins, minerals, and water provide the ingredients for proper body growth and function. Performance is greatly affected if these nutritional needs are not adequately supplied from our diet.

CARBOHYDRATES

Carbohydrates are made up of the elements carbon, hydrogen, and oxygen. They are comprised of sugars and starches found in your diet. Starches are complex sugars that have to be reduced to simple sugars before the body can use them as an energy source. Normally about 55 percent of the calories contained in your diet come from carbohydrates. The athlete's diet, however, may include as much as 60 to 70 percent carbohydrates.

Carbohydrates are stored in the body in the form of glycogen, large molecules made up of many simple sugars. They are stored in the liver and muscle tissues in limited amounts. Their importance as an energy fuel for exercise is essential for all types of running.

Wheat, corn, potatoes, peas, and beans are a few examples of foods that are high in starch. Candy, cake, honey, or fruits contain large amounts of sugar. If more carbohydrates are consumed in our diet than are needed, they are converted to fat.

FATS

Fats, like carbohydrates, are made up of carbon, hydrogen, and oxygen. They are large molecules that are capable of supplying large amounts of energy. Fats make up approximately 25 to 30 percent of the total calories in your diet. They are stored in muscle cells, around organs of the body, and, as adipose tissue, underneath the skin. Fats are very important in your diet; they act as carriers of the fat-soluble vitamins A, D, E, and K. Fats also make our food taste good and, because they are slow to digest, keep our hunger satisfied longer. Butter, vegetable oils, cheese, meat, and eggs are good sources of fat in your diet.

PROTEIN

Proteins are more complex than fats or carbohydrates. In addition to carbon, hydrogen, and oxygen elements in their structure, they also include nitrogen. Proteins are made up of simple units called amino acids. The number of different amino acids arranged in the structure of proteins indicates what kind of proteins they are. Proteins are the building blocks of the body and form a vital part of all cells.

Proteins are used for the formation of enzymes, antibodies, and some hormones found in the body. They serve as regulators for water balance and acid-base balance of the blood and tissue. The daily requirement for protein does not vary from athlete to nonathlete. About 15 percent of your calories consumed are in the form of protein; about 1 gram of protein is needed per kilogram (2.2 pounds) of body weight. Good sources of proteins are meats, fish, dairy products, and eggs.

FUEL FOR EXERCISE

Energy is supplied to the body when the fuel sources of carbohydrates, fats, and proteins are broken down chemically by the body. As we learned in Chapter 1, the most efficient means of providing energy from these nutrients is with the use of oxygen during aerobic work. During aerobic exercise the body supplies energy to the muscle at the same rate the muscle is using energy. If the energy expenditure exceeds the rate of supply, anaerobic production takes over, resulting in an oxygen debt and a buildup of lactic acid. Anaerobic work cannot be sustained for any great length of time because the body needs a constant supply of energy and oxygen to keep it going.

When glycogen is used as the source of fuel, it is first changed to glucose (Figure 7-1), a simple sugar. Glucose is capable of supplying energy both aerobically and anaerobically. However, anaerobic breakdown of glucose is incomplete, producing less energy, and results in the production of lactic acid.

Fats are used as an energy fuel when reduced to fatty acids (Figure 7-1). Fatty acids are capable of producing large amounts of energy during aerobic work. Because of the chemical structure of fats, they can only be broken down with the use of oxygen, meaning they are only used during aerobic metabolism.

Protein is not normally used as a major energy source while running. Protein contains nitrogen in its structure; this nitrogen reduces protein's energy yielding capability. Nitrogen has to be removed before energy can be liberated. Protein is more important as a building block for new tissue than as an energy fuel.

The major energy fuels used by the body while running are fats and carbohydrates. The percentage of these fuels used will depend on several factors:

1. Type of running: whether it is of short or of long duration, of high or of low intensity.
2. Condition of the runner: highly trained or untrained.
3. Content of diet: high or low amounts of carbohydrates.

FIGURE 7-1. *Breakdown of energy fuels.*

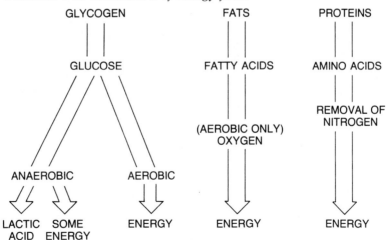

TABLE 7-2. *Calorie breakdown of energy fuels.*

Fuel	*Calories per gram	*Calories per liter O_2 consumed	Availability for running
CARBOHYDRATE	4.02	5.05	Limited
FAT	8.98	4.74	Unlimited
PROTEIN	5.20	4.46	Insignificant Use

*Physiological Values.

4. State of health: certain diseases such as diabetes may affect the body's choice of fuel.

In order to compare fat, carbohydrate, and protein as possible energy fuels, refer to Table 7-2. If you look at a particular quantity of each nutrient we see that fat yields more calories than the others. We must keep in mind that these fuels have to be broken down by the body; this process takes oxygen. Note that carbohydrate produces more calories than fat or protein. It would seem that carbohydrate would be the best source of energy while running; however, because protein is available only in limited amounts, the body tries to conserve the amount being used. Fat is more abundant and will yield more energy for a given amount used; therefore, the body will switch over

FIGURE 7-2. *Percentage of fats and carbohydrates used as energy fuel in a 2 hour run.*

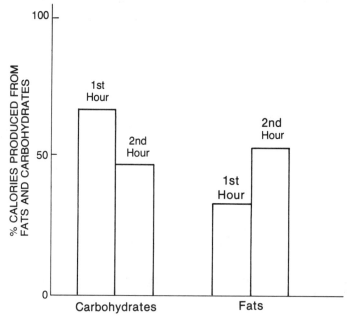

from carbohydrate to fat during long runs. At the beginning of a run and during short bouts of work lasting five minutes or less, the major fuel used is carbohydrate. If the run is continued over a couple of hours, as in a marathon, the body will switch over to fat (Figure 7-2). This changeover in fuel automatically takes place as the glycogen stores are lowered. If glycogen stores are close to being empty, the runner will have to slow down or stop. At this point runners commonly complain of "hitting the wall" or "running out of gas." Even though there is plenty of fat to supply the energy, the fat cannot be used, because fat needs carbohydrate present or it cannot be metabolized. This type of fatigue differs from that associated with sprinting. Fatigue from sprinting results from large amounts of lactic acid building up in the muscle tissue, not from the depletion of carbohydrate stores.

Training influences the amount of glycogen and fat stored in the muscle cell. The higher than normal energy use while training results in more fat and carbohydrate being stored in the muscle. Training also increases the amount of oxygen that can be consumed by the muscle, allowing for more energy production from the energy fuels.

VITAMINS

Vitamins are organic food substances that are needed by the body to help in regulating metabolism. Vitamins help in converting fat and carbohydrate into usable energy. They also assist in producing bones and other tissues of the body. Vitamins are required by the body in minute quantities and are normally supplied by your diet. The use of vitamin supplements is usually not necessary for the athlete, and massive doses of certain vitamins can be actually harmful.

Vitamins are divided into two groups, those that are soluble in fat (A, D, E, K,) and those soluble in water (B-complex and C).

Fat Soluble Vitamins

Fat soluble vitamins are stored by the body and are not needed on a daily basis from your diet. Because some of these vitamins can be harmful when stored in large quantities, dietary supplements are not needed.

Vitamin A. This vitamin is associated with vision in dim light and needed for healthy skin and for the maintenance of cell membranes. This vitamin has little direct relationship to muscular exercise, but is essential for good health. The body is capable of storing excess amounts of vitamin A in the liver. Large dosages of vitamin A may be toxic and may result in dry skin and swelling over the long bones of the body. Good sources of this vitamin in your diet include green vegetables, meat, fish, and butter.

Vitamin D. Vitamin D is sometimes called the sunshine vitamin because it can be produced by the body when exposed to sunlight. This vitamin is necessary for solid bones and teeth. It helps in the absorption of calcium from our diet. Vitamin D like vitamin A can be harmful to the body if taken in excess. Evidence suggest that excess amounts of vitamin D may cause normally soft tissues of the body to harden or calcify. There is no evidence that this vitamin when taken in excess has any effect on athletic performance. Sources of vitamin D in your diet include tuna, salmon, eggs, milk, and cream.

Vitamin E. Many claims have been made about vitamin E and performance. Some have claimed it will improve endurance capacities, act as a guard against heart disease, and increase your sexual potency. Regardless of these claims, any positive effect of vitamin E on performance has not been shown.

One of the properties of vitamin E is its antioxidant capabilities, meaning it opposes breakdown by oxidation. Because of this characteristic it is sometimes added to foods in order to protect other vitamins from being destroyed. Only minute quantities of vitamin E are needed by the body; therefore, it is almost impossible for you to be deficient in vitamin E. Rich sources of vitamin E are wheat germ oil, whole grains, and eggs.

Vitamin K. This vitamin is necessary for the formation of prothombin, a substance essential in blood clotting. Vitamin K supplements have not been shown to enhance athletic performance. Regular dietary sources are not needed in our diet because certain intestinal bacteria produce vitamin K. However, it may be found in green leafy vegetables, egg yolks, and liver.

Water Soluble Vitamins

Water soluble vitamins (B-complex and C) are not stored by the body and need to be supplied to our body on a daily basis from our diet. Because these vitamins are soluble in water, they may be destroyed in food preparation. Overcooking should be avoided. Taking excess amounts of these vitamins will not be toxic, but will result in an increase in the vitamin richness of the urine. Some researchers, nevertheless, recommend that athletes in heavy training increase the amount of water soluble vitamins in their diets.

Vitamin B-Complex. These vitamins are essential in making energy available for muscular exercise. They are important in the metabolism of fats, carbohydrates, and amino acids. B vitamins are also used for the proper functioning of the nervous system and are sometimes prescribed for people under stress.

During training the need for these vitamins increases; however, athletic performance is not improved by excessively supplementing an already nutritionally adequate diet with B-complex vitamins.

B-complex vitamins include B_1 (thiamine), B_2 (riboflavin), B_5 (niacin), B_6 (pyridoxine), B_{12} (cyanocobalamin), B_7 (biotin), B_9 (folic acid), pantothenic acid, and choline. Foods rich in B-complex vitamins are whole grains, meat, liver, milk, and eggs.

Vitamin C. Vitamin C or ascorbic acid is probably the best known vitamin of all. This vitamin is needed for the maintenance of bones and teeth and for the formation of collagen, a substance used in skin, tendon, cartilage, and scar tissue formation. It is important for the healing of injuries, but will not reduce the possibility of having an injury. It also aids in the absorption of iron from your diet, absorbtion vital to red blood formation.

Lack of vitamin C makes you less tolerant of exercise and can decrease performance. Some research suggests that vitamin C supplements may be beneficial, but will not increase physical performance above normal levels. Vitamin C should be contained in your diet on a daily basis; important sources include citrus fruits, juices, and vegetables.

Athlete	Dietary Supplement
ELLISON GOODALL	Multivitamins, minerals, vitamin C, liver tablets
CHUCK SMEED	Multivitamins, sometimes vitamins B, E, C
JOHN LODWICK	Vitamin C, liver, B-complex, minerals
BENJI DURDEN	High potency vitamins with minerals
KEVIN McCAREY	Multivitamins, B_{12}, C, liver, minerals
BILL ROGERS	Vitamins C, B-complex, iron, magnesium (all taken intermittently)
MIKE ROCHE	Multiple vitamins, C, E, B, bee pollen
STEVE PLASENCIA	Vitamin C sustained release, multiple minerals, liver, multiple vitamins
ROBERT HODGE	Vitamin C plus Theragram Multivitamins
AMBY BURFOOT	Vitamins C, E, B-complex, iron
FRANK SHORTER	Multivitamins
KEN MOORE	Vitamin C (1 gram twice a day), vitamin E (400 I.U. in A.M.), iron (ferrous sulfate in P.M.)
PAUL GEIS	Vitamin C (4 grams)
ALBERTO SALAZAR	Multivitamins, C, E, B
ALEX KASICH	Competitive Edge Formula
JON ANDERSON	Multiple vitamins, C, minerals
CHARLIE VIGIL	Calcium, multivitamins, minerals
MARGE ROSASCO	Iron, vitamin C, B-complex
NANCY CONZ	Iron, multiple vitamins
MARC NENOW	None
BILL ANDBERG	Multivitamins, vitamin E, vitamin C
RON TABB	Vitamin B, B-complex, B_{12}, vitamin C, multivitamin
TOM FLEMING	None
HERB LINDSAY	Competitive Edge Formula supplied to Athletes West athletes
RAY FLYNN	Vitamin C, up to 1 gram daily, 400 units vitamin E, iron
JON SINCLAIR	Multivitamins
PHILIP COPPESS	Vitamins B, E, C, multivitamins
DICK BEARDSLEY	Vitamins C, B_{12}, One-a-Day, trace minerals, iron

In summary, vitamin supplements are not usually needed; however, if you feel that you need a vitamin supplement, select one that contains the recommended daily allowances, and take only one per day. Megavitamins (or taking more than are needed) should be avoided.

MINERALS

Minerals, like fat-soluble vitamins, are stored by the body; therefore, many are not needed on a daily basis. Minerals are essential for normal bodily functions and act as regulators for physical performance. They are needed in varying quantities by the body. Some of the minerals needed are: iron, calcium, phosphorus, sodium, potassium, iodine, fluorine, magnesium, copper, sulfur, zinc, manganese, cobalt, molybdenum, selenium, chlorine, and bromine.

The addition of mineral supplements to our diet will not enhance running performance, although performances will be affected if deficiencies exist. Some athletes may be deficient in iron or calcium, depending on their diets and training regimens. Female runners may need iron supplements to replace the iron lost during the menstral flow. Males usually are not deficient in this mineral. Iron is an important mineral found in red blood cells and is a part of hemoglobin, which is responsible for carrying most of the oxygen transported by the blood. Iron is also needed for the myoglobin (important for storing oxygen) found in muscle cells. Deficiencies in iron cause anemia; weakness, paleness, and the feeling of fatigue are symptoms. Good sources of iron are liver, green leafy vegetables, raisins, whole grain cereals, and egg yolks.

Calcium is another mineral that is sometimes deficient in an athlete's diet. Dairy products supply most of our calcium requirements. Ninety-nine percent of all the calcium found in the body is in the bones and teeth. Calcium is important for muscle contraction and blood clotting. Calcium deficiency may be responsible for causing muscle cramps (although research has never documented this as fact).

The need for calcium varies; the young athlete needs almost twice as much calcium as an adult. Dairy products and green leafy vegetables are excellent sources of calcium.

During times of extreme fluid loss from sweating, sodium and chloride may be needed to replace the salt lost in perspiration. Most of the time just adding a little extra salt to your food more than adequately supplies this requirement. It is very unlikely that other minerals would be deficient or lacking from your diet; therefore, mineral supplements are not needed.

CARBOHYDRATE LOADING

Throughout the years scientists have tried to increase the performance capabilities of athletes. Of primary interest has been "hitting the wall" during endurance running. Fatigue of this kind limits athletic performance in sports that require relatively high intensities of effort over long periods of time. Fatigue resulting from prolonged heavy work is usually associated with drops in blood sugar and muscle glycogen levels.

During low intensity work which requires less than 50 percent of a runner's maximal capacity, fat is the main source of fuel. Most runners, however, train and race at higher intensities, 75 to 85 percent of their work capacity, meaning that most of the energy is being supplied from glycogen stores in the liver and muscles. Since glycogen is stored in limited amounts, the possibility exists of running out of this fuel source; when this happens, runners "hit the wall."

Normally your diet contains about 50 to 55 percent carbohydrates. This amount has been found to be inadequate in restoring the glycogen levels in the muscles after repeated days of training (Figure 7-3). If glycogen levels are low, performance is greatly affected. Researchers have found that by reducing the level of glycogen in the muscle and increasing the carbohydrates contained in the diet, the body is capable of overcompensating for the depletion. "Carbohydrate loading" or overcompensating results in higher than normal amounts of carbohydrates being stored as glycogen in the muscle. This helps decrease the chance of premature exhaustion during running lasting an hour or more. "Glycogen loading" is of little value in runs of less than one hour because the stores are usually adequate.

Carbohydrate loading is not for everyone and should not be used more than 2 to 3 times a year. People who require

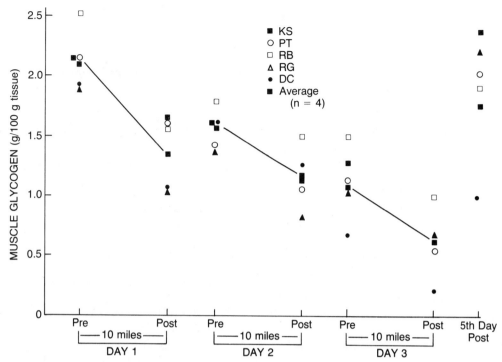

FIGURE 7-3. *Effects of repeated days of distance running on the glycogen content in the leg muscle.*

Adapted from Costill, D. L., Bowers, R., and Sparks, K., "Muscle glycogen utilization during prolonged exercise on successive days," *J. Appl. Physiol.,* 1971.

special diets, such as diabetics, should not try carbohydrate loading. The time it takes to restore the glycogen content in the muscle varies from person to person (Figure 7-3). Some athletes require 24 hours; others require 48 to 72 hours for the overcompensation to occur. Because of this fact carbohydrate loading should first be tried in practice or before an unimportant competition. Experimenting before big races may cause the results to backfire.

The principle behind carbohydrate loading is to first deplete the glycogen content in the muscle to near zero level. This can be done by running without a change in diet or by running and lowering the amount of carbohydrate contained in your diet. In both methods, carbohydrates are then increased for 3 or 4 days, and work is reduced to allow your body to store larger than normal levels of glycogen. Regardless of the technique used for depletion, the following guidelines should be followed when carbohydrate loading:

1. Be sure to record your body weight each day.

2. Glycogen depletion should be done by running, not by fasting or starving yourself.

3. Carbohydrates should not be eliminated completely from the diet during the depletion phase of carbohydrate loading.

4. Glycogen loading is not necessary for events lasting less than 1 hour.

5. Glycogen loading should not be used more than 3 times per year.

The technique of carbohydrate loading is very important; the following program is an example of one method that has been found effective in producing the overcompensating results for muscle glycogen content.

DAY 1   Exercise hard and long to deplete the glycogen content. The diet should be lower than normal in carbohydrates (do not eliminate all carbohydrate); increase the intake of fats and proteins during this time.

DAY 2   Intensity of the workout should be less, but the duration should be moderately long to use up the stored glycogen. A lower than normal intake of carbohydrates should be maintained; protein intake may be higher during this time.

DAY 3   Same as Day 2. Be sure to keep a record of your body weight. Your weight should be lower than normal, because as glycogen is depleted, water will also be lost.

DAY 4   The workout duration and intensity should be light. Carbohydrates, such as breads, cereals, sweets, and pasta, should become a major portion of your diet.

DAY 5   Same as Day 4. Rest is very important.

DAY 6   The workout should be very little. Body weight should be back to near normal. A meal high in carbohydrates should be consumed the night before a race to allow time for digestion and effectiveness.

DAY 7   On the day of the race the athlete should allow sufficient time for the pre-event meal to empty from the stomach, 3 to 4 hours for most people. Do not try to take in large amounts of carbohydrates within an hour of competition, because the high concentrations of sugar may cause an osmotic effect where water is actually drawn out of the body. The body weight is usually higher than normal due to the water that is stored with the glycogen. Increases in glycogen content may be 200 to 300 percent greater than normal if proper loading has taken place.

The practice of carbohydrate loading has been shown to increase performance; however, it is not completely without risk. The following is a list of recent clinical findings that suggest possible side effects from carbohydrate loading:

1. A change of dietary carbohydrate and glycogen content of the muscle may be associated with causing blood in the urine when coupled with dehydration.
2. Low carbohydrate diets may cause lightheadedness or even blackouts.
3. Because of the added weight, the athlete may experience sluggishness or muscle tightness when glycogen loaded.
4. The increased glycogen and water stored in the heart muscle during glycogen loading may cause changes in the electrocardiography of the athlete.
5. High carbohydrate diets may induce alterations in fat metabolism during exercise.

Carbohydrate loading is not for everyone; careful planning and monitoring should always be done. Because of the possible risks it is not recommended on a regular basis; all runners should be aware of the undesired side effects.

Most of the athletes surveyed said they did not carbohydrate load. Almost all of them, however, did have a high carbohydrate meal the day before competition. Carbohydrate loading may not be as effective for these runners because of the mileage they do each day. Most of these runners are training with 12 to 20 miles per day. Training of this magnitude causes the body to adapt by storing more glycogen naturally, making carbohydrate loading unnecessary. Carbohydrate loading may be more beneficial for athletes that are training with less mileage. How do runners feel about carbohydrate loading before competition?

Athlete	Do you "carbohydrate load"?
PAUL GEIS	No
ALBERTO SALAZAR	No
ALEX KASICH	No
JON ANDERSON	Only in an unscientific way. I do not deplete.
KEN MOORE	Yes, in a lackadasical fashion.
FRANK SHORTER	No
AMBY BURFOOT	Yes
ROBERT HODGE	No
LIONEL ORTEGA	No
STEVE PLASENCIA	No
MIKE ROCHE	I have tried it, but only in an 8 mile race. I felt good, but the race was too short for it to have an effect.
BILL ROGERS	Generally yes, but not the week long diet.
KEVIN McCAREY	Yes
BENJI DURDEN	Yes, but not a true depletion.
JOHN LODWICK	Mildly
CHUCK SMEED	No
ELLISON GOODALL	No
KIRK PFEFFER	No
GARY FANELLI	No
TONY STAYNINGS	No
HANK PFEIFLE	Yes
DAVE BABRIACKI	No
DOUG BROWN	No, my races are too short to benefit.
JOHN FLORA	No
JEFF GALLOWAY	Yes. I don't deplete, just eat a few more carbos before a race.
STEVE FLANAGAN	Yes, but I don't fully deplete.
DICK QUAX	No
DON KARDONG	Yes, but not all the time.
JEFF WELLS	Yes, sorta.
HENRY MARSH	No
LEE FIDDLER	Yes

LAURIE BINDER	Yes, but only for a marathon.
SUE STRICKLAND	No. I don't think women need to carbo load.
PATTI LIONS CATALANO	Yes
GRETE WAITZ	No
LORRAINE MOLLER	Yes. I have had good results both ways.
DONNA BURGE	Yes
CHARLIE VIGIL	No
MARGE ROSASCO	I don't deplete and carbo load; for a longer race I will eat extra carbohydrates, but for shorter races I eat just a regular diet.
NANCY CONZ	No
MARC NENOW	No
BILL ANDBERG	Yes, for marathon only.
TOM FLEMING	No
MARY DECKER	No
HERB LINDSAY	No
RAY FLYNN	No
RON TABB	Yes
JON SINCLAIR	No
PHILIP COPPESS	Yes
DICK BEARDSLEY	Yes

The timing of the pre-race meal is of utmost importance, because performance can be impaired if the athlete has eaten too close to race time. Eating too close to competition causes discomforts, such as belching, bowel disorders, gas in the stomach, or nausea. The emotional stress of competition, moreover, may cause an upset stomach.

The pre-race meal should be eaten 3 to 4 hours before the race to allow adequate time for digestion. The fat content of the meal should be kept to a minimum, since fat slows down the digestive process. The following foods should be avoided because of their irritating effect on the stomach and their gas forming properties.

Foods to avoid	Foods to use
Spicy foods	Juices
Bulky foods	Cheese
Fats	Potatoes
Raw fruits	Rice
Beans	Noodles
Cabbage	Spaghetti (no spicy meat sauce)
Onions	Roasted or broiled meats (small portion)
Radishes	Macaroni
Chili	

Bland diets are usually recommended and cause no trouble for most people. Everyone is different; some foods affect different people in different ways, so eat what works best for you.

The pre-race meal is important for most runners. The type of foods selected have to agree with their systems and at the same time provide the nutrition needed by the body. Athletes were asked what they included in a pre-race meal and responded in the following ways:

Patti Lions Catalano: I don't have a special pre-race meal, but I do eat more carbos, such as bread, pasta, and potatoes.

Sue Strickland: I have a special pre-race meal. It's crazy; I love baked potatoes with parmesan cheese, or pasta al pesto, and ice cream.

Laurie Binder: I eat a special pre-race meal before marathon races only. It includes whole wheat bread, salad (tossed), vegetables, and either pasta without meat or a rice dish.

Lee Fiddler: I eat little or nothing before races.

Henry Marsh: My pre-race meal includes fruits and pasta.

Jeff Wells: I don't have a special meal, but I do eat mostly pastas and ice cream.

Don Kardong: I avoid red meat 24 hours before competition. I don't eat on the morning of a race.

John Flora: The morning before the race I eat a piece of toast or two Hershey candy bars and drink water.

Dave Babriacki: I eat lots of carbos before competition.

Tony Staynings: I eat small amounts of bread and drink water before competition.

Gary Fanelli: I usually eat a light meal containing carbohydrates—dried fruits, dates, raisins, or figs.

Kirk Pfeffer: I eat a balanced diet before competition.

Chuck Smeed: I don't have any special meal, but I always eat light and try to eat 3 hours before competition.

John Lodwick: I enjoy pancakes before a race (at least 5 hours before). I always try to include carbohydrates and some kind of sweets in the last meal before a race.

Kevin McCarey: I don't eat the morning of a race. The night before I always eat a complex carbohydrate meal.

Bill Rogers: I usually eat carbohydrates like bread, rice, potatoes, macaroni and cheese, lasagna, pizza, cake or pie, and ice cream, and drink milk or Pepsi.

Mike Roche: No meat, no salad, just foods I know will eliminate in time with no problems. I like to eat very little before races (12 hours before).

Steve Plasencia: In the morning I usually eat toast and drink a cup of tea, if I compete early in the day. If I compete late in the afternoon or at night, I have a bland lunch, avoiding grease and heavy spices, and no orange juice.

Robert Hodge: Before a long race I eat a meal high in carbohydrates the night before and nothing except coffee the morning of the race.

Amby Burfoot: I don't have a special pre-race meal, but I usually eat pasta, potatoes, rice, or any other carbos.

Frank Shorter: I eat carbohydrates and drink two cups of coffee for a pre-race meal.

Ken Moore: I eat a special meal before competition; it includes toast and tea with honey, eaten 3 hours before the race.

Alex Kasich: If a race is early in the morning, I usually have nothing. Otherwise, I may have some toast and hot tea.

Charlie Vigil: I don't eat anything special, just normal diet.

Marge Rosasco: I try to eat light and easily digestible foods such as a big salad and some bread. If the race is a marathon, I eat more carbohydrates the night before. I don't eat breakfast on the day of the race, just a cup of weak tea.

Nancy Conz: I always try to eat well, vegetables, bread, maybe fish—no meat, pizza, or anything too salty or fatty.

Tom Fleming: Nothing special, maybe a little more bread with my meal and a couple of extra glasses of water.

Mary Decker: I don't carboload, but I usually eat only carbos as a pre-race meal.

Herb Lindsay: For an early morning race, toast with Morning Thunder tea. Nothing as special for other races, but I usually do consume tea, especially for longer races.

Ray Flynn: I don't eat anything special, but I try to eat something light 5 to 6 hours before a race.

Ron Tabb: I usually eat a special meal high in carbohydrates—spaghetti, pasta, bread, and cookies.

Philip Coppess: I don't eat anything special, but I try to drink plenty of water.

Alberto Salazar: On the day of the race I eat peaches and toast.

Paul Geis: My pre-race meal includes pancakes and peaches.

Jon Anderson: I usually have toast and tea as a pre-race meal.

As you can see, a variety of foods are consumed before competition. Each athlete has to know what his or her body can tolerate. Most of the diets are very bland, and meat is limited.

DIET FOLLOWING A LONG RUN OR MARATHON

The post-race meal is important and will help in speeding up recovery. The body needs nutrition after a long run; it has depleted much of its energy fuel and water content. Timing is important for this meal; it should not be eaten within an hour of competition in order to avoid the possible side effects of nausea or stomach cramping. The foods eaten should be easily digestible, such as fresh fruits, bread, puddings, fruit juices, cheese, and other dairy products. Fluid replacement is also essential, and an effort should be made to replenish the fluid lost from sweating. Every athlete should consume a well balanced meal as soon as possible.

MISCONCEPTIONS ABOUT DIET

Many misconceptions about eating have been handed down from coach to athlete over the years. The following are ideas that are sometimes regarded as fact:

MISCONCEPTION: Protein is the primary source for energy when running.

FACT: In a well nourished athlete, fats and carbohydrates are the major fuels needed for running.

MISCONCEPTION: No candies, sweets, pastries, or cakes should be eaten during training because they "cut your wind."

FACT: Sweets are excellent sources for the carbohydrates needed to replace the extra energy that has been used while running. However, these foods should not replace other foods that have more nutritional value. The term "cut your wind" is not a valid statement; sometimes foods eaten too soon after running can cause pressure of the stomach against the diaphragm, making it difficult to breath.

MISCONCEPTION: Fats, fried foods, and oily dressings should not be eaten during training.

FACT: The body needs a certain amount of fats to act as carriers of vitamins A, D, E, and K. Vegetable oils and other unsaturated fats may be substituted for animal fats to help in controlling cholesterol intake.

Fats slow down stomach emptying and should be reduced in the pre-race meal.

MISCONCEPTION: Milk causes "cotton mouth" and "cuts your wind."

FACT: Saliva flow and condition are related to body fluids and are not affected by milk or by the type of food eaten. Emotions may also affect saliva flow before competition; the mouth may feel dry, or the saliva may be thick.

MISCONCEPTION: Alcoholic beverages are good for replacing the fluids that have been lost during a long run.

FACT: The body needs fluid after running. Alcoholic beverages are not the best form of fluid replacement, because they can actually increase dehydration. Alcohol also affects the central nervous system and may impair coordination.

MISCONCEPTION: Drinking fluids during practice is a sign of weakness.

FACT: Fluid loss may be very high during long runs on hot days. As the body becomes dehydrated, performance is decreased, and serious illness may result. "Spartanlike" training is not a sign of weakness, but a sign of poor judgment.

MISCONCEPTION: Steak is the best food for the pre-race meal.

FACT: Meat contains fat as well as protein and is harder to digest than a more bland diet. If meat is contained in the pre-race meal, it should be broiled, not fried, and only small portions should be eaten.

MISCONCEPTION: Sugar and dextrose tablets may be taken for quick energy right up to the start of competition.

FACT: High concentrations of sugar taken at one time will tend to draw fluids into the stomach and intestines, increasing the possibility of dehydration. Too much sugar may also cause cramps, gas, diarrhea, and nausea. The wise runner will not be a victim of fad diets. Good judgment on the part of the coach and athlete will assure proper eating for good nutrition.

REFERENCES

Asprey, G., Alley, L., Tuttle, W., "Effect of eating at various times on subsequent performances in the 440 yard dash and half-mile run, "*Research Quarterly* 34(3) (1963), 267–270.

Bergetsom, J., Hermansen, L., Haltman, E., and Saltin, B., "Diet, muscle glycogen and physical performance," *Acta. Physical,* 71 (1967), 140–150.

Bogert, J. L., Briggs, G. M., and Calloway, D. H., *Nutrition and physical fitness,* 10th ed. (Philadelphia: W. B. Saunders, 1979).

Buskirk, E., and Haymes, E., "Nutritional requirements for women in sports," Women and Sports: A National Research Conference, ed. E. Harris (Pennsylvania State University, 1972), 339–371.

Costill, D. L., Bowers, P., Branam, G., and Sparks, K., "Muscle glycogen utilization during prolonged exercise on successive days," *J. App. Physiol.,* 31 (1971), 834–838.

Costill, D. L., and Fox, E. L., "Energetics of Marathon Running," *Med. Science Sport,* 1 (1969), 81–86.

Cramdon, J. H., Lund, C. C., and Dill, D. B., "Experimental human scurvy," *New England Journal of Medicine,* 223 (1940), 353–357.

Egana, E., Johnson, P. E., Bloomfield, R., Bromha, L., Meiklejohn, A. P., Whittenberger, J. M., Darling, R. C., Heath, C., Graybeith, A. M., and Consolazio, J., "The effects of diet deficiency in the vitamin B complex on sedentary men," *Am. J. Physiol.,* 127 (1942), 731–740.

Higdon, Hal, ed, "The complete diet for runners and other athletes," *Mt. View, CA World Publications,* (1978).

Haltman, E., and Bergstrom, J., "Muscle glycogen synthesis in relation to diet studied in normal subjects," *Act. Med. Scand.,* 182 (1967), 109–117.

Katch, F. II, and McAndle, W. D., *Nutrition, weight control and exercise* (Boston: Houghton Mifflin, 1977).

Marks, J., *A guide to vitamins: Their role in health and disease* (Baltimore: University Park Press, 1975).

National Research Council Committee on Dietary Allowances, *Recommended dietary allowances* (Washington DC: National Academy of Sciences, 1974).

Williams, M., *Nutritional aspects of human performance and athletic performance* (Springfield, Illinois: Charles C. Thomas, 1976).

Injury Treatment
and Prevention

THE RUNNING STRIDE

The running stride is a coordinated action of the entire body and consists of a support and nonsupport phase. The support phase can be divided into foot strike, midstance, and toe-off, while the nonsupport phase includes flight, follow through or back kick, forward swing, and foot descent (Figure 8-1).

Foot strike begins when the foot first touches the ground and body weight starts to be supported. There are basically three types of foot strikes. Sprinters usually land first on the ball of the foot and the toes. Distance runners tend to strike the ground with the heel or with the foot flat, followed by the forefoot.

Midstance starts when the foot is fixed and weight bearing; it continues until the heel begins to rise during the toe-off, where the forward push moves the body in the direction of the force.

The flight phase of the nonsupport portion of the stride is when neither foot is in contact with the running surface. The follow-through of the nonsupported leg starts as the trailing foot leaves the ground and continues in the backward motion. The forward swing occurs when the nonsupported leg moves forward past midstance of the supported leg. The foot descent is when the foot lowers toward the ground in preparation for foot strike.

There are many variations in running form or stride. Runners should not try to copy someone else's form, because it may not be natural or mechanically sound for them. Variations in anatomical structure, muscle strength, posture, and physical capacities make each runner different. Changing stride length, arm carriage, or foot strike sometimes places stress on other parts of the body, causing injury.

A runner's feet may collide with the ground as many as 1500 times per mile at a force of several times his or her body weight (depending on the pace and the running terrain). This force is absorbed by the running shoe and is transmitted to all parts of the body.

If injury results from overtraining, improper mechanics, or poor equipment, the runner is sometimes reluctant to seek medical attention for fear that the doctor will suggest that he or she stop running. If some injuries are not given medical attention, they become worse, and the result is more loss of training time than would have occurred if early treatment had been done.

FIGURE 8-1. *Phases of the nonsupport and support during the running stride.*

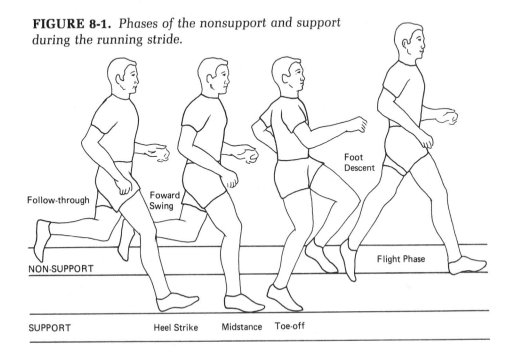

TYPES OF INJURIES

Runners are subject to all sorts of injuries. The majority of running injuries fall into four categories: (1) fatigue or stress fractures; (2) ligament sprain of the foot, ankle, and knee; (3) muscle pulls and strains; and (4) tendonitis of the leg and foot. Many of these injuries can be avoided if precautions are taken to assure that proper training techniques and warmup are being used. The incidence of injury is directly proportional to the mileage of each runner. Although all runners can encounter the same injuries, the highly competitive runner usually has more of the serious injuries.

Many running injuries involve the ankle joint and foot, because the constant pounding while running places stress on the ligaments, tendons, and bones. Two special terms, supination and pronation, have been used to describe the motion of the foot during the running stride. The actions of these movements help absorb the shock during heel strike and stabilize the foot during pushing off (Figure 8-2). The foot is supinated (the sole of the foot is turned inward during heel strike) in most runners. This means that most of the impact is on the outside surface of the heel and foot. The foot then begins to pronate (the sole of the foot turns outward) as it bears more weight during the support phase of the running stride.

Many injuries are caused by oversupination or overpronation of the foot. The bones that are absorbing the shock in the ankle and leg become misaligned. Poor mechanics of the foot and ankle are responsible for most running injuries.

Injuries of the Ankle and Foot

The ankle and foot are prone to many types of injuries because of the constant stress imposed by the pounding during running. Some of the less serious injuries may be treated by a coach, trainer, or by the athlete, but a more serious injury that is continually recurring should be treated by a physician.

Blister. Almost everyone who has been running for a time will get a blister, a collection of fluid underneath the skin. This fluid may be clear, or bloody if more severe. Blisters are caused by the excessive rubbing of one part of your running

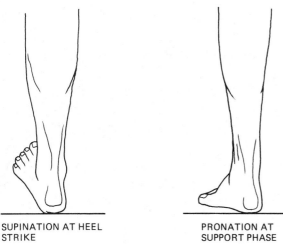

SUPINATION AT HEEL STRIKE

PRONATION AT SUPPORT PHASE

HILL RUNNING EXAGGERATES PRONATION OF THE FOOT

FIGURE 8-2. *Supination and pronation of the foot during the running stride.*

shoe, and should always be treated in order to avoid possible infection. The treatment of a blister will depend on its condition. If the blister is not open or has not been ruptured, you may place a pad that has been cut to fit around the injured tissue, protecting it from further pressure. However, if the danger exists of further tearing of tissue or spreading the blister, necessary steps may be needed to drain the fluid from the blister, thus relieving the pressure caused by the fluid. The following steps should be followed in draining the fluid from a blister:

1. Clean the area around the blister by washing it with soap and water, then wipe the area with alcohol.
2. Insert a sterile needle underneath the top layer of skin about 1/8 inch from the edge of the blister.
3. Using a sterile gauze pad, apply pressure directly over the blister, forcing the fluid out.
4. After the fluid has been drained, place a sterile pad over the blister to prevent it from refilling or getting dirty.
5. After the blister has dried up and the tenderness is gone, cut away the loose skin as close to the perimeter of the blister as possible.

Many times the blister will break and the skin will be torn loose. If this happens, the following guidelines can be taken for the care of a blister:

1. Clean the blister and surrounding area with soap and water (antiseptic soap preferred).
2. Apply antiseptic and a mild ointment such as zinc oxide to the exposed tender skin.
3. Lay the flap of torn skin back over the area from which it came.
4. Place a sterile bandage over the blister to protect it from further contamination.
5. After the new skin has hardened, remove the dead skin by trimming close to the perimeter of the blister.

Blisters should not be taken lightly; infection can result within a few hours. If this happens, seek medical attention immediately.

Calluses. Calluses are thick accumulations of skin that occur from abnormal skin stress. Many times calluses result from shoes that don't fit properly. As the thick callus develops, the skin loses some of its elasticity, causing possible tears or cracks.

Calluses can be treated by simply rubbing in cream that contains lanolin to soften the skin. Emery callus files can also be used to keep the callus from forming by eliminating the buildup of thick skin.

Callus prevention is much the same as blister prevention. Wear two pairs of socks and make sure your shoes are long enough and wide enough to eliminate the rubbing. A worn out pair of shoes can cause calluses, as well as blisters, to form.

Plantar Fasciitis (Heel Spur Syndrome). The most common cause for heel pain in runners is plantar fasciitis. The plantar fascia is attached to the calcaneus or heel and extends toward the toes of the foot where it attaches to each of the five toes (Figure 8-3). From the support phase on to the toe-off phase of the running stride, the plantar fascia plays an integral role in the supination of the foot for pushing off.

Plantar fasciitis is caused from overtraining or abnormal pronation of the foot, resulting in inflammation of the plantar fascia at the point of attachment to the heel. In severe cases of plantar fasciitis a calcium deposit or heel spur may develop on the calcaneus, causing considerable pain. Diagnosis and treatment will depend on the severity of the injury.

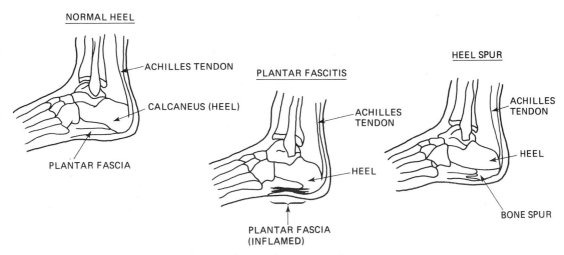

FIGURE 8-3. *Heel pain due to plantar fasciitis and heel spur.*

To relieve the symptoms, many runners try heel pads, plastic heel cups, ice, rest, aspirin, taping, steroid injections, or a combination of several of these. However, these methods do not help in correcting the underlying problem causing the inflammation and pain. If the problem is a mechanical one, a heel wedge or orthopedic device may be needed to correct the abnormal pronation of the foot. Surgery is sometimes used in severe cases to remove any bone spur that may exist.

Athletes should avoid hills, hard running surfaces, and any activities that require hyperextension of the toes or excessive pushing off with the toes. Runners should be encouraged to wear well constructed shoes that have a supportive heel cup and a flared heel. This will provide more stability of the foot and helps in distributing the force of impact over a larger area of the foot.

Ankle Sprains. The ankle sprain is one of the most common injuries involved in running. Irregular running surfaces and improper lacing of shoes account for most of the sprained ankles. Ligaments bind the bones of the ankle together to provide stability of the ankle joint. When the ankle is sprained the ligaments have been stretched or torn, allowing fluid to rush into the area, causing swelling and pain. Prompt and proper treatment is dependent upon early diagnosis and classification of the injury.

Ankle sprains are classified as first, second, or third degree sprains. First degree sprains are not very serious, with minimal swelling and little functional loss of the ankle. Second degree sprains involve partial tearing of the ligament, accompanied by swelling, tenderness, and some loss of ankle function. A third degree sprain is when the ligament has been completely torn. Swelling, discoloration, and loss of joint function is evident (Figure 8-4).

Most ankle sprains are to the outside or lateral ligaments of the ankle (Figure 8-5). The anterior talofibular ligament is the weakest of the lateral ligaments and accounts for most ankle sprains. Sprains involving the inside or medial aspect of the ankle are less common to runners than lateral sprains.

The treatment of ankle sprains is aimed at reducing the symptoms. Regardless of the severity of the sprain, the initial treatment is elevation of the foot, application of a compression bandage, and ice. This helps in reducing the pain and swelling of the ankle. An X-ray should be taken to make sure a fracture is not present.

First degree sprains are treated with rest, ice, compression, and perhaps temporary wrapping for greater support. Second degree sprains need to be protected by a cast, splint, tape, or wrap, until the ligament is strong enough for movement and resistive exercises. The severe third degree sprain may have to be surgically repaired to assure proper recovery. However, casting and rest may prove to be sufficient.

As the symptoms of pain and swelling decrease, the rehabilitation program can start with ankle exercises. The following exercises can be used to strengthen the ankle after injury.

FIGURE 8-4. *Third degree sprains of the lateral and medial sides of the ankle.*

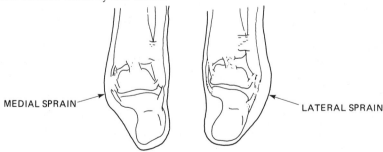

MEDIAL SPRAIN   LATERAL SPRAIN

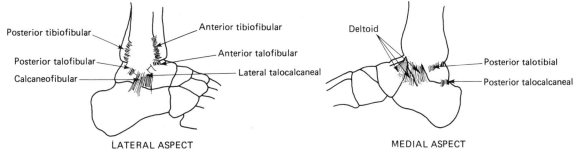

Posterior tibiofibular
Anterior tibiofibular
Deltoid
Posterior talofibular
Anterior talofibular
Posterior talotibial
Calcaneofibular
Lateral talocalcaneal
Posterior talocalcaneal

LATERAL ASPECT   MEDIAL ASPECT

FIGURE 8-5. *Ligaments of the ankle.*

1. *FOOT CIRCLES* - Make small circles with the foot, without forcing range of movement; gradually enlarge these circles until full range of motion can be made without pain.
2. *ALPHABET WRITING* - While sitting on a table with the knee straight and the ankle extended over the edge, draw the alphabet in capital letters with the foot.

These exercises help in rehabilitating range of motion in the ankle. When these exercises can be done without pain, resistive exercises can be started with gradual weight bearing.

1. *TOWEL EXERCISES* - While sitting on a chair, place the foot on a towel; pull the towel up under the foot using your toes. A weight may be placed on the other end of the towel to increase resistance.
2. *PICK-UP EXERCISES* - Pick up marbles or other small objects by grasping them with the toes.
3. *TOE RAISES* - Stand with the feet shoulder width apart; slowly raise up onto your toes as high as possible and slowly return back down to the starting position. If there is no pain, additional resistance may be added by using a wedge or by adding weights on the shoulders.

Walking and easy jogging may be started with the active exercises. The athlete should avoid sprinting and should not run on irregular surfaces or around curves on a track.

The following suggestions can be followed to reduce the chance of ankle sprains:

1. Wear proper fitting running shoes that are not worn out.
2. Warm up slowly by stretching (especially the heel cord exercises).
3. Avoid running curbs, curves, or rocky surfaces.
4. Used ankle wraps when ankle instability is evident.
5. Include exercises that will strengthen the ankle ligaments, tendons, and muscles.

Stress Fractures. Stress fractures are small hairline fractures caused by stress, overuse, or anatomical abnormalities occurring mainly in the foot or leg as a result of the constant pounding during running. Stress fractures are sometimes hard to diagnose because they may not appear initially on an X-ray. Most stress fractures are associated with too much milage or with rapidly increasing milage in preparation for a marathon. Hill running, toe running, and running on hard surfaces are also causes for stress fractures. Runners who have flat feet, knock-knees, or Morton's toe are prone to stress fractures. These conditions cause excessive pressures or forces on the bones of the foot and leg. The symptoms of stress fractures are tenderness and swelling of the injured area.

The treatment of all stress fractures is complete rest from running. Splinting or casting is usually done to protect the fracture. In order to maintain conditioning, you may substitute swimming or cycling until the fracture is healed (4 to 6 weeks). A gradual program of easy jogging on flat, soft surfaces can begin after the cast or splint has been removed.

In order to prevent stress fractures, you must stick to a sensible training program. Excessive milage should not be done before the body is ready for higher milage. It is important that your running shoes are in good condition and have proper supports and arches in them. Avoid running on slopes, hills, or on hard surfaces. If you have an anatomical problem that alters your running mechanics, you should seek professional advice for its correction before starting back to training.

Injuries of the Lower Leg and Knee

Injuries to the knee and lower leg are related to overuse syndromes or improper foot mechanics during the running stride. Poor foot mechanics compensate by transmitting the stress up the leg, resulting in greater stress to the leg and knee. Many times the treatments of these injuries do not get at the cause of injury. Therefore, after treatment of the symptoms, professional advice may be needed to correct the underlying problems.

Achilles Tendonitis. Achilles tendonitis is a significant problem in the track athlete and often causes the runner to lose an entire track season. Achilles tendonitis involves the tendon that extends down the back of the lower leg from the calf muscle (gastrocnemius) and attaches to the heel (calcaneus) (Figure 8-6). It is surrounded by a covering called the peritendineum, which may become inflamed during acute tendonitis.

FIGURE 8-6. Achilles tendonitis.

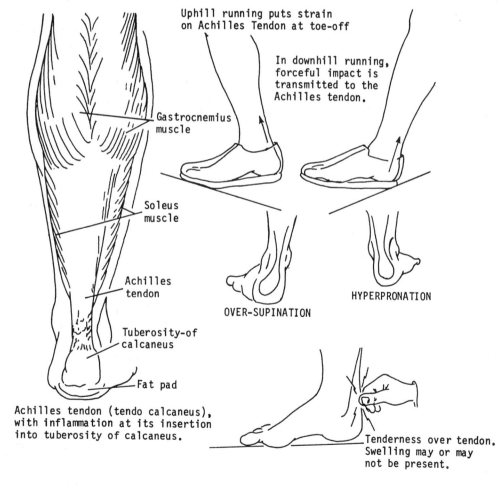

The Achilles tendon is responsible for extending the foot that produces the driving force during the toe-off phase of the running stride. Lack of flexibility in the lower leg places a greater than normal stress on the attachment of the tendon to the heel, which can result in the tearing or inflammation of the tendon. Achilles tendon problems are more prevalent in middle-aged runners than in young runners. This is probably due to loss of flexibility and tendon tensile strength with age. Sprinting, interval training, hill running, or mechanical factors such as hyperpronation or oversupination of the foot also contribute to the cause of Achilles tendonitis.

The three stages of Achilles tendonitis have been defined as acute, subacute and chronic, according to their seriousness and the duration of symptoms. In the acute stage of Achilles tendonitis, the peritendineum or covering of the tendon is involved and not the tendon itself, as in the more serious injury. The pain is usually present only during running and subsides with rest. The area of soreness is small and is located just above the back of the running shoe.

As the injury progresses to the subacute stage, the pain present during the initial part of the run may disappear for a time, during a sprint or in the early morning when you first get out of bed. The inflammation covers a greater area and may involve the tendinous tissue.

Chronic tendonitis involves inflammation of the tendon, either from overuse or from partial tearing. The area of pain is larger and the tendon may become thicker due to nodular formation associated with tendon degeneration.

Acute and subacute Achilles tendonitis can be treated with rest and ice, and in some instances anti-inflammatory drugs are given to relieve the symptoms. Injection of steroids into and around the tendon is dangerous because it may effect the tensile strength of the tendon, making it more susceptible to rupture. Splinting or casting the foot to protect it from further damage is common practice. Chronic tendonitis may require surgery to repair the torn or degenerated tissue.

Many runners try to "train through" acute cases of Achilles tendonitis by reducing mileage and treating with ice and anti-inflammatory drugs. In some cases this may be satisfactory, but the risk of further damage is always present. If the pain does not subside with reduced mileage, complete rest is needed. Swimming or running in water helps to maintain conditioning during this time. After the pain is gone, a gradual program of running may be started. It may be necessary to place a wedge in the heel of your running shoe to relieve some of the tension placed on the Achilles tendon. Sprinting, hill running, and track running should be avoided until complete recovery has taken place.

Avoid running on uneven terrain or hills if possible. If interval training is being started, work into increasing the intensity over several days or weeks to eliminate the possibility of overstressing the Achilles tendon. Make sure your running shoes provide proper support in the arch and heel. If a mechanical problem exists, such as hyperpronation or over-supination of the foot, orthopedic devices may be needed to correct the underlying problem causing Achilles tendonitis.

Stretching exercises are important in preventing injury from muscle tightness. Achilles tendon stretches, lower leg stretches, and hamstring stretches are good exercises to use on a daily basis to help prevent injury. Middle-aged runners especially should be aware of the importance of maintaining good flexibility.

Shin Splints. Shin splints cause pain on the inside front of the lower leg or shin. The pain is the result of straining or tearing the tibialis muscle from the tibia or shin bone (Figure 8-7). Shin splints are usually caused by overtraining, especially in poorer conditioned runners who increase their mileage too quickly, run on hard surfaces, or wear improper running shoes.

Shin splints can also result from muscle imbalance between the gastrocnemeus muscle of the back of the lower leg and the tibialis muscle on the front of the leg. The gastrocnemeus is responsible for pulling the foot downward during the toe-off phase and the tibialis muscle pulls the foot upward during the recovery phase of the running stride. An imbalance between these opposing muscles places a strain on the tibialis which can result in injury. Severe, recurring shin splints should be X-rayed to check for possible fractures.

Initial treatment includes rest, ice packs, or ice massage applied to the shin area. The ice has an anesthetic effect, giving some relief from the pain. Taping or wrapping the shin may also help relieve the pain. Resting from running for 7 to 10 days will allow for healing. During this time, swimming or running in the pool will help maintain physical condition.

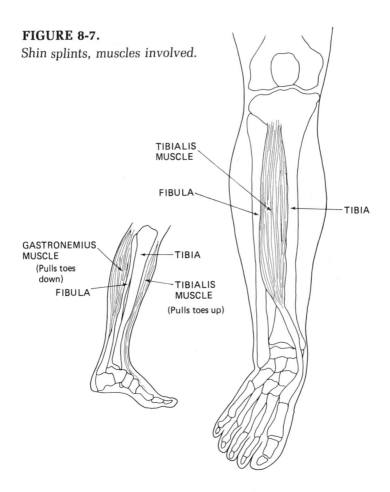

FIGURE 8-7.

Shin splints, muscles involved.

TIBIALIS MUSCLE

FIBULA

TIBIA

GASTRONEMIUS MUSCLE
(Pulls toes down)

TIBIA

FIBULA

TIBIALIS MUSCLE
(Pulls toes up)

When the pain subsides, the return to running should be gradual and on soft level surfaces to reduce strain. Orthopedic devices may be needed to correct hyperpronation of the foot, or arch supports may be sufficient in relieving stress on the shin.

Avoid running on slopes, around tight curves, or on hard surfaces. A good flexibility and strengthening program for the legs should be done in the pre-season. Proper warmup with stretching is always important in reducing injury (Figure 8-8).

Lateral Knee Pain. Lateral knee pain is associated with deviations in the proper mechanics of running. Flat feet or weak ankles that cause the foot to hyperpronate during the running stride are causes for many of the problems in the knee. These conditions allow the foot to roll medially or inwardly. When

FIGURE 8-8. *Flexibility exercises for shinsplints and Achilles tendonitis.*

Strengthening Exercise

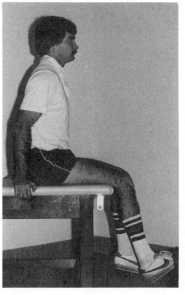

Achilles Tendon Stretcher

(Variation)

Achilles Stretcher Using Wedge

Toe-Lifts

Lower Leg Stretch

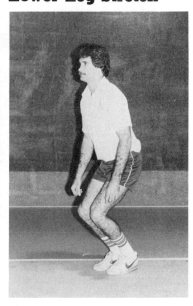

this happens, forces are transmitted to the inside of the ankle. To compensate for this pressure on the ankle, a lateral force is transmitted to the outside of the knee and the thigh (Figure 8-9). This lateral force causes greater stress on the muscle tendons and ligaments supporting the knee, resulting in inflammation and soreness.

Treatment for lateral knee pain is the application of ice to the lateral side of the knee over the points of tenderness. Anti-inflammatory medications are sometimes used as part of the treatment to relieve the symptoms; however, use of steroid injections is discouraged.

Correction of the underlying problem is essential or the symptoms will reappear when training resumes. If you have flat feet, an arch support under the longitudinal arch of the foot can be used, or orthopedic devices may help in correcting

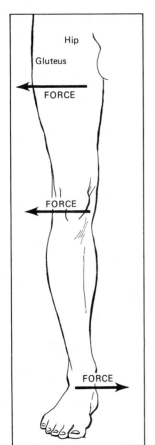

FIGURE 8-9 *As the foot rolls medially, force is exerted medially at the ankle. Opposite compensatory forces are exerted at the knee and hip.*

FIGURE 8-10. *Patella alignment of normal and abnormal knee.*

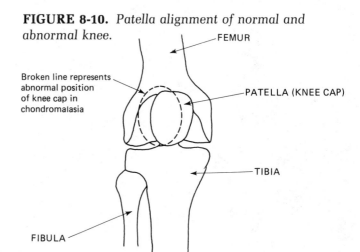

the problem of hyperpronation. Excessive wear on the soles of running shoes and loose fitting heel supports can also lead to knee soreness.

Avoid running on slopes; the foot is more likely to be pronated. Wear well constructed shoes that have a good arch support and a firm fitting heel support. Stretching the thigh, hamstring, and lower leg muscles before running helps to eliminate the muscle tightness that may cause knee problems.

"Runner's Knee" Chondromalacia. One of the most frequent knee injuries to runners is that of "runner's knee" or chondromalacia, pain under the kneecap, which is aggravated by hill running or stair climbing. This painful condition affecting the back of the kneecap (patella) is caused when imperfect alignment exists between the patella and the femur of the thigh, causing injury to the cartilage that lines the back side of the kneecap.

There are several causes for chondromalacia. Being "knock-kneed" places more stress on the knee, forcing the kneecap out of alignment (Figure 8-10). Poorly developed thigh muscles also can cause the kneecap to be pulled to one side. Excessive pronation of the foot produces internal rotation of the leg, forcing the kneecap laterally out of the patellar groove of the femur, thus irritating the cartilage of the patella. This excessive pronation of the foot may be related to running surfaces rather than anatomical misalignment. Running on the side of a road or hill puts the foot into greater pronation, causing the kneecap to track more laterally. Being flat footed or having differences in leg length also cause "runner's knee." Regardless of the cause, medical advice should prevail for the treatment of chondromalacia.

The treatment of chondromalacia depends on the primary cause for irritation. Immediate treatment includes the application of ice packs on the knee for 5 to 7 minutes or until the skin begins to turn red. This should be done for the first couple of days to reduce swelling and inflammation. Aspirin or other anti-inflammatory drugs may be administered under medical supervision to alleviate pain. During this time the knee should be rested until the pain stops. After the pain has subsided, a progressive resistance exercise program can be started to strengthen the quadriceps (especially the vastus medialis muscle), Figures 8-11a & b. The exercises should be done with

FIGURE 8-11a. *Exercises for the treatment of chondromalacia.*

(Phase I) Straight Leg Lifting Strengthens Quadriceps

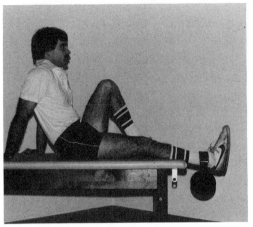

Starting Position

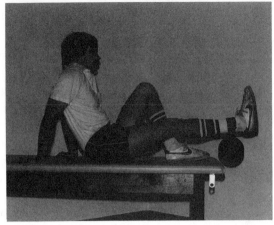

Ending Position

(Phase II) Actively Strengthening Quadriceps

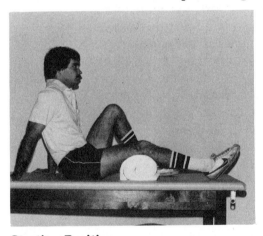

Starting Position

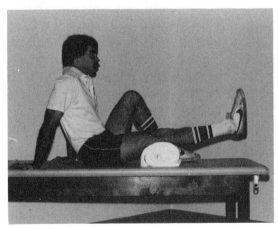

Ending Position

FIGURE 8-11b. *Exercises for the treatment of chondromalacia.*

(Phase III) If no pain is noticed with Phase II, a gradual isotonic program can be started with progressive resistance.

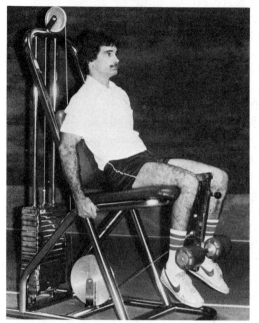

Starting Position

Ending Position

The Hamstring Muscles Should Be Strengthened Along With The Quadricep Muscles. This Should Be a Progressive Progam.

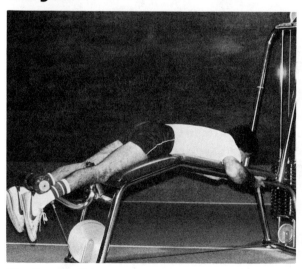
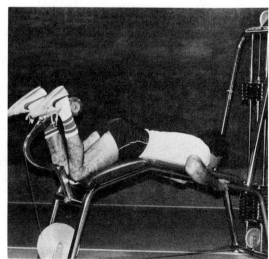

Starting Position

Ending Position

the knee fully extended; progression should be slow with 1 to 2 pounds resistance, lifted 10 times with 2 sets. Over several weeks the resistance can be increased to 8 to 10 pounds. To gauge progression, the ultimate goal is 50 percent of the weight that can be lifted by the healthy leg. Once this can be done, the athlete can lift the leg with the knee slightly flexed, progressing from 10 to 30 degrees at first and progressing to 90 degrees if no pain is present. After this is accomplished with no pain, the runner is ready to do isotonic or isokinetic exercises using the hamstring muscles. Running can resume when 80 percent of the strength in the healthy leg has been gained by the injured leg. A gradual running program can be started as long as there is no pain. After each run, ice should be applied immediately to the knee. After several hours, moist heat may be applied.

Knee wraps, braces, or straps may be used to relieve symptoms. Orthopedic devices may be used to correct excessive pronation of the foot and internal rotation of the leg. However, these devices should be used under professional guidance. Surgery is seldom done for chondromalacia and would be considered only in very severe cases.

If there is no anatomical misalignment of the kneecap, the athlete should take measures to prevent runner's knee by using a stretching and strengthening program for the muscles of the upper leg. Running shoes should not be worn if wear has taken place. Running surfaces should be flat, and hill running kept to a minimum. Orthopedic devices should be worn only if necessary.

Low Back Pain and Hamstring Muscle Injury

Runners often complain of low back pain. Many times this pain is a result of postural deviations that become evident during running or overuse. The underlying cause of back pain must be determined for proper treatment. The causes for back pain are many; those commonly associated with running are discussed here.

Low Back Strain. Many injuries of the low back are difficult to diagnose because of the complexity of causes. Low back strain involves damage to some part of the muscle tendon unit that is involved in holding the body erect. A strained back is usually caused by a violent contraction beyond the strength of the muscle. Symptoms include tenderness over the involved muscles, pain during muscle contraction, or even muscle spasm in the whole muscle group.

Low Back Sprain. Low back sprain is an injury to some part of a ligament. The difference between a strain and a sprain is sometimes difficult to determine; however, the mechanisms of the injury are usually the same. Muscle spasm may be present during a sprain, making the diagnosis difficult. In all cases, an X-ray should be taken to rule out serious injury such as a rupture of ligaments, a fracture of the vertebra, or a herniated disc.

The treatment of the strained or sprained back includes rest, bracing the injured back, ice, and later heat massage. Sometimes physicians may prescribe muscle relaxants, anti-inflammatory drugs to relieve the tension of the muscles involved. If the back strain or sprain is chronic, physical therapy and protection (which usually means rest) is employed.

Avoid hill running, especially downhill running, hard surfaces, and wearing worn-out shoes. Always do proper stretching as a part of your warmup. Runners also need to work on the development of abdominal muscle strength to provide a balance between abdominal and lower back muscles. Weak abdominal muscles may result in posture deviations such as lumbar lordosis or curvature of the spine.

Sciatica (Posterior Thigh Pain). The sciatic nerve is a large nerve branching from the spine and pelvic area and extending down the back of the leg. If this nerve becomes inflamed (sciatica) or pinched, pain will result. Runners who are affected by sciatica may feel localized backache, soreness, pain on movement, numbness, or tingling sensations running down the back of the leg and knee.

Most runners who complain of sciatica have a curvature of the spine called lumbar lordosis. This condition causes pressure on the sciatic nerve as it branches from the spine. Lumbar lordosis may result from weak abdominal muscles and tight back muscles, causing the pelvis to tilt slightly. In severe cases a herniated or degenerated disc may be causing pressure on the sciatic nerve.

The treatment will depend on the extent and cause of the injury. An X-ray should be taken to determine proper diagnosing. Running should be limited or stopped until the pain has subsided and normal movement is restored. Exercises should be done to lessen the lumbar lordosis by strengthening the abdominal muscles. Massage and heat applied to the lower back area will help in relaxing muscle tension.

Strengthening exercises and exercises for increasing flexibility are essential in preventing injuries to the back. A program for muscle development in the abdominal muscles is encouraged, with stretching exercises recommended for the low back. Avoid improper lifting with the back at all times.

Hamstring. A common injury to runners, especially sprinters, is hamstring muscle strains. Muscle fatigue, poor posture, inflexibility and poor running mechanics contribute to hamstring injury. The amount of pain and length of treatment will depend on the severity of muscle injury or damage.

Hamstring strains are treated with rest and the application of ice for the first 24 to 48 hours to stop any bleeding. After the hemorraging or bleeding has stopped, whirlpool bath therapy may be started. Severe strains should be iced and referred to a physician in case surgical repair is needed. Treatment may also include gentle stretching exercises of the hamstrings. Recovery takes from a few days to several months, depending on the severity of the strain and the damage to the tissue.

Proper warmup and stretching help eliminate muscle strain. Balance between the strength of the hamstrings and quadricep muscles will help in controlling coordinated muscle action. Muscle conditioning in the off-season is recommended for all runners.

ORTHODIC DEVICES

Many running injuries are caused by anatomical problems of the feet. These problems may not be of significance when walking, but during running they may cause stresses on the ankles, knees, hips, and lower back, leading to painful injuries. Sometimes the stresses caused by anatomical misalignment of the feet and ankles can be corrected by the use of orthodic devices.

An orthodic device can be thought of as a type of "shim" placed in the shoe to correct the position of the foot so it can function more naturally. Orthodics come in various sizes and shapes, and are made of various materials. The wearing of these devices may be temporary during the diagnosis or treatment of certain injuries, or may be permanent for the correction of an anatomical misalignment that will not correct itself. Orthodics can be effective in compensating for oversupination or hyperpronation of the foot.

Orthodics should be custom fitted for each individual; they should be made from a cast of the foot taken in the neutral position (Figure 8-12). Good results may be achieved if a correct analysis of the leg-heel-forefoot is made, a proper casting technique is used, and a precise fabrication is done to insure proper fit. If the device is not properly fitted by a professional, it may cause more problems than the ones already evident.

Prescription orthodic devices are rather expensive and may not be needed for minor injuries. Exercises or inexpensive supports may be sufficient; you may want to change your running shoes. However, with recurring injuries, a physician probably will prescribe orthodics.

FIGURE 8-12. *Technique of fitting orthodic devices.*

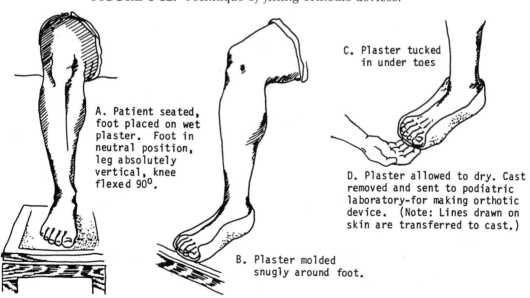

A. Patient seated, foot placed on wet plaster. Foot in neutral position, leg absolutely vertical, knee flexed 90°.

B. Plaster molded snugly around foot.

C. Plaster tucked in under toes

D. Plaster allowed to dry. Cast removed and sent to podiatric laboratory-for making orthotic device. (Note: Lines drawn on skin are transferred to cast.)

THE RUNNING SHOE

There are many types of running shoes on the market, making it difficult to choose the "right" shoe. The running shoe is probably the runner's most important piece of equipment. Running shoes should not be selected because of price, color, or popularity. No shoe is ideal for everyone, and the selection should be yours. Many shoes look alike from the outside, but may be poorly constructed. Some of the differences are in the materials used in making the shoe. The heel should be made of a firm material, usually plastic, not cardboard, and the heel wedge should be soft and wear resistant. The midsole should be flexible, and the inside of the shoe should have supports and smooth seams. Other features of a good running shoe (Figure 8-13) are:

1. A flared heel that is beveled or rounded for greater stability.
2. A well molded back to prevent irritation to the Achilles tendon.
3. A well padded tongue.
4. A high rounded toe box at least 1.5 inches high.
5. Well fitted arch supports.
6. A raised heel with a wedge, made of a soft material for shock absorption at heel strike, built into the sole.
7. An outer sole that is durable and that provides traction.
8. A comfortable fit.

Proper fitting should be done by someone experienced in fitting running shoes. Once the "right" shoe has been selected, there are several guidelines that need to be followed for proper care of the shoes.

1. Do not wash the shoes in a washing machine, because the shoes will lose their shape.
2. Do not dry the shoes in a dryer.
3. Do not remove the arch or heel supports.
4. Do not participate in other sports, such as tennis, racquetball, or basketball, in your running shoes.
5. Do not wear badly worn running shoes.

FIGURE 8-13. *Characteristics of a good running shoe.*

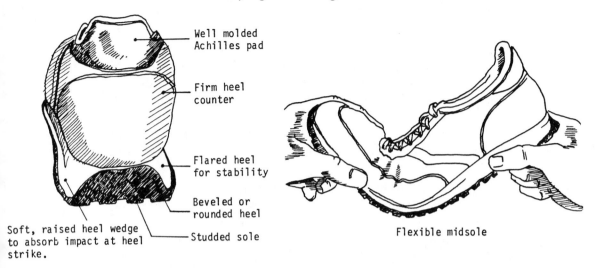

Well molded Achilles pad

Firm heel counter

Flared heel for stability

Beveled or rounded heel

Soft, raised heel wedge to absorb impact at heel strike.

Studded sole

Flexible midsole

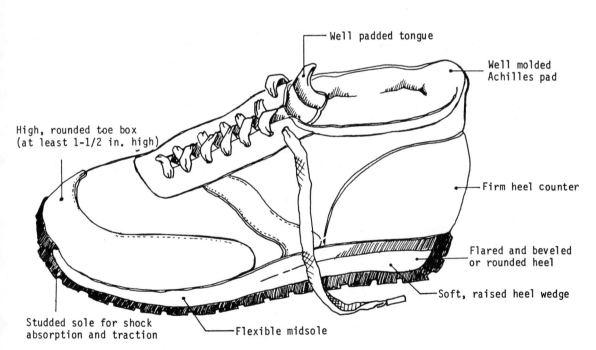

Well padded tongue

Well molded Achilles pad

High, rounded toe box (at least 1-1/2 in. high)

Firm heel counter

Flared and beveled or rounded heel

Soft, raised heel wedge

Studded sole for shock absorption and traction

Flexible midsole

If proper attention is given to the selection and care of your running shoes, minor injuries may be avoided. One thing to remember is that regardless of your running ability, the running shoe is just as important to the beginner as it is to the super star.

RUNNING INJURIES ARE FOR REAL

As the intensity and duration of training increase, runners are more prone to getting an injury. Even when the best training shoes are worn, and rest and diet are proper, injuries still occur. Running becomes very stressful on joints and muscles even in the best athletes of the world. It takes its toll on the runner who pushes 100 to 150 miles per week, just as it can on the jogger who is putting in 10 to 20 miles per week. Look at the injuries reported by athletes who train for top level competition.

Kevin McCarey: As a result of training, Kevin has had sciatic nerve problems and chronic hamstring tightness. His treatment is stretching, heat packs, a whirlpool before a run, and ice after the run.

Bill Rogers: Bill has experienced several injuries throughout his career. Shin splints were a problem in high school and college; these were treated by rest, running on grass, wearing better cushioned shoes, whirlpool, and hydroculator heat. Tendonitis in the knee joint and muscle pulls have also been a problem; treatment for these injuries consisted of aspirin for the inflammation, ice before running, swimming in a heated pool, whirlpool, and gentle stretching. Recovery from these injuries meant slower training and running on flat terrain—no hills. Bill has also had foot problems, the most serious being a neuroma on the right metatarsal. Aspirin, ultrasound, shoe change, and change in training (no speed) with ice treatments before and after each run helped in solving the problem.

Henry Marsh: Shin splints and knee problems have been the worst injuries for Henry. He cures his shin splints with rest and aspirin; his knee problems, however, resulted in knee surgery.

Mike Roche: Mike has had several problems; tendonitis (Achilles and knee) required aspirin, heat, and ice treatment. Sciatic nerve and back problems were helped by taking aspirin, resting and doing sit-ups to strengthen the abdominal muscles and to help in stretching the back and hamstring muscles.

Frank Shorter: Frank, like many other runners, has had problems with his feet and ankles. Ankle tendonitis and the development of a bone spur which resulted in surgery are among some of his problems resulting from training.

Jeff Wells: Jeff has been plagued with Achilles tendonitis. His treatment was ice, hydrotherapy, ultrasound, pools, and stretches. As a result of hard training he has had stress fractures which required rest for rehabilitation.

John Lodwick: John's most serious injury was a ruptured plantar fascia that required rest and heat before runs and ice after training.

Doug Brown: Doug also had plantar fascia problems that resulted in cortisone and vitamin B-12 injections coupled with ultrasound and massage.

Mike Pinochi: Mike has experienced a number of problems, sciatic nerve, back, pulled muscles, knee problems, bursitis nueromas and ischial tuberosity osteitis. Rest, aspirin, ice, and heat treatment along with a rehab program of weights, swimming, and massage were used by Mike.

Don Kardong: In the last fifteen years Don has had two cortisone treatments, one for a knee bursitis and one for a pelvis injury. Otherwise, he uses rest, ice, or new shoes to solve most of his minor injuries.

Benji Durden: Benji has had blisters and tendonitis problems in his left ankle. He usually just reduces his training intensity and uses ice, along with increased strengthening and stretching exercises.

Kirk Pfeffer: Kirk has had some serious training injuries which resulted in two knee surgeries and the removal of his lateral meniscus. He has also had hip bursitis that was treated by cortisone injection.

Laurie Binder: Laurie, like many runners, has had problems with blisters and uses Vaseline to reduce friction. She has also had heel problems (bursitis) which were treated with ice, massage, reduced speed work, and grass runs.

Gary Bjorklund: Gary has had surgery to remove an extra bone in his foot. The surgery required rest and extensive time for recovery. Achilles tendonitis and sciatic nerve problems were treated with rest, aspirin, ice, and extra stretches.

Jeff Galloway: The most serious injury Jeff has had was an Achilles tear that required over 2 months' rest.

Alberto Salazar: Alberto has had several injuries, including strained muscles treated by ultrasound, ice, and DMSO. He also had a stress fracture of the ankle, treated by ice, massage, and aspirin.

Ken Moore: The most serious problem Ken has experienced has been tendonitis near the insertion of the hamstring at the point of the hip. Treatment of this injury involved rest, ultrasound, whirlpool, and stretches.

Lorraine Moller: Besides blisters, Lorraine has had a more serious condition involving the Achilles tendon. A calcaneal spur had to be removed surgically to allow more freedom of movement for the Achilles tendon, which was shortened and thickened. The probable cause of this injury was a lack of flexibility and mobility of the spine. Most of Lorraine's injuries have been on her right side.

Donna Burge: Donna has had Achilles tendonitis, knee problems, and hip problems associated with her training. Her knee problems were treated with aspirin, ice, and the use of DMSO; her tendonitis was treated with aspirin, ice and heat alternated, and DMSO; and her hip problems were treated with ice and DMSO.

Grete Waitz: Grete has had a variety of injuries, including Achilles tendonitis, shin splints, knee problems, and back problems, that have required physical treatment.

Sue Strickland: Sue has Achilles tendon problems which resulted in Achilles tendon tear. She was treated by having her foot placed in a cast for six weeks to keep it immobile. After she had the cast removed, she went on a walking program for an additional six weeks and could not resume training for several months. To relieve some of the stress placed on the Achilles tendon, Sue wears a slight heel lift in her running shoes.

Patti Lions Catalano: Strained hamstring muscles have been the most serious problems Patti has experienced. She uses whirlpool and massage treatment, does some light jogging, and wears warm sweats.

Jon Anderson: John has experienced some very serious problems, such as bilateral retrocalcaneal bursitis and tendonitis, which required surgery in September, 1977 and again in January, 1978. He has also had occasional sciatica that he feels is due to laxity in his sit-ups, stretching, and weight workouts.

Charlie Vigil: Charlie has had problems with blisters, his sciatic nerve, and his back. Instead of running, he spent some days biking, hiking, or swimming for sciatic nerve problems. He says he really needs to see a "bona fide" chiropractor. He treats blisters by cleansing the area and taping it well.

Herb Lindsay: Herb has had sciatic nerve problems and strained muscles. Rest, diathermy, stretches, and alternative exercises seem to help him in getting back on the road.

Tom Fleming: Tom has problems with bursitis in the heel area and the lower foot. This type of injury can be very plaguing; resting and taking anti-inflamatory medicine are about all he can do.

Nancy Conz: Nancy has had problems with blisters, pulled muscles, shinsplints, and knee injuries. She has also had stress fractures of the feet. Problems usually show up after a marathon; resting and cutting back on training usually do the trick for her. She has never had to have surgery for running related injuries.

Marge Rosasco: Marge has had only one *real* injury that affected her conditioning program—a neuroma in the foot. This type of injury is not something that will go away by itself; some days it hurts, some days it doesn't. She tried Sport-thotics that were unsuccessful because they were too stiff and caused other problems.

Jon Sinclair: The most serious problem Jon has experienced has been chondromalacia. He rested and worked on a weight program for his knees; the program helped strengthen the quadricep muscles.

Ron Tabb: Ron has had just about every injury common to runners—blisters, Achilles tendonitis, sciatic nerve, back problems, shinsplints, knee problems, and bone spurs. He has had surgery on both feet to repair the plantar fascia.

Mary Decker: Mary has had sciatic nerve problems that required rest and chiropractic care, Achilles tendonitis that required surgery and rest, and shinsplints, more specifically compartment syndrome, that required surgery. Wearing special running shoes helps solve some of her problems.

Dick Beardsley: "I haven't had any injuries until just recently. My Achilles tendon has been hurting lately; I've been icing it, taking aspirin, and cutting my mileage down with no hard speed work.

REFERENCES

Brody, D. M., "Running Injuries," *Clinical Symposia,* 32:4 (CIBA Phar. Co., 1980).

Clancy, W. C., Deidhart, D., and Brand, R. L., "Achilles tendonitis in runners: A report of five cases," *Am. J. Sports Med.,* 4:2 (1976), 46–57.

Dehaven, K. E., Dolan, W. A., Mayer, P. J., "Chondromalacia patellae in athletes," *Am. J. Sports Med.,* 7:1 (1979), 5–10.

Fox, J. M. et al, "Degeneration and rupture of the Achilles tendon," *Clin. Orthop.,* 107 (1975), 221–224.

Garrick, J. G., "The frequency of injury, mechanism of injury and epidemiology of ankle sprains," *Am. J. Sports Med.,* 5:6 (1977), 241–242.

James, S. L., Bates, B. T., Osternig, L. R., "Injuries to runners," *A. J. Sports Med.,* 6:2 (1978), 40–50.

James, S. L., Brubaker, G. E., "Running mechanics," *JAMA,* 221 (1972), 1014–1016.

Klafs, C. E., Arnheim, D. D., *Modern Principles of Athletic Training* (St. Louis: Mosby, 1969).

Levine, J., "Chondromalacia patellae," *Physician and Sportsmed.,* 7:8 (1979), 39–49.

McCluskey, G. M., Blackburn, T. A., and Lewis, T., "Prevention of ankle sprains," *Am. J. Sports Med.,* 4:4 (1976), 151–157.

McCluskey, G. M., Blackburn, T. A., and Lewis, T., "A treatment for ankle sprains," *Am. J. Sports Med.,* 4:4 (1976), 158–161.

Nelson, C. M., "Rehabilitation emphasis should be on exercise," *Physician and Sportsmed.,* (September 1976), 93–96.

Newell, S. G., and Miller, S. J., "Conservative treatment of plantar fascial strain," *Physician and Sportsmed.,* (November 1977), 68–73.

Outerbridge, R. E., Dunlop, J., "The problem of chondromalacia patella," *Clin. Ortho. and Related Res.,* 110 (1975), 177–196.

Ramig, D., Shadle, J., Watkins, C. A., Cavolo, D., and Kreutzberg, J. R., "Biomechanical foot faults as related to chondromalacia patellae," *Bulletin of Sports Med., A.P.T.A.,* 3:2 (1979), 11–12.

Rubin, B., and Collins, H. R., "Runner's knee," *Physician and Sportsmed.,* 8:6 (1980), 49–58.

Snook, G. A., "Achilles tendon tenosynovitis in long distance runners," *Med. Sci. Sport and Exer.,* 4 (1972), 155–158.

Stanitski, C. L., McMaster, J. H., Scranton, P. E., "On the nature of stress fractures," *Am. J. Sports Med.,* 6:6 (1978), 391–396.

Starkey, J. A., "Treatment of ankle sprains by simultaneous use of intermittent compression and ice pack," *Am. J. Sports Med.,* 4:4 (1976), 142–144.

Veith, R. G., Matsen, F. A., Newell, S. G., "Recurrent anterior compartment syndromes," *Physician and Sportsmed.,* 8:11 (1980), 80–88.

Walsh, W. M., Blackburn, T., "Prevention of ankle sprains," *Am. J. Sports Med.,* 5:6 (1977), 243–245.

Drugs and Sport

Henry Chambers, M.D.

The use of drugs in sports is a very timely and controversial issue. There can be no doubt that some drugs will aid in an athlete's performance. However, the price that they extract over the long term is not commensurate with the added few seconds to one's performance. There are currently many drugs that are of questionable use to the athlete, and there are drugs that are potentially very harmful. The use of drugs as an adjunct to sports is known as an ergogenic (literally "work producing") aid. This is also known in some circles as *doping*.

Many, if not most, of the ergogenic aids in running are used widely without any regard to the proof or disproof of their efficacy or their danger. Often ergogenic aids become popular because a certain runner or weight lifter stated that he attained the world record because he, for example, chewed twenty packs of purple gum before the Olympics. At the next local 10 kilometer race everyone is chewing purple gum. While this clearly is a facile example, most of the use of these ergogenic aids is based on similar "scientific" investigation.

There are many drugs, both legal and illegal, used by athletes today. Many feel compelled to use them, and others simply enjoy them. The athlete is now in a position in which he or she sees fellow competitors using ergogenic aids and fears that these pills will make the difference in the race's outcome. It is a difficult proposition that the young athlete, coach, trainer, parent, and physician face. The International Olympic Committee has issued a list of doping substances for which they test before and after competition. An athlete who is caught with one of these substances in his or her bloodstream will be eliminated from further competition and may even be banned from amateur athletics. One of the best ways to deal with the pressures of drug use is to be educated as to the potentially dangerous effects of drugs on the human body. Stimulants, such as amphetamines, caffeine, analgesics (painkillers), anabolic steroids, alcohol, and marijuana, are sometimes used by athletes who believe they get that "extra edge" in competition. Ergogenic aids that are considered to be physiologic are those substances that the body normally uses. These include "blood doping" and oxygen.

BLOOD DOPING

Blood doping gained notoriety in the popular press when Lasse Viren was accused of employing it as an ergogenic aid after he won the 5,000 K and 10,000 K races in the 1972 Olympics. Blood doping consists of removing 500 to 1,000 cc of your blood prior to the final month of training and then, just prior to the competition, reinfusing (transfusing) yourself with that blood. Viren denied using this tactic, but others have tried it. This technique supposedly increases the oxygen carrying capacity of the bloodstream by adding more red blood cells. While this is theoretically possible, many studies doubt the validity of the tactic, and most studies note that transfusions are fraught with hazards.

OXYGEN

Oxygen use in marathon running is not very practical since it is difficult to carry much of a supply while running. There are some arguments that oxygen may be useful in short-term exercise, but it is obvious that after a few breaths in a marathon, the benefits of the oxygen would be gone.

AMPHETAMINES

Amphetamines ("speed," "bennies") are probably the most abused drugs in sports. These are stimulants which make an athlete more alert and quicker for a short time. They also alter the athlete's perception of fatigue so that he or she may run longer. In actuality, only the effects of fatigue are masked. The runner may ignore pain and injury and may risk crippling himself. These drugs also make an athlete more aggressive and hostile. Most of the literature on amphetamines states that there is no effect on athletic performance, especially in aerobic or long distance running.

CAFFEINE

Caffeine is certainly one of the most widely used drugs in America, by athletes and nonathletes alike. There has been a recent interest taken in caffeine's effect on athletic performance. The authors of this book conducted research in 1978 at the University of Colorado and found that caffeine aids the athlete in three important ways:

1) Caffeine, by slightly increasing the stomach acidity, increases the rate at which the energy providing contents of the stomach are used;
2) Caffeine and its metabolites in the body combine to relax smooth muscle tissue (particularly the bronchioles of the lungs), thereby providing for slightly increased ventilation; and
3) It affects the fats normally stored in the body.

As these fats are stored, they are useless to the exercising athlete. However, upon the ingestion of caffeine, a phenomenon occurs whereby the inactive fat is transformed into active utilizable free fatty acids. This occurrence is very beneficial to the exercising athlete since fats are preferentially utilized by muscles during the stress of exercise. The use of free fatty acids as an energy substrate initially precludes the use of carbohydrates in the form of glycogen and glucose. Glycogen is the last energy substrate that can be used by an athlete. The longer that the glycogen can be "spared" or unused, the longer the athlete can exercise.

Although caffeine would seem to be the ultimate ergonenic aid, there are many problems with its use. The effects of caffeine are usually not appreciable until at least 90 minutes of exercise have elapsed. There are many side effects of caffeine including heart arrythmias and gastrointestinal disturbances. There have also been reports of death from as few as 1000 milligrams (an average cup of coffee contains 150 milligrams) of caffeine. Because the delivery of caffeine to the bloodstream from coffee, tea, and soft drinks exhibits much variability, you cannot be sure of the dosage administered.

ANALGESICS (PAIN KILLERS)

The use of analgesics (pain killers), both narcotic and non-narcotic, is very distressing. Narcotic analgesics include codeine, morphine, methadone, heroin, and Dilaudid, among others. Besides being on the International Olympic Committee's banned substance list, the addictive quality of the narcotic analgesics and their ability to mask pain are clearly very dangerous. Pain is an important adaptive response—nature's way of telling you that something is injured. The inability to recognize painful stimuli permits the athlete to incur perhaps crippling damage to his body. Non-narcotic analgesics include aspirin, non-steroidal anti-inflammatory drugs (NSAID) such as Naprosyn and Motrin, and topically applied agents such as DMSO and the spray-on freezing agents. The non-narcotic analgesics are not as effective as narcotic analgesics in eliminating pain, and are therefore somewhat less dangerous. There is a role in sports for the use of anti-inflammatory drugs, such as prescribed NSAI drugs and aspirin in the treatment of injury, but not that of a pain suppressor.

The use of the spray-on freezing agents is potentially

dangerous because of the risk of frostbite as well as, once again, the masking of pain. Dimethyl sulfoxide (DMSO) is a very controversial and popular analgesic. The press and a few doctors are lauding its ability to eliminate pain and tenderness in soft tissue (muscle, tendon, and ligament) injuries. Most of the studies of the drug are based on testimonials rather than experimental research. A recent double blind controlled study showed that there was no difference in pain, swelling, or tenderness between the experimental and the control group, thereby indicating the uselessness of the drug. Many side effects were noted in this study, including rash, burn, blisters, and an unpleasant garlicky taste and smell. DMSO is not a useless drug; it has many uses in medicine, but sports medicine is not one of its beneficiaries.

ANABOLIC STEROIDS

Anabolic steroids are synthetic drugs that are analogs of the male sex hormone, testosterone. Since testosterone is the natural hormone used by the body to increase muscle bulk and strength, you might assume that if you augment your body's steroids with synthetic steroids, your bulk and strength will increase. While there is no doubt that steroids increase bulk, there is not much reliable evidence that steroids increase strength, and you certainly do not need bulk for bulk's sake. The American College of Sports Medicine issued a position paper in 1978 on the use and abuse of anabolic steroids. In it they stated that there is no scientific evidence that steroids "bring about any significant improvements in strength, aerobic endurance, lean body mass, or body weight." They also list the many adverse effects of steroids, such as liver damage and a decrease in testicular size and function with a decrease in sperm production. It is unknown at this time whether or not these effects are reversible. Many women are currently taking steroids, and the effects on their bodies, especially in regard to the menstrual cycle and the production of cancerous cells, are not completely understood.

Because research results concerning anabolic steroids are very confusing and incomplete at this time, it is difficult for runners to decide whether or not to use them. Many runners, including world-class athletes, do. The amateur runner is expected to make a decision when all of the evidence is not yet in. However, there are definite contraindications to the use of steroids, and certainly the risks greatly outweigh any possible gains.

ALCOHOL AND MARIJUANA

Alcohol and marijuana are drugs in wide use today. Obviously the overuse of these drugs to the point of inebriation would hinder any athlete's performance, but there are many who use these drugs to allay anxiety before an important match or race. Some marathoners use alcohol, especially beer, as a source of energy and as a rehydration fluid. However, the amount of readily accessible calories in beer is minimal. Alcoholism is a tremendous problem in our society, and since alcohol does not help your athletic performance, it is better left out of your training diet.

Marijuana is still illegal, and the amount of research on this much used drug is limited. A study by Steadward and Singh in 1975 showed that there was no difference in the vital capacity, expiratory flow rate, and handgrip between subjects who smoked a placebo and subjects who smoked marijuana. Since marijuana reportedly makes one less competitive, it's of little use as an ergogenic aid.

VITAMINS: NEEDED OR NOT?

The addition of vitamins to one's diet seems an innocuous way to increase an athlete's performance. There are no studies that indicate that more than the recommended daily allowance of any vitamin will make one a better athlete. In fact, one does not even need to take a daily multivitamin if balanced daily meals are consumed. Healthfood stores often make unfounded but convincing claims for individual vitamins and food additives. Too much of some vitamins can be very detrimental to an athlete's performance and may even be harmful to one's health.

Much has been written about "vitamin B_{15}," the new

"wonder drug." It is not actually a vitamin, nor is it "pangamic acid," as the Russians claim. It is N, N dimethyl glycine (DMG), a normal intermediate of choline metabolism. The Russians were apparently the first to use this drug, and their success in track was ascribed to this use. It is not currently on the market, because the Food and Drug Administration, considering it illegal and possibly dangerous, is still studying it. Further research is necessary in more extensive and controlled human performance experiments.

HYPNOSIS AND TRANCENDENTAL MEDITATION

Sports psychology is a relatively new area of sports medicine. Little is known of the effect of the mind on athletic performance, although it is intrinsically obvious to most of us that the contestant who, all other things being equal, "wants it the most" will win. The athlete who can "psyche himself up" or be "psyched up" by a coach can often perform at unexpected levels. The jockeying for position and the talk during a marathon race are both psychological ploys used by the runner to gain an edge. Hypnosis and Trancendental Meditation are used by many runners to help them concentrate and allay anxiety. There is apparently little harm and much benefit from employing psychological ergogenic aids.

SUMMARY

There is enough doubt and controversy surrounding the use of ergogentic aids that extreme caution must be exercised when considering their use. There is much pressure on the athlete of today to perform at a level pleasing to himself, his coach, his parents, or his sponsor. The young astute athlete will no doubt notice some use of drugs by his competitors and might feel compelled to use drugs to remain competitive. One must be aware of ethical and legal considerations raised by the use of ergogenic aids, as well as the possible health hazards they entail.

REFERENCES

"Alcohol and athletes—a round table," *Physician and Sportsmed.*, 7 (July 1979), 39–55.

Barnes, L., "B$_{15}$: The politics of ergogenicity," *Physician and Sportsmed.*, 7 (November 1979), 17–18.

Chandler, J. and Blair, S., "The effect of amphetamines on selected physiological components related to athletic success," *Med Sci Sport and Exer.*, 12 (1080), 65–69.

Costill, D. L. and Sparks, K. E., "Rapid fluid replacement following thermal dehydration," *J. Appl. Physiol.*, 34 (1973), 299–303.

Costill, D. L., Dalsky, G. P., and Fink, W., "Effects of caffeine ingestion on metabolism and exercise performance," *Med. Sci. Sport and Exer.*, 10 (1978), 155–158.

Ekblom, B., Goldbarg, A. N., and Gullbring, B., "Response to exercise after blood loss and reinfusion," *J. Appl. Physiol.*, 33 (1973), 175–180.

Karpovitch, P. V., "Effect of amphetamine sulfate on athletic performance," *JAMA*, 170 (1959), 558–561.

Kedra M., Pitera, A., Poleszak, J., and Horubala, G., "Effect of caffeine on the composition of blood lipids," *Polish Med. J.*, 74 (1967), 825–831.

Marks, V., and Kelly, J. F., "Absorption of caffeine from tea, coffee, and Coca Cola," *Lancet*, 827 (1973).

Mafenson, H. C., and Greensher, J., "Drugs in sports," *New York State J. of Med.*, 80:1 (January 1980), 57–60.

Percy, E. C., "Ergogenic aids in athletics," *Med. Sci. Sport and Exer.*, 10 (Winter 1978), 298–303.

Percy, E. C., "Chemical warfare: drugs in sports," *West J. Med.*, 133 (December 1980), 478–484.

Percy, E. C., and Carson, J. D., "The use of DMSO in tennis elbow and rotator cuff tendonitis: a double-blind study," *Med. Sci. Sport and Exer.*, 13 (1981), 215–219.

"Position statement on the use and abuse of anabolic-androgenic steroids in sports," *Am. Coll. Sports Med. Bull.*, 13 (Jan 1978), 1.

Smith, G. M., and Beecher, H. K., "Amphetamine sulfate and athletic performance," *JAMA*, 170 (1959), 542–547.

Steadward, R. D., and Singh, M., "The effect of smoking marijuana on physical performance," *Med. Sci. Sport and Exer.*, 7 (1975), 309–311.

Sweeny, G. D., "Drugs—some basic concepts," *Med. Sci. Sport and Exer.*, 13 (1981), 247–251.

Runners' Biographies

We would like to thank the athletes mentioned in this chapter for their contributions to this book. They have presented some practical ideas about training and racing. This section introduces you to the runners and emphasizes some of their personal achievements.

Personal Profile

Date of Birth:	6–8–11
Height:	5'7"
Weight:	130 lbs.
Hometown:	Concord, New Hampshire
Current Address:	Anoka, Minnesota
Children:	4; Grandchildren: 4
High School:	Concord High School, New Hampshire
College:	University of New Hampshire
College Coach:	Paul Sweet
Club Affiliation:	T.C.T.C.
Current Coach:	Self
Ran First Race:	Concord, New Hampshire 1926—finished 2nd in 3 Mile YMCA run. 34 year layoff after college; returned to running at age 55.

William Andberg

Running Profile

International Intercollegiate
   Championship Cross Country Team
Snowshoe Champion (1931–1933)

U.S. Age Group Records (70–74)

20 Km	1:27:42	(1981)
½ Marathon	1:35:42	(1981)
25 Km	2:00:24	(1981)
30 Km	2:25:55	(1981)

Favorite Distance

Up to ½ marathon, because I seem
to cramp up in longer runs.

Personal Records

880 yds	2:27.2	Age 64 (WR)
1,500 M	4:53.5	Age 63 (WR)
1 Mile	5:18.8	Age 64
2 Mile	10:41.0	Age 64
5,000 M	17:42.6	Age 60
10,000 M	37:12.0	Age 62
15 Km	1:04:29.0	Age 70
9 mi	1 hour	Age 60
880 yds	run	
20 Km	84:42.0	Age 67
½ Marathon	1:35:40.0	Age 70
25 Km	2:22:04.0	Age 70
30 Km	2:25:53.0	Age 70
Marathon	2:51:44.0	Age 57
	3:30:25.0	Age 70
Best 10 Km	42:19.0	Age Group
Performance		70–74

Photo by Gregory Yamamoto

Jon Anderson

Personal Records

1,500 M	3:50.2	(1977)
2 Mile	8:45.4	(1977)
3,000 M	8:09.6	(1972)
5,000 M	13:45.6	(1972)
10,000 M	28:34.2	(1972)
6 Mile	27:40.0	(1973)
Steeplechase	9:00.9	(1970)
15 Km	45:05.0	(1981)
12 Mi	1 hour	(1977)
618 yd	run	
20 Km	1:01:40.0	(1971)
½ Marathon	1:05:40.0	(1982)
Marathon	2:12:03.0	(1980)

Personal Profile

Date of Birth:	10–12–49
Height:	6'2"
Weight:	160 lbs.
Hometown:	Eugene, Oregon
Current Address:	Eugene, Oregon
Married:	wife Yvonne
Children:	Clark, Erica
College:	Cornell University
College Coach:	Jack Warner
Club Affiliation:	Nike
Current Coach:	Bill Bowerman, Dick Brown
Number of Years Running:	16

Running Profile

NCAA All American 6 Mile (3rd) (1970)

Heptagonal Cross Country Champion (1970)

Olympic Team 10,000 M (1972)

Boston Marathon Champion (1973)

Nike/OTC Marathon Champion (1975)

Member U.S. Cross Country Team (1977)

Antwerp (Belgium) Marathon Champion (1981)

Honolulu Marathon Champion (1981)

Favorite Distance—Marathon

I had the marathon (Boston) as a goal when I was a freshman in college (1967–68). My first effort (2:23:44) in 1971 was a successful one—then Boston 1973! So my success has provided much incentive. One tends to enjoy what one is good at.

Personal Profile

Date of Birth:	7–22–52
Height:	5′9″
Weight:	138 lbs.
Hometown:	Granada Hills, California
Current Address:	Valencia, California
Married:	wife Tamara
Children:	Jonathon, Kristen
College:	Brigham Young University
Club Affiliation:	Sub–4 Track Club
Current Coach:	Self
Nickname:	"Bab"
Number of Years Running:	15

Running Profile

National Junior College Record
   Holder in 3 Mile, 10,000 M,
   Distance Medley
National 20 Km Champion
Member U.S. Cross Country Team
   (1976)
California Road Racer of the Year
   (1979, 1980)

David Babriacki

Favorite Distance—

5,000 M and ½ Marathon.

Personal Records

440 yds	:51.0	(1974)
880 yds	1:52.0	(1974)
1 Mile	4:00.2	(1975)
1,500 M	3:42.0	(1975)
2 Mile	8:29.0	(1976)
3,000 M	7:58.0	(1976)
3 Mile	13:13.0	(1976)
5,000 M	13:43.0	(1976)
10,000 M	28:25.0	(1981)
20 Km	59:39.0	(1980)
½ Marathon	1:02:56.0	(1980)
Marathon	2:16:48.0	(1980)

Dick Beardsley

Personal Records

Mile	4:18	(1982)
2 Mile	8:53	(1982)
5,000 M	13:25	(1982)
10,000 M	28:37	(1980)
Steeplechase	9:26	(1977)
15 Km	44:44	(1981)
12 miles 396 yds	1 hour run	(1982)
20 Km	59:55	(1981)
½ Marathon	1:03:30	(1982)
25 Km	1:15:10	(1981)
Marathon	2:08:53	(1982)

Personal Profile

Date of Birth:	3–21–56
Height:	5'11"
Weight:	130 lbs.
Hometown:	Wayzata, Minnesota
Current Address:	Rush City, Minnesota
Married:	wife Mary
High School:	Wayzata
College:	University Minnesota– Waseca South Dakota State
College Coach:	Dr. John Fulkrod/Scott Underwood
Club Affiliation:	New Balance Track Club
Current Coach:	Bill Squires
Number of Years Running:	8

Running Profile

All Conference & All Region Track & Cross Country at U.M.W.
All American Marathon U.M.W.
Member of Runner–up Division II Cross Country Championship at S.D.S.U.
Grandmas Marathon Champion (1981, 1982)
Co-Winner London Marathon (1981)
Runner up at Boston Marathon (1982)

Favorite Distance–

20 K and Marathon
I seem to get rolling after 10 miles or so into a race. I utilize my strength in the longer distance.

Personal Profile

Date of Birth:	4–22–51
Height:	5'10"
Weight:	140 lbs.
Hometown:	Twig, Minnesota
Current Address:	Boulder, Colorado
Married:	wife Rhonda
High School:	Proctor High School, Proctor, Minnesota
College:	University of Minnesota
College Coach:	Roy Griak
Club Affiliation:	University of Chicago Track Club
Current Coach:	Ted Haydon
Number of Years Running:	20
Nickname:	"BJ"

Running Profile

Big Ten Champion (Track & Cross Country) (9 times)

NCAA All American (Track & Cross Country) (4 times)

NCAA 6 Mile Champion (1971)

Pan American Team (10,000 M) (1971, 1975)

Olympic Team (10,000 M) (1976)

US vs. France/US vs. W. Germany/US vs. USSR (1970)

US vs. Africa (1971)

US vs. Africa (1975)

USA Representative to Midnight Run Sao Paulo, Brazil (1975)

USA vs. USSR vs. Canada (1977)

USA Representative to Trinidad (5,000 M, 10,000 M) (1977)

USA Representative to Japan (Kobe, Hiroshima, Tokyo) (1977)

Fukouka Marathon, Japan (1979, 1981)

Garry Bjorklund

Personal Records

440 yds	:50.3	(1969)
880 yds	1:54.0	(1971)
Mile	4:02.2	(1971)
2 Mile	8:28.0	(1976)
3,000 M	7:46.0	(1976)
3 Mile	13:07.0	(1977)
5,000 M	13:35.0	(1976)
6 Mile	27:22.0	(1971)
10,000 M	27:49.0	(1976)
15 Km	44:09.0	(1978)
Marathon	2:10:20.0	(1980)

Favorite Distance—

15 Km Roads; 3,000 M Track
On the roads I like the 15 Km because it requires the mixture of speed and toughness that makes a good 15 Km runner. I believe it is as fair a test as a runner will find, because it requires speed, strength and concentration.

On the track I like the 3,000 M distance because, for me, it is very exciting. The pace is similar to that of running a mile, but it requires a different kind of mental toughness because of the extra distance.

Doug Brown

Personal Profile

Date of Birth:	3–1–52
Height:	6′2″
Weight:	155 lbs.
Hometown:	Eugene, Oregon
Current Address:	Eugene, Oregon
Married:	wife Carolyn
Children:	Christopher, Lindsay
High School:	Notre Dame High School
College:	University of Tennessee
College Coach:	Stan Huntsman
Club Affiliation:	Athletics West
Current Coach:	Stan Huntsman, myself
Nickname:	"The Dog"
Number of Years Running:	16

Running Profile

All American NCAA Champion
Steeplechase (1973)
All American NCAA Champion
Steeplechase (1974)
AAU Steeplechase Champion (1973)
United States Olympic Team
Steeplechase (1972)

Personal Records

1,500 M	3:45.1	(1978)
1 Mile	4:03.0	(1976)
3,000 M	7:58.7	(1978)
5,000 M	13:33.9	(1978)
10,000 M	27:54.2	(1978)
Steeplechase	8:19.3	(1978)
15 Km	44:29.0	(1979)
½ Marathon	1:04.45.0	(1979)

Favorite Distance—10K
Because it feels good.

Amby Burfoot

Personal Profile

Date of Birth:	8–19–46
Height:	6′0″
Weight:	142 lbs.
Hometown:	New London, Connecticut
Current Address:	New London, Connecticut
Married:	wife Susan
Children:	Daniel, Laura
College:	Wesleyan University
College Coach:	Elmer Swanson
Club Affiliation:	Thames River Road Runners
Current Coach:	Self
Number of Years Running:	20

Running Profile

All American NCAA Cross Country
(1966)
All American NCAA Cross Country
(1967)
Boston Marathon Champion (1968)
Manchester, Connecticut 5 Mile
(winner 9 times)

Personal Records

440 yds		:57.5
880 yds		2:02.5
1 Mile		4:12.0
2 Mile		8:45.0
10,000 M		29:20.0
12 mi 55 yds	1 hour run	
Marathon		2:14:28.0

Favorite Distance—Marathon
Because I've had the most racing
success at the distance.

Patti Lions Catalano

Personal Profile

Date of Birth:	4–6–53
Height:	5′5″
Weight:	106 lbs.
Hometown:	Quincy, Massachusetts
Current Address:	Dedham, Massachusetts
Married:	husband Joe
Team Affiliation:	B.A.A.
Current Coach:	Joe Catalano
Nickname:	"Clyde"
Number of Years Running:	6

Running Profile

American Record Holder Marathon (2:27:51)
World Record Holder 30 Km (1:44:25)
Boston Marathon (2nd) (1980)
Cascade 15 Km Champion (1980)
Peachtree 10 Km Champion (1980)
Montreal Marathon Champion (1980)
Bonne Bell 10 Km Champion (1980)

Personal Records

440 yds	:65	
880 yds	2:19	
1 Mile	4:50	(1980)
3,000 M	9:35	(1980)
5,000 M	16:24	(1980)
10,000 M	32:06	(1981)
15 Km	49:33	(1981)
20 Km	68:26	(1980)
½ Marathon	1:14:14	(1980)
30 Km	1:44:25	(1981)
Marathon	2:27:51	(1981)

Favorite Distance—Marathon

Because it is the best event.

Nancy Conz

Personal Profile

Date of Birth:	5–1–57
Height:	5′9″
Weight:	116 lbs.
Hometown:	Southampton, Massachusetts
Current Address:	Easthampton, Massachusetts
Married:	husband Paul
Club Affiliation:	New Balance Track Club
Number of Years Running:	6

Running Profile

American Record Holder 25 K (1:30:26) (1980)
American Record Holder 20 K (1:08:44) (1982)
American Record Holder 1 hour run (10 miles 1290 yds)
Avon International Marathon Champion (1981)

Personal Records

1 Mile	4:51	
2 Mile	10:13	
3,000 M	9:26	
3 Mile	15:45	
5,000 M	16:19	
10,000 M	33:10	
15 Km	51:50	
10 miles 1290 yds	1 hour run	(AR)
20 Km	1:08:44	(AR)
½ Marathon	1:13:48	
25 Km	1:26:34	
Marathon	2:33:23	

Favorite Distance—

As for racing, I can't say I have a favorite distance, but I tend to like the longer races better because I seem to be more competitive there. I don't have a lot of speed necessary to run really fast 10 K's and so on.

Philip Coppess

Personal Profile

Date of Birth:	9–2–54
Height:	5'11"
Weight:	145 lbs.
Hometown:	Oxford Junction, Iowa
Current Address:	Clinton, Iowa
Married:	wife Deb
Children:	Cory, Vickie, Gregory
High School:	Oxford Junction
Club Affiliation:	New Balance Track Club
Current Coach:	Kevin Ryan

Running Profile

Drake Relays Champion (1981)
Americals Marathon Champion (1981)
Rocket City Marathon Champion (1981)
RRCA 30 Km Champion (1982)

Personal Records

440 yds	:54	(1972)
880 yds	1:59	(1972)
1 Mile	4:20	(1981)
2 Mile	9:00	(1981)
10,000 M	29:29	(1981)
15 Km	44:35	(1982)
20 Km	1:02:27	(1982)
½ Marathon	1:05:29	(1981)
30 Km	1:36:23	(1982)
Marathon	2:13:27	(1981)

Favorite Distance—15 Km or 10 Mile
These races are long enough for
some good surges and short enough
to go all out.

Personal Profile

Date of Birth:	7–17–47
Height:	5'7"
Weight:	140 lbs.
Hometown:	Exeter, New Hampshire
Current Address:	Hackensack, New Jersey
Married:	wife Sue
High School:	Ridge High School, New Jersey
College:	Harding College, Arkansas
College Coach:	Ted Lloyd, Gordon Scoles
Club Affiliation:	Athletics West
Current Coach:	Self
Nickname:	"Craw"
Number of Years Running:	21

Running Profile

NAIA Hall of Fame

NAIA All American (1968, 1969)

Arkansas Record Holder (Mile, 1,500, 2 Mile, 3 Mile, 6 Mile)

Pan American Team 1,500 M (Bronze Medal) (1971)

U.S.A. Tour to Iran, Afganistan, Pakistan, Turkey (1973)

U.S.A. vs. U.S.S.R.—Germany (1969)

U.S.A. vs. U.S.S.R.—Pan African (1971)

Favorite Distance—Mile

Probably because the mile is the most prestigious of all running events. To be successful at it you must have speed and strength. You must train like an 800 meter and a 5,000 meter runner. I want to be respected anytime I step to the starting line in any event—400 M to marathon.

Photo by Harry Johnson

Jim Crawford

Personal Records

440 yds	:49.4/48.8	(Relay 1969)
880 yds	1:50.8	(1975)
1 Mile	3:57.7	(1971)
1,500 M	3:39.9	(1978)
2 Mile	8:29.4	(1973)
3,000 M	7:50.0	(1978)
5,000 M	13:35.4	(1978)
10,000 M	28:32.5	(1978)
Steeplechase	8:54.0	(1973)
15 Km	45:13.0	(1979)
½ Marathon	1:06:27.0	(1976)
Marathon	2:57:00.00	(1978)

John Dimick

Personal Profile

Date of Birth:	9–20–49
Height:	5'8½"
Weight:	130 lbs.
Hometown:	Brattleboro, Vermont
Current Address:	Brattleboro, Vermont
Married:	wife Lynne
Children:	Elizabeth, Michael
College:	University of Vermont
College Coach:	Wm. Neddle/Ed Kosiak
Club Affiliation:	Green Mt. Athletic Assoc.
Number of Years Running:	20

Personal Records

440 yds	:52.0
880 yds	1:57.0
1 Mile	4:12.0
2 Mile	8:54.0
5,000 M	13:53.0
10,000 M	30:18.0
½ Marathon	1:05:00.0
30 Km	1:31:00.0
Marathon	2:11:52.0

Favorite Distance—Marathon
It gives guys with moderate speed but endurance a chance to be equally competitive.

Running Profile

Road Runners National Marathon
 Champion
AAU Team to Puerto Rico (1976)
USTFF National 10 Mile Champ
Vermont Sports Caster/Writer Athlete
 (1978)

Personal Profile

Date of Birth:	8–28–51
Height:	5'10½"
Weight:	145 lbs.
Hometown:	Tacoma, Washington
Current Address:	Stone Mountain, Georgia
Married:	wife Barbara
College:	University of Georgia
College Coach:	Forrest "Speck" Towns
Club Affiliation:	Racing South
Number of Years Running:	19

Running Profile

AAU Marathon Team Champions (1976)
Olympic Team—Marathon (1980)
Orange Bowl Marathon Champion (1981)
Nike Marathon Champion (1981)
Houston Marathon Champion (1982)
Montreal Marathon Champion (1982)

Benji "Zonker" Durden

Personal Records

440 yds	:50+	(1968)
880 yds	1:56.7	(1970)
1 Mile	4:13.7	(1976, 1982)
2 Mile	8:55.0	(1976)
5,000 M	14:10.8	(1981)
10,000 M	28:36.0	(Road)
Steeplechase	9:04.5	(1977)
15 Km	43:28.0	
20 Km	1:01:43.0	(1978)
½ Marathon	1:03:11.0	(1982)
25 Km	1:16:17.0	(1980)
Marathon	2:10:41.0	(Olympic Trials 1980)

Favorite Distance—15 Km

Because normally the 10K is too short for me to be extremely competitive by national standards, but the extra 5K lets me close up on the "horses." I'm best at the Marathon, but it takes too much to run one and takes too long to recover. I would probably like 25–30 Km races, but these are very infrequent so I have little to go on here.

Personal Profile

Date of Birth:	3-21-49
Height:	6'0"
Weight:	155 lbs.
Hometown:	Carrollton, Georgia
Current Address:	Stone Mountain, Georgia
Married:	wife Jenny
College:	Furman University
College Coach:	Bill Kelshing/ John West
Club Affiliation:	Racing South Competitive Team
Current Coach:	Self with advice from Benji Durden and Mike Caldwell
Number of Years Running:	19

Lee Fiddler

Running Profile

MVP Cross Country and Track
  Furman University
All State Cross Country
State Collegiate 3 Mile Champion
Peachtree Road Race (2nd) (1974)
Olympic Trials Marathon—3 times
BAA Marathon (11th) (1975)
Peachbowl Marathon Champion
  (1976)

Favorite Distance—15-10 Mile
It's long enough for me to be fairly
competitive, but it does not require
the long taper and recovery of a
marathon.

Personal Records

440 yds	:56.0	(1972)
880 yds	2:04.4	(1976)
1 Mile	4:17.0	(1971)
2 Mile	9:05.7	(1971)
3 Mile	13:59.7	(1977)
5,000 M	14:40.0	(1979)
10,000 M	30:03.0	(1976)
15 Km	46:18.0	(1981)
20 Km	63:58.0	(1981)
½ Marathon	1:06:33.0	(1979)
25 Km	1:24:24.0	(1979)
Marathon	2:15:03.0	(1980)

Steve Flanagan

Personal Records

440 yds	:49.8	(1970)
880 yds	1:50.8	(1970)
1 Mile	4:05.0	(1970)
3,000 M	8:10.0	(1974)
2 Mile	8:48.0	(1974)
3 Mile	13:36.0	(1976)
Steeplechase	9:00.0	(1976)
10,000 M	29:07.0	(1976)
15,000 M	45:41.0	(1978)
½ Marathon	1:06:52.0	(1981)
Marathon	2:18:36.0	(1976)

Personal Profile

Date of Birth:	6–15–48
Height:	5'11"
Weight:	151 lbs.
Hometown:	Brooklyn, Connecticut
Current Address:	Boulder, Colorado
Married:	wife Cheryl
Children:	Shalane
College:	Connecticut University
College Coach:	Bob Kennedy
Club Affiliation:	Frank Shorter Racing Team
Current Coach:	Self
Occupation:	Business Teacher

Running Profile

New England 880 Champion (1970)
New England 1,000 yd Champion (1970)
Member International Cross Country Team (Wales) (1976)
Member International Cross Country Team (Dusseldorf) (1977)
Member International Cross Country Team (Limerich, Ireland) (1979)

Favorite Distance—10 Km
It provides best opportunity to race, recover, and prepare for the next one.

Personal Profile

Date of Birth:	7–23–51
Height:	6'1"
Weight:	152 lbs.
Hometown:	Bloomfield, New Jersey
Current Address:	Bloomfield, New Jersey
Married:	wife Barbara
High School:	Bloomfield High School
College:	William Paterson College of New Jersey
Club Affiliation:	Tom Fleming's Running Room Track Club
Number of Years Running:	14

Running Profile

NAIA All American Cross Country (1970)

NCAA All America (3 times in track and once in Cross Country) (1972, 1973)

New Jersey College Athlete (1972)

AAU National 30 Kilometer Champion (1977)

American Record Holder 30 Kilometers (1978)

Boston Marathon—6 times top ten (1973, 1979) (2nd, 2nd, 3rd, 6th, 10th, 4th)

Fukuoka Marathon (4th) (1977)

New York Marathon Champion (1973, 1975)

Pending American Record Holder 50 Kilometers (2:52:29) (1982)

Favorite Distance—20 Miles

You can go all out for 1 hour and 40 minutes and stop before the "dreaded" wall. I have always raced well at 20 miles distance.

Tom Fleming

Personal Records

440 yds	:52.6	(1973)
880 yds	1:56.9	(1975)
1,500 M	3:51.4	(1977)
2 Mile	8:41.6	(1977)
3 Mile	13:40.8	(1977)
10,000 M	29:08.0	(1978)
15 Km	45:16.0	(1978)
12 mi 145 yds	1 hour run	(1977)
20 Km	1:00:35.0	(1977)
½ Marathon	1:04:07.0	(1979)
25 Km	1:16:09.0	(1977)
30 Km	1:30:59.0	(1978)
Marathon	2:12:05.0	(1975)

Ray Flynn

Personal Records

880 yds	1:48.3	(1981)
1 Mile	3:49.77	(1982)
1,500 M	3:33.5	(1982)
3,000 M	7:50.1	(1981)
5,000 M	13:34.7	(1982)
10,000 M	28:31.0	(1982)

Favorite Distance—Mile

It is the event for which I am most suited at this time. It is exciting and unpredictable, long enough to make it a contest of strength as well as speed, but not too long to hold the spectators' attention throughout.

Personal Profile

Date of Birth:	1–22–57
Height:	5′11½″
Weight:	142 lbs.
Hometown:	Longford, Ireland
Current Address:	Johnson City, Tennessee
Not Married	
High School:	St. Mel's, Longford, Ireland
College:	East Tennessee State University
College Coach:	Dave Walker
Club Affiliation:	New Balance Track Club
Current Coach:	Self
Number of Years Running:	10

Running Profile

Athlete of the Year Ohio Valley Conference (1978)

All American NCAA Track Indoors (1978)

All American NCAA Track Outdoors (1978)

9th All Time Fastest Mile in World (3:49.77)

4th All Time Fastest Mile Indoors (3:53.6)

Irish Champion 5,000 M (1982)

Irish Record Holder 1,500 M, Mile, 2,000 M

Mobil Oil Grand Prix Champion (1982 indoors)

Jeff Galloway

Personal Profile

Date of Birth:	7–12–45
Height:	5′11″
Weight:	135 lbs.
Hometown:	Atlanta, Georgia
Current Address:	Atlanta, Georgia
Married:	wife Barbara
Children:	Brennan
College:	Wesleyan University
College Coach:	Elmer Swanson
Club Affiliation:	Phidippides
Number of Years Running:	24

Running Profile

College All American
United States Olympic Team (1972)
United States National Team (1973)
United States Cross Country Team (1974)

Personal Records

1 Mile	4:11
2 Mile	8:31
5,000 M	13:41
6 Mile	27:21
10,000 M	28:29
10 Mile	47:49
Marathon	2:16:35

Favorite Distance—Marathon
I have 98% slow twitch fibers.
During my best years, I ran
marathons in hot weather.

Don Kardong

Personal Profile

Date of Birth:	12–22–48
Height:	6′3″
Weight:	150 lbs.
Hometown:	Bellevue, Washington
Current Address:	Spokane, Washington
Married:	wife Bridgid
High School:	Seattle Prep
College:	Stanford University University of Washington
College Coach:	Marshall Clark
Club Affiliation:	Club Northwest
Occupation:	Writer
Number of Years Running:	18

Running Profile

Member Stanford's 2nd Place NCAA
  Cross Country Team (1968)
NCAA 3 Mile (4th) (1970)
NCAA Cross Country (3rd) (1970)
AAU Cross Country (3rd) (1970)
PAC 8 3 Mile (2nd) (1971)
Olympic Trials 10 K (6th) (1972)
Olympic Trials Marathon (6th) (1972)
Member International Cross Country
  Team, Chepstow, Wales (1974)
Member U.S. Track Team to the
  Peoples Republic of China (1975)
U.S. Olympic Team (Marathon) (1976)
Montreal Olympic Marathon (4th) (1976)
Peachtree Road Race Champion (1976)
Honolulu Marathon Champion (1978)

Personal Records

880 yds	1:53.0
1 Mile	4:01.9
2 Mile	8:32.0
3 Mile	12:56.6
5,000 M	13:35.0
10,000 M	28:56.0
Marathon	2:11:16.0

Personal Profile

Date of Birth:	1–5–55
Height:	6′1″
Weight:	150 lbs.
Hometown:	Hermitage, Pennsylvania
Current Address:	Eugene, Oregon
Not Married	
High School:	Hickory High School
College:	West Virginia University
College Coach:	Stan Romanoski
Club Affiliation:	Athletics West
Current Coach:	Dick Quax
Nickname:	"Kash" or "Goose"
Number of Years Running:	14

Running Profile

NCAA All American Cross Country (16th) (1975)

U.S.T.F.F. National Champion Cross Country (1975)

AAU 15 Km National Champion (1978)

U.S. Olympic Trials Marathon (1980)

U.S. Olympic Trials 10 K Finalist (1980)

New York City Marathon (9th) (1981)

American Record 30 K (1982)

Favorite Distance—15 K; Marathon
These distances seem to be where my potential is best, although I enjoy competing at all distances.

Alex Kasich

Personal Records

440 yds	:53.8	(1976)
880 yds	1:54.0	(1976)
1 Mile	4:05.1	(1976)
2 Mile	8:39.9	(1976)
5,000 M	14:03.4	(1980)
10,000 M	28:43:22	(1982)
15 Km	44:57.0	(1980)
20 Km	1:01:38.9	(1979)
½ Marathon	1:04:46.0	(1979)
25 Km	1:18:52.0	(1982)
30 Km	1:33:56.0	(1982)
Marathon	2:13:20.0	(1981)
50 Mile	7:03:36.0	(1977)

Photo by Duomo/Sutton

Herb Lindsay

Personal Records

440 yds	:52.0	(1972)
880 yds	1:54.0	(1974)
1 Mile	3:59.0	(1976 relay)
2 Mile	8:37.0	(1976)
3 Mile	13:12.0	(1976)
5,000 M	13:36.0	(1980)
10,000 M	28:16.0	(1982)
Steeplechase	9:01.0	(1974)
15 Km	43:16.0	(1981)
20 Km	58:46.0	(1981)
½ Marathon	1:01:47.0	(1981)

Personal Profile

Date of Birth:	11–12–54
Height:	5′9″
Weight:	152 lbs.
Hometown:	Reed City, Michigan
Current Address:	Boulder, Colorado
Married:	wife Theresa
High School:	Reed City High School (1973)
College:	Michigan State University
College Coach:	Jim Gibbard
Club Affiliation:	Athletic West–Nike
Current Coach:	Self with input from runners and coaches
Running Competitive:	since 1969

Running Profile

Big Ten Indoor 2 Mile Champion (twice)

All American Cross Country (3 times)

All American Track (Indoors 3 times)

Runner Magazine Road Racer of the Year 1980 and 1981

American Record Holder 20 Kilometers

American Record Holder ½ Marathon (1:01:47)

American Record Holder 10 miles (45:58.9)

American Record Holder 25 Kilometers (1:14:08.2)

Favorite Distance– 15–20 Km

It's long enough to reduce the "threat" of track speed and short enough to reduce the "threat" of strong Marathon competitors.

John Lodwick

Personal Profile

Date of Birth:	3–16–54
Height:	6'4"
Weight:	155 lbs.
Hometown:	Eugene, Oregon
Current Address:	Eugene, Oregon
Married:	wife Judy
Children:	Hannah
College:	Rice University, Dallas Seminary
College Coach:	Bob May/Harry Johnson
Club Affiliation:	Athletic West
Current Coach:	Dick Brown
Numer of Years Running:	11

Running Profile

Top 10 Southwest Conference Cross Country (1972, 1973, 1974)

Top 10 U.S. Marathon (1976, 1978, 1979, 19781)

Boston Marathon (8th) (1978)

Boston Marathon (4th) (1981)

Boston Marathon (3rd) (1982)

Nike Marathon (3rd) (1979)

Favorite Distance—Marathon

Three reasons—I've enjoyed success at it; there is a more relaxed pace; and I enjoy the challenge in the area of endurance.

Personal Records

440 yds	:53.0	(1972)
880 yds	1:52.6	(1972)
1 Mile	4:08.0	(1976)
2 Mile	9:04.0	(1979)
5,000 M	13:58.0	(1979)
10,000 M	29:34.0	(1982)
15 Km	45:00.0	(1980)
½ Marathon	1:05:35.0	(1978)
Marathon	2:10:54.0	(1979)

Kevin McCarey

Personal Profile

Date of Birth:	6–27–54
Height:	5'8"
Weight:	126 lbs.
Hometown:	Eugene, Oregon
Current Address:	Eugene, Oregon
Not Married	
High School:	Cathedral Prep. Queens, New York
College:	Villanova University
College Coach:	James "Jumbo" Elliot
Club Affiliation:	Athletic West
Current Coach:	Dick Brown
Numer of Years Running:	14

Running Profile

All American NCAA (Indoors) 2 Mile (1975)

All American NCAA Distance Medley (1976)

ICUA 6 Mile Champion (1975)

Olympic Trials Marathon (6th) (1980)

London Marathon (5th) (1982)

Personal Records

880 yds	1:53.8	(1975)
1 Mile	4:06.2	(1975)
2 Mile	8:35.2	(1975)
5,000 M	13:48.0	(1982)
10,000 M	29:06.0	(1982)
½ Marathon	1:03:23.0	(1981)
Marathon	2:13:17.0	(1980)

Favorite Distance—2 Mile

Because I attended Villanova University, I will always be a track runner at heart. I enjoy the crowd participation indoors, their closeness to the track, and even the physical contact of racing on an 11 lap to a mile track.

Henry Marsh

Personal Profile

Date of Birth:	3–15–54
Height:	5'10"
Weight:	160 lbs.
Hometown:	Bountiful, Utah
Current Address:	Bountiful, Utah
Married:	wife Suzanne
Children:	James, Danielle
College:	Brigham Young University
College Coach:	Sherald James
Club Affiliation:	Athletic West
Current Coach:	Bill Bowerman
Number of Years Running:	12

Running Profile

NCAA All American Steeplechase (3 times)

NCAA All American Cross Country (2 times)

Olympic Team (10th) (1976)

American Record Holder Steeplechase (8:21.2) (1977)

National Champion Steeplechase (1978, 1979, 1981, 1982) (4 times)

United States Olympic Team (set American Record 8:15.68) (1980)

Ranked #1 in World 1981

Undefeated and Fastest Time in World 1982

Personal Records

880 yds	1:53.0
1,500 M	3:44.6
1 Mile	4:02.0
2 Mile	8:32.0
5,000 M	14:03.0
10,000 M	29:10.0
Steeplechase	8:15.68

Favorite Distance—Steeplechase

Because it is not so long that you get bored, yet long enough to involve distance running tactics.

Stan Mavis

Personal Profile

Date of Birth:	2–26–55
Height:	6'2"
Weight:	150 lbs.
Hometown:	Greensburg, Indiana
Current Address:	Boulder, Colorado
Married:	wife Lynn
High School:	Greensburg High School
College:	Michigan State University
College Coach:	Jim Gibbard
Club Affiliation:	Athletic West
Current Coach:	self (advice from Frank Shorter)
Occupation:	Credit Manager, Frank Shorter Sportswear

Running Profile

American Record Holder ½ Marathon (1:02:16) (1980)

Top 10 Track and Field Road Races (1980)

Olympic Trial Finalist 10,000 M (10th)

Pacific Conference 10,000 M (1981)

Personal Records

440 yds	:49.5
880 yds	1:51.0
1 Mile	4:02.6
2 Mile	8:27.0
5,000 M	13:43.0
10,000 M	28:13.0
15,000 M	44:18:0
20,000 M	61:40.0
½ Marathon	1:02:16.0
Marathon	2:16:24.0

Personal Profile

Date of Birth:	9–18–55
Height:	5'9"
Weight:	146 lbs.
Hometown:	Grand Rapids, Michigan
Current Address:	Wellesley, Massachusetts
Married:	wife Paula
Children:	Nicolle
College:	University of Michigan
College Coach:	Ron Warhurst
Club Affiliation:	Brooks Racing Team
Current Coach:	Bill Squires
Number of Years Running:	13

Running Profile

All American Cross Country (1974, 1975, 1976)

All American Track (1976)

Big Ten Champion Steeplechase (1974, 1976)

Big Ten Champion 10,000 M (1977)

Ranked by Track and Field for Road Racing (7th 1978, 7th 1979, 3rd 1980, 3rd 1981)

American Record Holder for Road Races 15K 43:11, 20K 58:26

Former American Record Holder for Road Races 10K 28:24, 25K 1:14:29

Boston Marathon Champion 1983

Favorite Distance—15–20 Km
Because it combines strength and speed; very comfortable race difference.

Greg Meyer

Personal Records

440 yds	:50.8	(1977)
880 yds	1:50.8	(1977)
1 Mile	3:59.1	(1978)
2 Mile	8:32.0	(1978)
5,000 M	13:35.0	(1982)
10,000 M	28:24.0	(1979)
Steeplechase	8:28.0	(1980)
15 Km	43:11.0	
20 Km	58:26.0	
½ Marathon	1:03:10.0	
25 Km	1:14:29.0	
Marathon	2:10:59.0	

Lorraine Moller

Personal Profile

Date of Birth:	6-1–55
Height:	5'8½"
Weight:	124 lbs.
Hometown:	Putaruru, New Zealand
Current Address:	Auckland, New Zealand
College:	Denielen Teacher's College
Club Affiliation:	New Balance/ Lynndale College
Current Coach:	Dick Quax
Number of Years Running:	13

Running Profile

Ranked 2nd in World (1981)

Avon Marathon Champion (1980, 1982)

Commonwealth Games 3rd (1,500, 3,000 M)

Nike OTC Marathon Champion

Personal Records

440 yds	:56.0
800 M	2:03.6
1,500 M	4:14.7
Mile	4:38.2
3,000 M	8:55.0
2 Mile	9:58.0
5,000 M	15:28.0
10,000 M	32:47.0
Marathon	2:29:35.0

Kenny Moore

Personal Profile

Date of Birth:	12-1–43
Height:	6'0"
Weight:	145 lbs.
Hometown:	Eugene, Oregon
Current Address:	Eugene, Oregon
Not Married	
College:	University of Oregon
College Coach:	Bill Bowerman
Club Affiliation:	Oregon Track Club
Current Coach:	Bill Bowerman
Occupation:	Writer
Number of Years Running:	23

Running Profile

PAC-8 Steeplechase Champion (1965, 1966)

PAC-8 3 Mile Champion (1965)

AAU Cross Country Champion (1967)

Olympic Team (14th Marathon) (1968)

American Record Holder Marathon (2:13:27) (1969)

AAU Marathon Champion (1971)

Olympic Team (4th Marathon) (1972)

Personal Records

440 yds	:52.8
880 yds	1:55.0
1,500 M	3:47.0
1 Mile	4:03.2
2 Mile	8:43.2
3 Mile	13:44.0
Steeplechase	8:49.4
5,000 M	13:44.0
10,000 M	27:47.4
15,000 M	43:59.0
Marathon	2:11:35.8

Favorite Distance—

Marathon—it is the best for my blend of ability and temperament.

Marcus James "Mark" Nenow

Personal Profile

Date of Birth:	11–16–57
Height:	5'9"
Weight:	130 lbs.
Hometown:	Anoka, Minnesota
Current Address:	Lexington, Kentucky
Not Married	
High School:	Anoka High School
College:	University of Kentucky
College Coach:	Don Weber
Club Affiliation:	Todds Road Stumblers
Current Coach:	Self
Number of Years Running:	6

Running Profile

All American Cross Country

All American Track (10 K)

Southeast Conference Champion (5 K and 10 K)

Olympic Trials (1980) (10 K 11th)

World Cross Country Team (1981)

World University Games (1981)

U.S. Team vs. USSR (1981)

3rd Fastest American Ever—10 K (27:36.7)

Personal Records

1,500 M	3:50	(1982)
3,000 M	7:58.0	(1981)
5,000 M	13:46.0	(1982)
10,000 M	27:36.7	(1982)
½ Marathon	1:03:09.0	(1981)

Favorite Distance—10,000 M

I enjoy the track more than anything right now, and that's my best track distance. I feel confident at 10,000 M.

Lionel Ortega

Personal Profile

Date of Birth:	7–30–54
Height:	5'7"
Weight:	134 lbs.
Hometown:	Albuquerque, New Mexico
Current Address:	Exeter, New Hampshire
Married:	wife Esmeralda
Children:	Lionel Jr., Merisol
High School:	West Mesa High School
College:	University of New Mexico
College Coach:	Hugh Hackett
Club Affiliation:	Athletics West
Current Coach:	Self
Number of Years Running:	12

Running Profile

NCAA All American Cross Country (1975)

Western Athletic Conference Indoor 3 Mile Champion (1976)

Texas Relays 10,000 M Champion (1976)

Nike Marathon Champion (1978)

Personal Records

440 yds	:54	(1975)
880 yds	2:01	(1979)
1 Mile	4:09	(1976)
2 Mile	8:54	(1976)
5,000 M	13:59	(1979)
10,000 M	29:06	(1976)
15 Km	46:02	(1979)
20 Km	1:01:36	(1978)
½ Marathon	1:05:09	(1981)
Marathon	2:14:24	(1978)

Favorite Distance—20 Km

I am consistent at this distance and feel very relaxed compared to any other distance.

Kirk Pfeffer

Running Profile

Big Eight Cross Country Champion
(1976)
Big Eight Cross Country Champion
(1978)
Olympic Marathon Trials (7th) (1976)
Mission Bay Marathon Champion
(1977)
New York Marathon (2nd) (1979)
Fukuoka Marathon (7th) (1980)
San Diego ½ Marathon Champion
(1981)
Junior World Marathon Record
(2:17:44)
Fastest American Overseas Marathon
(2:10:29)
Track and Field Road Racing (4th)
(1979)
Track and Field American Marathon
(2nd) (1979)

Personal Profile

Date of Birth:	7–30–56
Height:	6'3"
Weight:	140 lbs.
Hometown:	San Diego, California
Current Address:	Boulder, Colorado
Married:	wife Kim
Children:	Zachary, Samatha, Ashley, Elizabeth
High School:	John C. Crawford High School
Junior College:	Grossmont Junior College
College:	University of Colorado
College Coach:	Bob Larsen/Dean Brittenham
Club Affiliation:	ASICS Tiger
Current Coach:	Bob Larsen
Occupation:	Student, University of Colorado

Personal Records

440 yds	:54.0
1 Mile	4:05.0
2 Mile	8:45.0
5,000 M	13:52.0
10,000 M	28:19.0
15,000 M	43:26.0
20,000 M	59:13.0
½ Marathon	1:02:14.0
Marathon	2:10:29.0

ank Pfeifle

Personal Profile

Date of Birth:	2–21–51
Height:	6'0"
Weight:	140 lbs.
Hometown:	Kingfield, Maine
Current Address:	Kennebank, Maine
Married:	wife Beth
Children:	Kristen, Mitchell, Brooke
College:	University of Vermont
College Coach:	Bill Nedde
Club Affiliation:	Running East
Nickname:	"Fife"
Number of Years Running:	14

Running Profile

USTFF All American (6 miles) (1975)
New England TAC Cross Country
  Champion (1980)
Runner of the Year in Maine 1981
Team East National Sports Festival (1982)
Olympic Marathon Trials (1980)
Ranked 3rd USA ½ Marathon (1978)

Personal Records

440 yds	:53.0
880 yds	1:54.7
1 Mile	4:20.3
3,000 M	8:03.4
5,000 M	14:11.1
10,000 M	28:46.0
15 Km	45:16.0
20 Km	60:41.0
½ Marathon	1:04:37.0
30 Km	1:35:36.0
Marathon	2:16:41.0

Favorite Distance—10 Mile

Because you have to carry 10,000
meter speed for another 4 miles and
that becomes a matter of strength.
Those who don't have it fade, and it
is fun to have them drop off behind you.

ike Pinocci

Personal Profile

Date of Birth:	11–25–54
Height:	5'9½"
Weight:	131 lbs.
Hometown:	Fremont, California
Current Address:	South Lake Tahoe, California
Not Married	
Junior College:	Odessa Junior College
College:	Oklahoma State University
Club Affiliation:	Sub–4
Number of Years Running:	15

Running Profile

Junior College All American Cross
  Country (2 times)
U.S.T.F.F. 10 Km (5th)
Barcelona Marathon Champion (1982)
Boston Marathon (10th) (1980)

Personal Records

440 yds	:53.6	(1975)
880 yds	1:59.8	(1976)
1 Mile	4:11.6	(1979)
2 Mile	9:01.0	(1976)
5,000 M	13:52.0	(1976)
10,000 M	29:17.0	(1981)
Steeplechase	9:27.0	(1976)
15 Km	44:51.0	(1982)
½ Marathon	1:04:31.0	(1982)
Marathon	2:13:36.0	(1981)

Favorite Distance—Marathon

Time element; can complete with top
runners internationally because of
distance; it's a challenge.

Steve Plasencia

Personal Profile

Date of Birth:	10–28–56
Height:	5'11"
Weight:	150 lbs.
Hometown:	Minneapolis, Minnesota
Current Address:	Eugene, Oregon
College:	University of Minnesota
College Coach:	Roy Griak
Club Affiliation:	Athletics West
Current Coach:	Dick Quax
Number of Years Running:	10
Nickname:	"Hess"

Running Profile

NCAA All American Track (1975)
NCAA All American Track (1977)
NCAA All American Cross Country (1977)
NCAA All American Cross Country (1978)
Drake Relays Champion (1978)
Texas Relays Champion (3 mile) (1975)
Peking Invitational (5,000 M)
World Cross Championships (1980)
National Team East Germany (1982)
National Team Tokyo/China (1980)

Personal Records

440 yds	:52.6
880 yds	1:56.1
Mile	3:58.3
1,500 M	3:41.3
2 Mile	8:30.1
3,000 M	7:49.0
5,000 M	13:25.0
10,000 M	28:41.0
15,000 M	45:10.0

Favorite Distance—5,000 M
It combines strength and speed. Working in only one area becomes boring, so training for both keeps me sharp.

Miguel Santiago "Mike" Roche

Personal Profile

Date of Birth:	6–27–53
Height:	5'8½"
Weight:	135 lbs.
Hometown:	Crawford, New Jersey
Current Address:	Framingham, Massachusetts
High School:	Crawford High School
College:	Rutgers University
College Coach:	Frank Gagliano
Club Affiliation:	Puma
Number of Years Running:	15

Running Profile

ICUA Steeplechase Champion (1975)
NCAA All American Steeplechase (1975)
Olympic Team Steeplechase (1976)
Steeplechase Champion Prefontaine Meet (1977, 1978)
Peachtree Road Race Champion (1978)
International Cross Country Team (1978)

Personal Records

440 yds	:51.8
880 yds	1:54.0
1 Mile	4:04.0
2 Mile	8:38.0
5,000 M	13:45.0
10,000 M	28:53.0
Steeplechase	8:30.1
15 Km	43:35.0
10 Mile	46:57

Favorite Distance—Steeplechase
This seems to be my strongest event on a national basis. On the roads 10 K to 10 miles are my most effective distances.

Personal Profile

Date of Birth:	12–23–47
Height:	5′8½″
Weight:	128 lbs.
Hometown:	Newington, Connecticut
Current Address:	Sherborn, Massachusetts
Not Married	
College:	Wesleyan University, Middleton, CT
College Coach:	Elmer Swanson
Club Affiliation:	Greater Boston Track Club
Current Coach:	Self
Occupation:	Retailer
Nickname:	"Will-ha the Cruel"
Number of Years Running:	18

Bill Rodgers

Personal Records

440 yds	:58.0	(1981)
880 yds	2:00.0	(1968)
1 Mile	4:16.2	(1981)
1,500 M	4:00.0	(1982)
2 Mile	8:53.6	(1975)
3 Mile	13:26.0	(1976)
5,000 M	13:42.0	(1978)
10,000 M	28:04.0	(1977)
15,000 M Road	43:25.0	(1981)
12 Mile 1,351 yds	1 hour run	(1977)
20,000 M track	58:15.0	(1977)
½ Marathon	1:03:08.0	(1977)
25,000 M Track	1:14:12.0	(1977)
30,000 M Road	1:29:04.0	(1976)
Marathon	2:09:27.0	(1979)

Running Profile

Boston Marathon Champion (1975)

Olympic Team (Marathon) (1976)

Boston Marathon Champion (1977)

Fukuoka Marathon Champion (1978)

Boston Marathon Champion (1978)

Boston Marathon Champion (1979)

Marge Rosasco

Personal Profile

Date of Birth:	4–6–48
Height:	5′3¾″
Weight:	107 lbs.
Hometown:	Baltimore, Maryland
Current Address:	Fallston, Maryland
Married:	husband Steve
Children:	stepsons—Steve, Mark
High School:	Merganthaler (Baltimore)
Club Affiliation:	Brooks Racing Team
Current Coach:	Self coached, advised by Jim Sutton
Number of Years Running:	12

Running Profile

RRCA National Champion 20 Km (1979)

RRCA National Champion 10 Miles (1982)

Baltimore Road Runners Club Female Runner of the Year (1978–1981)

South Atlantic AAU Female Long Distance Runner of the Year (1976–1980)

Personal Records

10,000 M	34:37	(1981)
15 Km	54:23	(1982)
10 Mile	56:39	(1982)
20 Km	72:57	(1982)
½ Marathon	80:04	(1980)
30 Km	1:59:23	(1979)
Marathon	2:56:29	(1979)

Favorite Distance—10 Mile

I suppose as with most people, your favorite distance is the one you are most competitive at, and with me that is probably 10 miles. It's also the race distance I feel most comfortable with because the 10 Km is an all out sprint for me and I know it is going to hurt (I don't have much speed). At 10 miles the pace is more controlled the first few miles.

Personal Profile

Date of Birth:	8–7–58
Height:	6'0"
Weight:	144 lbs.
Hometown:	Wayland, Massachusetts
Current Address:	Eugene, Oregon
Married:	wife Molly
Children:	Antonio
College:	University of Oregon
College Coach:	Bill Dellinger
Club Affiliation:	Athletics West
Current Coach:	Bill Dellinger
Occupation:	Internal Marketing Blue Ribbon Sports
Number of Years Running:	11

Running Profile

NCAA Cross Country Champion (1978)
AAU Cross Country Champion (1979)
New York Marathon Champion (1980)
Olympic Team 10,000 M (1980)
7AC 10,000 M Champion (1981)
World Cup Team (1981)
New York Marathon Champion (1981)
Boston Marathon Champion (1982)
American Record Holder 5,000 M
American Record Holder 10,000 M
World Record Holder—Marathon

Alberto Salazar

Personal Records

440 yds	:54.0	
1,500 M	3:44.5	
1 Mile	4:01.9	
3,000 M	7:43.7	
2 Mile	8:24.0	
5,000 M	13:11.9	
10,000 M	27:25.6	
Marathon	2:08:13.0	(WR)

Frank Shorter

Running Profile

NCAA Cross Country (19th) (1968)
NCAA 6 Mile Champion (1969)
NCAA 3 Mile (2nd) (1969)
NCAA 3 Mile Indoor (2nd) (1969)
Heptagonal 2 Mile Champion (1969)
AAU 6 Mile, 3 Mile and Cross
  Country Champion (1970)
AAU 6 Mile and Cross Country
  Champion (1971)
AAU Indoor 3 Mile Champion (1971)
Fukuoka Marathon Champion (1971)
Olympic Team 10,000 M and
  Marathon (1972)
Olympic Marathon Champion (1972)
Fukuoka Marathon Champion (1972)
National Cross Country Champion
  (1972)
Fukouka Marathon Champion (1973)
National Cross Country Champion
  (1973)
Fukuoka Marathon Champion (1974)
AAU 10,000 M Champion (1974)
AAU 10,000 M Champion (1975)
Olympic Team Marathon (1976)
Olympics Marathon (2nd) (1976)

Personal Profile

Date of Birth:	10–31–47
Height:	5'10½"
Weight:	132 lbs.
Hometown:	Middletown, New York
Current Address:	Boulder, Colorado
Married:	wife Louise
Children:	Mark, Alex
High School:	Mt. Herman High School
College:	Yale University University of Florida Law School
College Coach:	Robert Gregengack
Club Affiliation:	Frank Shorter Racing Team
Current Coach:	Self
Occupation:	Businessman, Attorney
Number of Years Running:	23

Personal Records

1,500 M	3:45.0
1 Mile	4:02.5
2 Mile	8:26.0
3,000 M	7:51.0
3 Miles	12:51.9
5,000 M	13:26.0
10,000 M	27:45.9
½ Marathon	1:03:36.0
Marathon	2:10:30.0
	2:10:50.0
	2:11:30.0
	2:11:45.0
	2:11:52.0
	2:12:00.0
	2:12:19.0
	2:12:53.0
	2:13:08.0

Personal Profile

Date of Birth:	9–4–57
Height:	5'6½"
Weight:	127 lbs.
Hometown:	Ft. Collins, Colorado
Current Address:	Ft. Collins, Colorado
Married:	wife Wendy
High School:	Arvado West, Colorado
College:	Colorado State University
College Coach:	Jerry Quiller
Club Affiliation:	Brooks Racing Team
Current Coach:	Damien Koch
Number of Years Running:	11

Running Profile

All American NCAA Indoor Track (1979)

All American NCAA Cross Country (1979)

All American USTFA (1,500 M) (1979)

Member International Cross Country Team (1980)

National Cross Country Champion (1980)

Member U.S. Team (Chartre France Cross Country Race) (1981)

Rated by the Track and Field News as 4th best road racer in World (1981)

Member USA World Cross Country Team (1982)

Peachtree 10 Km Champion (1982)

Jon Sinclair

Personal Records

1,500 M	3:45.6	(1979)
1 Mile	4:04.8	(1979)
2 Mile	8:43.95	(1979)
5,000 M	13:43.0	(1981)
10,000 M	28:16.0	(1982)
15 Km	43:13.0	(1982)
10 Mile	47:02.0	(1981)
20 Km	58:58.0	(1981)
½ Marathon	1:02:22.0	(1981)
Marathon	2:13:29.0	(1981)

Favorite Distance—15 Km
It seems to fit my talents best.

Charles "Chuck" Smead

Personal Profile
Date of Birth: 8–4–51
Height: 5'9"
Weight: 143 lbs.
Hometown: Santa Paula, California
Current Address: Santa Paula, California
Married: wife Carol
Children: Isaac, Aaron
College: Humbolt State
College Coach: Jim Hunt
Club Affiliation: California Condors/ Converse
Number of Years Running: 17

Running Profile
All American Cross Country (College)
All American Track (twice National Champion Six Mile)
American Record Holder 50 Km Road (2:50:45)
Silver Medalist Pan-American Games Marathon
AAU National Champion 6 times (15 Km, 20 Km, 30 Km, 50 Km)

Personal Records

440 yds	:54.1	(H.S. 1968)
880 yds	1:56.2	(College 1973)
1 Mile	4:12.0	(College 1973)
1 Mile	4:07.0	(Road 1981)
2 Mile	8:59.0	(College 1973)
2 Mile	8:25.0	(Road 1981)
3 Mile	13:42.0	(College 1976)
10,000 M	28:35.0	(Switzerland 1980)
15 Km	45:20.0	(Cascade Runoff 1981)
12 miles 350 yds	1 hour run	(College 1976)
20 Km	1:01:29.0	(AAU 20 Km Mass. 1976)
½ Marathon	1:05:59.0	(Las Vegas 1981)
25 Km	1:17:45.0	(Ventura 1980)
30 Km	1:34:10.0	(Nike Marathon 1981)
Marathon	2:13:47.0	(Nike Marathon 1981)

Favorite Distance
I prefer longer races uphill because I don't have the leg speed for shorter races and seem to run well uphill.

Running Profile

NCAA All American (800 M) (1967)

AAU All American (2 Mile Relay) (1969)

AAU All American (2 Mile Relay) (1970)

AAU All American (2 Mile Relay) (1971)

USTFF 800 M Champion (1972)

USA Representative to St. Pierre Games, Martinique (1972)

USA Team vs. USSR (1972)

Olympic Trials (800 M) (1972)

World Record Holder 2 Mile Relay (1973)

American Record Holder (4 times 800 M) (1973)

AAU All American 2 Mile Relay (1974)

AAU All American 2 Mile Relay (1975)

USA Team vs. People's Republic of China (1975)

AAU All American 2 Mile Relay (1976)

International Track Association Pro Tour (1976)

Ken Sparks

Personal Records

440 yds	:47.4	(1973)
880 yds	1:47.1	(1973)
800 M	1:47.4	(1972)
Mile	4:03.6	(1974)
2 Mile	9:03.6	(1974)
10,000 M	31:46.0	(1973)
10 Miles	53:19.0	(1971)
Marathon	2:49:54.0	(1970)

Favorite Distance—800 M

I like this distance because it takes a lot of speed and short, intense concentration. You can race a lot without getting physically run down.

Personal Profile

Date of Birth:	1–25–45
Height:	5'10"
Weight:	150 lbs.
Hometown:	Greenfield, Indiana
Current Address:	Chagrin Falls, Ohio
Married:	wife Debbie
Children:	Chad, Kelly
High School:	Mt. Comfort High School, Indiana
College:	Ball State University
College Coach:	Dick Stealy/Dave Costill
Club Affiliation:	University of Chicago Track Club
Current Coach:	Ted Haydon
Number of Years Running:	30

Tony Staynings

Favorite Distance—3,000 M
Steeplechase
It requires both speed and strength.
But recently I gave up the event, and
now find any indoor track race, and
race of any distance, equally
enjoyable.

Personal Profile

Date of Birth:	7–21–53
Height:	5'6½"
Weight:	132 lbs.
Hometown:	Bristol, England
Current Address:	Bowling Green, Kentucky
Married:	wife Linda
College:	Western Kentucky University
College Coach:	Jerry Bean
Club Affiliation:	Sub-Four Track Club
Current Coach:	Dave Sennings
Number of Years Running:	15

Running Profile

Member British Olympic Team (1976)
Member British Olympic Team (1980)
Olympic Finalist 3,000 M
Steeplechase
All American Indoor/Outdoor Track
and Cross Country (9 times)
Member of English Team, 1978
Commonwealth Games
5th Fastest 3 Mile Ever Indoors (13:00)
British Record Holder 3 Mile Indoors,
1 Mile (4 times)

Personal Records

440 yds	:52.5	(1974)
880 yds	1:53.7	(1974)
1,500 M	3:42.5	(1977)
2 Mile	8:30.0	(1975, 1982)
3 Mile	13:00.2	(1981)
10,000 M	28:20.0	(1981)
Steeplechase	8:27.1	(1980)
½ Marathon	1:03:38.0	(1978)

Mary Decker

Personal Profile

Date of Birth:	8–4–58
Height:	5'6"
Weight:	110 lbs.
Hometown:	Flemington, New Jersey
Current Address:	Flemington, New Jersey
High School:	Orange High School
College:	University of Colorado
Club Affiliation:	Athletics West
Current Coach:	Dick Brown
Number of Years Running:	12

Running Profile

AIAW Cross Country Champion (1978)

Pan American Champion 1,500 M (1979)

United States Olympic Team 1,500 M (1980)

National Champion 1,500 M (1982)

World Record Holder Mile (4:18.08) (1982)

American Record Holder 3,000 M
  (8:29.71) (1982)

World Record Holder 5,000 M
  (15:08.26) (1982)

World Record Holder 10,000 M
  (31:35.3) (1982)

Personal Records

400 M	:53.8
800 M	1:58.3
1 Mile	4:18.08
1,500 M	3:59.4
3,000 M	8:29.71
5,000 M	15:08.26
10,000 M	31:35.3

Favorite Distance—Mile

It's traditional, most people can relate even without track experience. However, I find myself with tendencies towards longer distances. I enjoy them physically and find them easy.

Ron Tabb

Personal Records

440 yds	:51.0
880 yds	1:53.5
1 Mile	4:08.0
2 Mile	8:45.0
5,000 M	13:31.0
10,000 M	28:35.0
15 Km	46:03.0
20 Km	1:01:30.0
½ Marathon	1:04:05.0
Marathon	2:11:00.0

Favorite Distance—Marathon
I am more competitive at this
distance.

Personal Profile

Date of Birth:	8–7–54
Height:	5′6″
Weight:	116 lbs.
Hometown:	Lexington, Missouri
Current Address:	Eugene, Oregon
High School:	Lexington Senior High
College:	Central Missouri State University
College Coach:	Jim Pilkington
Club Affiliation:	Adidas U.S.A. Racing Team
Current Coach:	Dick Brown
Number of Years Running:	10

Running Profile

NCAA Division II Track All American
(2 times)
NCAA Cross Country All American (2
times)
Outstanding College Athletes of
America (1974)
Houston Marathon Champion (1978,
1980)
Boston Marathon (3rd) (1980)
Olympic Trials Marathon (4th) (1980)
New York Marathon (6th) (1979)
Member 1st American World Cup
Team (10th) (1979)

Pablo Charley Vigil

Personal Profile

Date of Birth:	1-25-52
Height:	5'8"
Weight:	128 lbs.
Hometown:	Craig, Colorado
Current Address:	Alamosa, Colorado
Not Married	
High School:	Craig High School
College:	Adams State College
College Coach:	Dr. Joe Vigil
Club Affiliation:	Phidippides
Current Coach:	Self and Dr. Joe Vigil
Number of Years Running:	12

Running Profile

NAIA National Cross Country Championship (3rd) (1974)
NAIA All American Track
NAIA All American Cross Country—2 times
United States International Cross Country Team (1978)
Revco Marathon Champion (1980, 1981)

Personal Records

440 yds	:57.0
880 yds	2:00.0
1 Mile	4:14.0
2 Mile	5:56.0
5,000 M	13:50.0
10,000 M	29:13.0
15 Km	44:44.0
Marathon	2:15:19.0

Jeff Wells

Personal Profile

Date of Birth:	5-25-54
Height:	5'11"
Weight:	135 lbs.
Hometown:	Eugene, Oregon
Current Address:	Eugene, Oregon
Married:	wife Gayle
College:	Rice University
College Coach:	Steve Straub/ Bobby May
Current Coach:	Athletic West
Number of Years Running:	10

Running Profile

All American Cross Country (1974, 1975)
All American Track (1975, 1976)
Southwest Conference Cross Country Champion (1973, 1974)
Southwest Conference 3 Mile Champion (1975)
Nike Marathon Champion (1977, 1979)
Honolulu Marathon Champion (1977)
Houston Marathon Champion (1976)
Stockholm Marathon Champion (1980)
Olympic Trials Finalist (1976, 1980)
2nd Boston Marathon (1978)
2nd Ranked U.S. Marathoner (1979)

Personal Records

1 Mile	4:05	(1976)
2 Mile	8:40	(1974)
5,000 M	13:31	(1978)
10,000 M	28:12	(1980)
½ Marathon	64:37	(1978)
Marathon	2:10:15	(1978)

Favorite Distance—Marathon
Best distance because pace feels the best.